T0100226

Arduino in Science

Collecting, Displaying, and Manipulating Sensor Data

Richard J. Smythe

Apress®

Arduino in Science: Collecting, Displaying, and Manipulating Sensor Data

Richard J. Smythe
Wainfleet, ON, Canada

ISBN-13 (pbk): 978-1-4842-6777-6   ISBN-13 (electronic): 978-1-4842-6778-3
https://doi.org/10.1007/978-1-4842-6778-3

Copyright © 2021 by Richard J. Smythe

This work is subject to copyright. All rights are reserved by the Publisher, whether the whole or part of the material is concerned, specifically the rights of translation, reprinting, reuse of illustrations, recitation, broadcasting, reproduction on microfilms or in any other physical way, and transmission or information storage and retrieval, electronic adaptation, computer software, or by similar or dissimilar methodology now known or hereafter developed.

Trademarked names, logos, and images may appear in this book. Rather than use a trademark symbol with every occurrence of a trademarked name, logo, or image we use the names, logos, and images only in an editorial fashion and to the benefit of the trademark owner, with no intention of infringement of the trademark.

The use in this publication of trade names, trademarks, service marks, and similar terms, even if they are not identified as such, is not to be taken as an expression of opinion as to whether or not they are subject to proprietary rights.

While the advice and information in this book are believed to be true and accurate at the date of publication, neither the authors nor the editors nor the publisher can accept any legal responsibility for any errors or omissions that may be made. The publisher makes no warranty, express or implied, with respect to the material contained herein.

Managing Director, Apress Media LLC: Welmoed Spahr
Acquisitions Editor: Natalie Pao
Development Editor: James Markham
Coordinating Editor: Jessica Vakili

Distributed to the book trade worldwide by Springer Science+Business Media New York, 1 NY Plaza, New York, NY 10014. Phone 1-800-SPRINGER, fax (201) 348-4505, e-mail orders-ny@springer-sbm.com, or visit www.springeronline.com. Apress Media, LLC is a California LLC and the sole member (owner) is Springer Science + Business Media Finance Inc (SSBM Finance Inc). SSBM Finance Inc is a **Delaware** corporation.

For information on translations, please e-mail booktranslations@springernature.com; for reprint, paperback, or audio rights, please e-mail bookpermissions@springernature.com.

Apress titles may be purchased in bulk for academic, corporate, or promotional use. eBook versions and licenses are also available for most titles. For more information, reference our Print and eBook Bulk Sales web page at http://www.apress.com/bulk-sales.

Any source code or other supplementary material referenced by the author in this book is available to readers on GitHub via the book's product page, located at www.apress.com/978-1-4842-6777-6. For more detailed information, please visit http://www.apress.com/source-code.

Printed on acid-free paper

Table of Contents

About the Author

Richard J. Smythe attended Brock University in its initial years of operation in southern Ontario and graduated with a four-year honors degree in chemistry with minors in mathematics and physics. He then attended the University of Waterloo for a master's degree in analytical chemistry and computing science and a doctorate in analytical chemistry. After a post-doctoral fellowship at the State University of New York at Buffalo in electro-analytical chemistry, Richard went into business in 1974 as Peninsula Chemical Analysis Ltd. Introduced in 1966 to time-shared computing with paper tapes, punched cards, and BASIC prior to Fortran IV at Waterloo, as well as the PDP 11 mini-computers and finally the PC, Richard has maintained a currency in physical computing using several computer languages and scripting codes. Professionally, Richard has functioned as a commercial laboratory owner and is currently a consulting analytical chemist, a civil forensic scientist as PCA Ltd., a full partner in Walters Forensic Engineering in Toronto, Ontario, and senior scientist for Contrast Engineering Limited in Halifax, Nova Scotia. A large portion of Richard's professional career consists of devising methods by which a problem that ultimately involves making one or more fundamental measurements can be solved by using the equipment at hand or using a readily available "off-the-shelf/out-of-the-box" facility to provide the data required.

About the Technical Reviewer

Roland Meisel holds a B. Sc. in physics from the University of Windsor, a B. Ed. from Queen's University specializing in physics and mathematics, and an M. Sc. in physics from the University of Waterloo. He worked at Chalk River Nuclear Laboratories before entering the world of education. He spent twenty-eight years teaching physics, mathematics, and computer science in the Ontario secondary school system. After retiring from teaching as the head of mathematics at Ridgeway Crystal Beach High School, he entered the world of publishing, contributing to mathematics and physics texts from pre-algebra to calculus in various roles, including technology consultant, author, interactive web files (which he conceived, created, published and edited), and photography. He remains active in several organizations, including the Ontario Association of Physics Teachers, the Ontario Association of Mathematics Educators, the Canadian Owners and Pilots Association, and the Wainfleet Historical Society.

He has always had a strong interest in technology, mail-ordering his first personal computer, an Apple II with a 1 MHz CPU and 16 kB of memory, from California in 1979. At leisure, he can be found piloting small airplanes, riding his bicycle or motorcycle, woodworking, reading, or playing the piano, among other instruments.

Acknowledgments

Acknowledgments begin with my late parents, Richard H. Smythe and Margaret M. Smythe (née Earle), who emigrated from the remains of London, England, after the war with their small family of three and eventually raised four siblings in Canada. Our parents instilled in us the need to be educated as much as possible in order for each of us to be self-sufficient and independent. That independence has led to the comfortable retirement of the middle two and to the youngest continuing in her chosen occupation for close to a decade past retirement and the oldest to still be actively engaged in the business of chemical analysis consulting and the practice of civil forensic science.

Along the way, numerous individuals have served as an inspiration while teaching and mentoring me, imparting knowledge, the art of rational thinking, tenacity, and in most cases valuable wisdom:

From Merritton High School in St. Catharines, Ontario:

Mrs. E. Glyn-Jones, mathematics; Mr. J. A. Smith, principal; and Mr. E. Umbrico, physics

From Brock University in St. Catharines, Ontario:

Prof. E. A. Cherniak, Prof. R. H. Hiatt, Prof. F. Koffyberg, and Prof. J. M. Miller

From the University of Waterloo in Waterloo, Ontario:

Prof. G. Atkinson

From the State University of New York at Buffalo:

Prof. S. Bruckenstein

It may also be said that the seeds for the growth and development of this work began when as a parent I made sure that both my daughters, Wendy and Christie, could read at a very early age and devised graphic teaching aids for them to learn and understand binary digital arithmetic.

ACKNOWLEDGMENTS

Acknowledgments would not be complete without recognizing the person who has allowed me the time required to write, in spite of life's everyday chaos in the country, my spouse, Linda. She has suffered through many years of papers, notes, books, breadboards, wires, electronic components, and desktop experiments scattered everywhere in our home and, when she wasn't looking, on the kitchen table! Thank you, my love.

Although my career consists of solving essentially chemistry-based problems and writing reports explaining how the problem came into existence and how to correct its effects or avoid its re-occurrence, I have never written a book. This work would not be possible without the help and guidance of editors at Apress, Ms. Natalie Pao, Ms. Jessica Vakili, and Mark Powers.

The Author's Preface to *Arduino in Science*

Arduino in Science is written to provide an introduction to the basic techniques that can be used by individuals to engage in experimental science. It is hoped that the manuscript can assist students and those new to or with limited backgrounds in electro-mechanical techniques or the physical sciences, to devise and conduct the experiments they need to further their research or education. It is also hoped that the manuscript will be useful where there are limited financial resources available for the development of experimental designs and experimental or educational programs.

Migrating or foraging animals and insects use daylight, near- infrared light, polarized light, celestial indicators, chemical traces in water, the Earth's magnetic field, and other aids to navigate over the Earth's surface in search of food or to return home to their breeding grounds. Astronomy, biology, chemistry, geology/geography, mathematics, physics, and other subjects through to zoology are human concepts and classifications entirely unknown to the travelers of the animal world. There are parallels between the animal kingdom's usage of multiple scientific phenomena of which they have no knowledge and current scientific investigations. A significant amount of new scientific knowledge is being revealed by investigators educated in one classifiable discipline using the unfamiliar experimental techniques from another. Although written by an analytical chemist, this manuscript is a compilation of introductory basic techniques applicable to any scientific discipline that requires the experimental measurements of basic physio-chemical parameters.

The author is an experimental analytical chemist who has worked with vacuum tubes, transistors, integrated circuits, main frame, mini-computers, microcomputers, and microcontrollers, while computing technology transitioned from BASIC, Fortran, and variations of C to iterations of the open source systems such as Python, Processing (the basis of the Arduino microcontroller integrated development environment (IDE) language), and Linux operating systems used in the Raspberry Pi. New and revised versions of languages, IDEs, and operating systems are available free of charge from the Internet and are constantly in a state of flux.

This work could be considered as being virtually obsolete as it is being written, but as with the science and technology that it describes, it is a starting point in an ever-changing subject. For the researcher and practicing scientist, the fundamentals of science are relatively constant and reasonably well understood, so a great deal of caution must be used when deciding that a concept or technique is "obsolete." The SCADA concept and its development significantly predate the PC. Some of the transistor and CMOS ICs and the 7400 series of integrated circuitry that are in heavy use today date from the 1970s. Many chemical analysis and physical measurement techniques, taught and in use today, date virtually from the Middle Ages.

SCADA is the acronym for supervisory control and data acquisition. SCADA software allows a computer to supervise an electro-mechanical process and do so by acquiring data from sensors that are monitoring the process being controlled. Many of the measurement techniques to be discussed can be considered as single element components that are now part of the developing technology being called the Internet of things (IOT) with the Node-RED connectivity open source software.

HMI is the acronym for human-machine interface. The HMI can be an electronic device or construct that provides an interface between a computer, an experimental setup, and a human operator. (A graphical user interface, GUI, may serve as an HMI.)

USB is the acronym for Universal Serial Bus that is, in reality, a written standard of specifications to which electro-mechanical hardware systems are expected to conform. The USB is a subsystem that lets a personal computer communicate with devices that are plugged into the Universal Serial Bus.

When a personal computer runs supervisory control and data acquisition software with a human-machine interface connected via the Universal Serial Bus system, then investigative science experiments or other processes, experimental apparatus, or equipment setups, either "in the field" miles away or "on the bench" next to the computer/workstation or laptop, can be monitored and controlled in "real time."

Laptops, stand-alone desktops, and cabled or wireless networked workstations together with Internet connections now allow unprecedented flexibility in laboratory or "in-field" monitoring of investigative science experiments.

The options available to the experimentalist for implementing SCADA systems can essentially be divided into three categories based upon the amount of development work required to achieve a fully functional system.

Complete, finished, working software systems that are able to measure and control virtually any electro-optical-mechanical system are available from manufacturers such as National Instruments and Foxboro. Commercially available fully functional, basic, software-only systems can be expected to cost in the range of several thousands of dollars.

The author chose to develop this manuscript on three much-lower-cost options for SCADA implementation in experimental setups.

A moderate-cost implementation strategy, involving the following list of resources, has been used to develop the exercises in this manuscript. These resources should also be adequate for further experimental development of new applications:

1) A PC with SCADA software. Numerous systems are available, and the DAQFactory Express and the base-level DAQFactory version of the system from AzeoTech have both been used in this manuscript (cost for DAQFactory base-level software approx. $250 CDN, 2008). There are freeware versions of SCADA systems available for those who are able to adapt the software and may require the extended flexibility.

2) A USB HMI. Again there are many devices available from many manufacturers, and the device chosen for this manuscript is the model U12 from LabJack Corporation. (U12 costs approx. $120. U3 was added later, which costs approx. $110 USD.) The LabJack devices are provided with software in the form of a working version of the DAQFactory program called "Express." The LabJack-supplied software is excellent with respect to its graphical display capabilities and for many applications in investigative sciences is more than adequate. The DAQFactory Express is however limited to ten lines of script code, five script sequences, and two display pages. For some of the topics discussed and project exercises described in this manuscript, the more extensive capabilities of a commercial version of the DAQFactory software may be required. If the software is to be purchased, the reader should start with the most basic program available and add upgrades as required.

3) The third option for experimentalists is the newest
and lowest-cost approach to the implementation of
a SCADA system that consists of the Raspberry Pi, its
Linux operating system, the Python programming
language with its matplot library, and the tkinter
graphical user interface. The Linux operating
system and Python and its modules are all open
source projects and hence free for download
from the Internet. The Raspberry Pi project has
made available the Raspberry Pi board that can
be purchased from many large electronics supply
houses such as DigiKey or Newark element14, to
name only two, for $35. The Raspberry Pi board
requires an HDMI-compatible TV or computer
monitor, mouse, and keyboard to form a fully
functional computing system. In addition to the
virtually no-cost software, the Raspberry Pi board
contains its own general-purpose input/output bus
in addition to its USB input/output connection and
hence contains its own HMI requiring no additional
circuitry or expense to be interfaced to external
electronics or experimental setups. The Raspberry
Pi board is manufactured with an Ethernet
connection and is thus network capable.

In 2008 an open source project called Arduino made available a series
of USB-connected microcontroller boards that allowed designers, artists,
hobbyists, and non-electronics specialists to interface electro-optical-
mechanical devices to a computer. The basic Arduino Uno Rev3 board
can be purchased from any of the major electronics supply houses for
$25. The software to program the microcontroller board is another open
source project and is freeware that can be downloaded from the Internet.

The Arduino board can be used with Windows or Linux-based operating systems and is fully supported with an online forum, many tutorials, and an extensive range of example programs and applications.

Experimental investigations using SCADA-type implementations can thus take the form of a complete commercially available package, useable as received with no required development time, as a lesser-cost system requiring a moderate amount of programming using the DAQFactory program and commercial HMI devices such as the LabJack series of interfaces or as an assemblage of very-low-cost hardware and open source software freely available for download from the Internet.

In addition to the software and hardware required to implement the monitoring and controlling system, additional ancillary equipment may be required in the form of the following list:

1) A solderless breadboard system, appropriate power sources such as battery or electronic regulated supplies, and access to various IC and passive electronic components are required.

2) For troubleshooting, a multimeter is required; and for more advanced work, an oscilloscope, either stand-alone or an oscilloscope program for a PC, may be required.

It is suggested that the reader, new to this technology, work through the manuscript in order of presentation so as to gain practice and confidence with software, wiring, and increasing project complexity. The basics of scripting software, hardware interfacing, electronics fundamentals, and IC usage will all progressively become more complex; and the basic knowledge and procedures established in the earlier exercises will not be repeated in the more advanced projects. All science is empirical in nature, and this manuscript is no different than real-life scientific work. The investigator must progress from the simple to the more complicated facets of the project at hand, verifying and validating each intermediate step in a multiple-stage measurement process.

The rate at which the individual can progress through the various topics presented will be dependent upon their knowledge of the basic physical sciences that form the core of the exercises. If difficulty is encountered, textbooks, online tutorials, and academic course outlines with exercises can be located to further aid in understanding the required base knowledge.

As the title states, this manuscript deals essentially with monitoring and measuring physical-chemical parameters with integrated circuitry and physical computational systems. In this work, inexpensive "off-the-shelf components" are used to monitor and control experimental setups that are able to measure data in the form of basic physio-chemical parameters of interest to investigators in many of the classified sciences, with in some cases astounding sensitivity, flexibility, accuracy, and precision.

Disclaimer

1) 110-volt electricity can be lethal and will start fires.

2) Soldering irons are hot enough to cause serious burns.

3) This document is for educational purposes only and presents concepts that are demonstrated through experimental formats. These experimental setups have not been tested for robustness and are not designed or intended for any form of implementation in field service. These concepts are the basis for education only and are intended as being starting points for further R&D into instrumental methods of monitoring experimental scientific apparatus for the purposes of gathering data or making physical measurements.

4)   The concept for this work came to the author in the mid-1960s, and in the interim years, various portions of this work were developed with the technology available at the time, while other concepts were found to be unworkable. Although formal assembly of this document was begun in 2008 and 2009 using the integrated circuitry, physical computing, and Internet information resources available at that time, the document continues to develop as it is being written using new integrated circuits, physical computing software, and online information sources. The continued availability of either software or electro-mechanical hardware can never be assured, and hence the practitioners of this or any science must learn the art of "a work-around."

Exercise Road Map

As noted in the Preface, this work is not intended to be a first or ab initio introduction to data collection. Although motivated or enthusiastic investigators can plunge right in and try to pick up needed knowledge and skills on the fly, the guide is aimed at those who have at least some experience in working with electronic hardware and computer software. A basic familiarity with simple electronics as well as some elementary programming in a structured language such as Python or C++ will shorten the time required to complete the various exercises.

The manufacturer's literature for most of the data collection hardware referred to in this guide provides guidance and elementary activities to help familiarize the new user with its implementation. Online sources can also provide numerous practical applications of the hardware at hand.

Once the experimenter is comfortable with the hardware and software exercises described in this work, the experimental measurement of many basic scientific parameters can be made in accordance with the methods detailed in the next book in this series, *Arduino Measurements in Science*.

This work is devoted to developing the techniques that can be used for making experimental physio-chemical measurements with equipment assembled from readily available components, materials, and most small desktop or portable computing systems. This manuscript is an attempt to provide written methodologies by which fundamental measurements can be made by investigators of varying levels of familiarity with electronics, electro-optical, and simple mechanical systems. A series of experimental measurement procedures are developed as a prelude for being able to make the basic measurements of parameters such as temperature, distance, light intensity, sound frequency, relative humidity, and other fundamental measurements in basic science.

Each of the chapters develops a method or technique that can ultimately be used to assemble a testing or measurement method or procedure consisting of the various methodologies developed.

Exercise Format

Experimental

Hardware

Software

Observations

Discussion

Code Listings

Project Management

When working through each of the exercises in the various chapters, the following procedures are suggested:

1) In preparation for the assembly of an experimental exercise or project described in a chapter, review the manuscript information and collect the published work relevant to the exercise such as manufacturer's data sheets for the components in use. This will serve to add to the depth of knowledge available to the investigator and may avoid component damage. Rough notes and drawings should be collected together into a notebook (either on paper or in an electronic format).

2) Begin assembling the hardware/electronics and corresponding software from the simplest unit operations of the project, debugging the individual modules and then verifying operational status until the entire project functions as designed.

3) Caution is required in reading schematic diagrams and attempting to duplicate their assembly as certain discrete components and integrated circuitry are constantly decreasing in physical size or are replaced with newer technology. The decrease in size means that identification markings on components are getting smaller also.

Resistance and capacitor markings may appear in several formats as combinations of numbers and letters with the magnitude symbol sometimes replacing the decimal point. Surface mount technologies (SMTs) have a three-digit code in which the first two digits are the value and the third is the power of 10 of the value multiplier.

Resistors' unit of measure is ohms, symbol Ω.

M is 10^6 or 1,000,000 ohms, and typical identifications may be 1.5 M or 1M5.

K is 10^3 or 1,000 ohms, and typical identifications may be 1.2 K or 1K2.

R is 10^0 or 1 or unit ohms, and typical identifications may be 100 R or just 100 as there is no decimal point to replace.

m is 10^{-3} or 1/1000 ohms, and 0.052 Ω is written as 52 mΩ.

Capacitance units in older works were mainly limited to micro- and picofarad designations, and the range of nano- was covered either by thousands of pico- or thousands of microfarads. Most current capacitor notation usage seems to adhere to the three main fractional designations listed in the following but has recently been expanded to include the Farad to avoid using thousands and millions of the micro- term when describing ultra- and super-capacitor devices.

Capacitors' unit of measurement is Farads, symbol F.

u is microfarad and is 10^{-6} Farads.

n is nanofarad and is 10^{-9} Farads.

p is picofarad and is 10^{-12} Farads.

The exercises in this book use very simple electrical circuits that will be assembled on a "breadboard" and connected to the LabJack HMI, DAQFactory Express system, Arduino microcontroller–DAQFactory combination, or directly to the Raspberry Pi or RPi-Arduino systems to provide an interface between the working electronic circuit and a computer-generated GUI. Each of these combinations allows the experimenter to exercise supervisory control, acquire data, or monitor a data stream trend, through a software, user interface screen. There is no better way to gain experience with electro-mechanical control systems than to mechanically assemble circuits and test and establish their functioning, before configuring software for data acquisition (DAQ) and hardware control. As a general rule, the hardware is assembled, tested, and validated before one moves on to interfacing and software development.

The following discussion uses the first of the exercises as an example of the general methodology that will be used for the rest of the exercises. Each exercise in this work is generally set out in the traditional laboratory format, and it is assumed that this general section has been read and is understood by the researcher.

When working with electrical signals from a sensor or experimental apparatus, ensure that the output voltage level does not exceed the input voltage capability of the electronic components being used to process the signal. Most discrete integrated circuitry is limited to 5 volts, some op-amps will operate at up to 18 volts, and most surface mount technologies operate at a nominal 3.3 volts.

As with all scientific endeavors, a logical progression should be made from the simplest to the more complex. When developing the software for the project at hand, the experimenter should begin with the code required to connect the apparatus to the computing and display circuitry.

The simplest form of electrical signal transmission uses a series connection for both analog and digital signals.

Analog voltage signals are often connected directly to the input pins of integrated circuits that provide some form of signal processing, while digital signals are connected to pins that sense whether the signal is high or low. In general terms, a large portion of sensor outputs are voltage based, but current sensing is also used in some sensor measurements.

Computational circuitry usually accesses external data through a "serial port." The serial port is often a specific addressable location in the computer memory that accepts incoming digital data according to a specific encoding called a protocol. The protocol specifies the meaning of the high-to-low or low-to-high transitions that make up the digital signal with respect to timing, data values, and signal processing control parameters. There are numerous scientific and industrial serial transmission protocols designed and optimized for specific applications, but the following exercises will be predominantly confined to the basics of serial data transmission.

The exercises can use the DAQFactory scripting language, Python, and the variant of C used in Arduino programming. All three programming languages have reserved keywords that cannot be used as variable names. Follow the variable naming rule suggestions in the appropriate documentation for the language in use. Create meaningful names by following traditional C styles such as MySignificantName, MySgnfcntNme, or My_Significant_Name. Do not use proper words such as "temperature" or "Temperature" or any other word that may be a proper word used within Python, DAQFactory scripting, C, or C++ programming code. Scripts that contained proper words used as variable names or channels for "clarity" by the author that failed to operate and produced baffling outputs suddenly performed flawlessly when the proper words were re-keyed with unique mixed upper- and lowercase characters. Follow the proper formal methodology built into the software at hand. In the DAQFactory software, creation of the channels first allows DAQFactory to populate the pop-up intelligent listing of channels, variables, and constants to cut down on error-prone typing. The primary step in all troubleshooting procedures involving written coded systems that do not work is to check all spelling. Names are case sensitive.

Keep detailed notes of what is being done, write down calculations, sketch schematics and rough mechanical drawings. This is, after all, science. The drawing conventions for mechanical systems and electronic circuits can be found in several reference texts.[1] The reader is encouraged to follow these conventions.

---

[1] 1) *Building Scientific Apparatus* 4th Edn., Moore, Davis, and Coplan, Cambridge University Press, ISBN 978-0-521-8785-6

2) *The Art of Electronics* 2nd Edn., Horowitz and Hill, Cambridge University Press, ISBN 0-521-37095-7

3) *Practical Electronics for Inventors* 3rd Edn., Scherz and Monk, McGraw Hill ISBN 978-0-07-177133-7

As an exercise is assembled from software control of the HMI to wiring of the circuitry on the breadboard, test each segment of the process. Work neatly; lay out the wiring parallel to the lines and rows of pins on the breadboard socket. Cross wires at right angles and only bend small copper wires to right angles with your fingers so as to achieve a relatively large radius of curvature. Recall that copper, although very ductile, "work hardens," so use new wire where possible or make sure that a wire is re-bent to large-radius, gentle curvatures, no more than half a dozen times at most. In the chemical engineering discipline, a manufacturing process is set up from a number of "unit operations." Each unit operation is usually a complete basic step involving a physical change or chemical transformation such as crystallization or precipitation that forms a component of a larger multistep manufacturing process. A unit operations concept can be applied to creating a basic supervisory control and data acquisition (SCADA) process. In essence each SCADA process can be considered to have, at a minimum, three components, a process to be controlled, a sensing and adjusting mechanism, and a central control authority.

To practice the unit operations concept in our first exercise, we should set up or configure our DAQFactory software to activate a channel. The channel will have been assigned a screw terminal output on the LabJack, and the terminal output will have been wired to the appropriate input pin on the integrated circuit driver. The output pins on the current driver IC will have been individually wired to the current limiting resistor (CLR) on the LED diodes being controlled by the system.

The first step in our testing procedure is to verify the appearance of +5 and 0 volts at the channel output pin on the LabJack with a digital voltmeter (DVM). The appearance of the +5 and 0-volt signal should be verified at pin number 3 on the CD4050 hex buffer chip current driver and at the higher-voltage end of the current limiting resistor on the LED. It is inherently assumed that if all the component parts of a system work, then the entire process will work. Remember that the assumption is just that!

Isolation

The USB is essentially a communications standard and as such has a limited ability to supply power. An HMI that can be used for this work is the LabJack that draws virtually all its power from the computer's main supply. The LabJack can source up to 450 mA. It is good practice for an external power supply to be used to power our experimental devices. In this manuscript, we are working on a bench or desktop and will do so with a self-contained power supply as will be encountered in any field or laboratory experimental setup. Some experimental setups in either laboratory or field will draw more than a half amp, and some will control line voltages and currents. Control of remote setups by the SCADA software over networks or from laptops may not be able to supply any current to the experimental equipment. To power the LED in the first exercise, we will use the HMI to control a "buffer" circuit of a CD4050 CMOS IC chip that will in turn be used to switch the LED power on and off. The control logic of a ONE or ZERO, created by the SCADA software and appearing at the I/O terminals of the HMI device in the form of +5 or 0 volts, is thus used to control the required current from an external 6-volt power supply.

An independent battery or highly regulated power supply is often required for measuring low-level analog signals. Investigators using the 5-volt supply of the USB will often find that the sensitivity of low-level analog signals is defined by the digital clock noise of the bus.

The systems being monitored and controlled in most real-world applications are self-powered and in fact may be linked to the computer and the SCADA software through a wireless link. When the USB is used for power, it is good practice not to load the computer power supply and hence draw only the minimum required current from the bus.

Some of the experimental setups to be explored will draw amps of current and hence cannot be driven by the computer power supply, so some of the exercises to follow must obviously be self-powered. In the later exercises, the power and flexibility of USB-connected microprocessors will be explored; and although these can be powered by the USB, they should be self-powered to stop the noise on the bus system being blended with the data signal output of the microprocessor. (USBs 1 and 2 can supply 500 mA and USB 3 900 mA.)

Software Scripting

Every script written should be fully documented. The name of the sequence or code, the purpose of the sequence, and possibly the date the code was written should all be placed at the head of the actual code in accordance with the details for naming and commenting as given in the various software language references. The heading should also outline what the code does, describe the algorithm in text, and define the variables used. Recall also that a variable must be declared in a scripted sequence, plus the sequence must be running for the variable to exist and be useable. DAQFactory has an auto-start option for a sequence, which will start the sequence when the page with the script-related icon's control screen is loaded, and if required the auto-start option can be used to automatically start a sequence that declares a set of variables for use in configuring a control screen or sequence.

The RPi and Arduino auto-start their operating system and defined software variable on the application of system power.

Integrated Circuitry and Surface Mount Technology (SMT)

Traditionally experimenters bought components for mounting on breadboards during testing and project development. The successful breadboard circuit could then be transformed into printed circuit boards with single- or double-sided etched patterns. The double-sided boards often used drilled holes to connect both sides of the board. However, as integrated circuits became significantly smaller, drawing less current, they became faster and significantly more sensitive and are now at the point at which many of these miniature ICs can neither be handled manually nor electrically connected into circuits, by the average researcher.

Smaller IC size has given rise to smaller component area and surface mount technology (SMT) that in turn has made circuit boards much smaller, easier to manufacture, and less expensive. The decrease in physical size and the development of SMT have added a layer of complexity for the experimentalist. Using the advantages gained by physically decreasing the size of the integrated circuits requires adapters to convert SMT components into compatible breadboarding formats.

Exercises in the following chapters predominantly use readily available ICs that are compatible with the common prototyping breadboard systems.

CHAPTER 1

Button Control of LED Illumination

The exercise in this chapter is virtually one of the simplest forms of computer control in that an LED device is powered on and off by clicking a button icon on the main system display screen or by running several lines of computer code. The graphical user interface (GUI) is the display screen that contains the icons of buttons, sliding controls, meters, digital numeric displays, graphical strip chart recorder displays, and other symbols, both active/passive and text based that can be used to monitor and control the process at hand. Clicking the screen button toggles the LED on and off, and the state of the system is determined visually, by whether or not the LED is illuminated. As the initial exercise in interfacing the SCADA software with the HMI and the breadboard electronics, the ability to control the application of power to simple electronic circuits from a display screen or keyboard is demonstrated.

In order to connect visually oriented digital software running on a "Windows"-based computer operating system to a "plug-in" rapid prototyping "breadboard" sitting on a bench top or embedded in an experimental environment, a digital electrical connection is required. A USB cable used to connect peripherals to host computers can be employed as the electrical signal transmission line connecting the host computer to the machine interface.

© Richard J. Smythe 2021
R. J. Smythe, *Arduino in Science*, https://doi.org/10.1007/978-1-4842-6778-3_1

The machine interface connection can be any one of a number of USB-compatible, programmable hardware devices, able to receive an input of digital code, interpret or recognize the intent of the code, and generate the required digital output signal.

In Figure 1-1, a selection of data acquisition or HMI devices able to provide the required input interpretation and generate the proper output signal are displayed.

Items 1 and 3 are from LabJack Corporation of Lakewood, CO, USA. The corporation produces approximately a dozen multifunctional data acquisition (DAQ) devices compatible with USB, Ethernet, and Wi-Fi systems. LabJacks are rugged, robust devices intended for hard industrial and laboratory applications with their heavy plastic protective cases and large screw terminal wiring connections. The two devices depicted are the lowest-cost U3-HV ($115 USD; see LabJack literature for a list of all the additional functions and features available) and the original LabJack multifunction DAQ device ($160 USD).

Item 2 is a Digilent Inc. chipKIT Uno32 (since retired) Arduino-compatible microcontroller. The illustrated device has been replaced by the chipKIT uC32, 3.3-volt Arduino-compatible microcontroller ($42 CDN). Items 4 and 5 are inexpensive mass-produced SMT Arduino-compatible microcontrollers from SparkFun Inc. ($20-$30 USD).

Each of the devices illustrated is able to receive either a single digital on/off signal or a coded instruction and generate the required output.

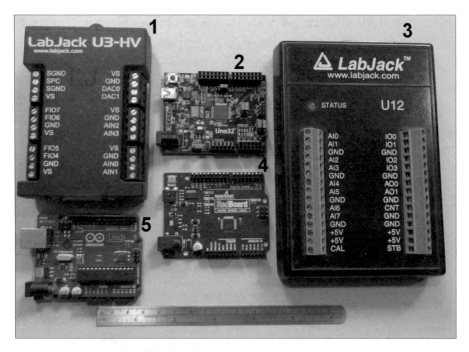

Figure 1-1. *Some HMI Devices*

Microcontrollers are currently manufactured by over a dozen companies with a large variety of features and a wide range of costs.

Experimental

The original control screen button illumination of an LED resident on an external independently powered, prototyping board was created and written in 2007 with the LabJack U12 as seen in Figure 1-1, item 3. Many years later with the availability of the low-cost microcontroller boards, items 2, 4, and 5 in Figure 1-1 can be used to do the same interface functioning. Although this exercise describes the use of the U12, any microcontroller board can be used as a replacement for the LabJacks in Figure 1-1. Details on the configuration of the DAQFactory control screen button to activate an Arduino to illuminate an LED are given in Chapter 11. In the "Experimental Downloading – Sending Data to the Microprocessor" section, three buttons are configured to turn the power on and off to an LED and to do so in a programmed sequence.

Hardware

A typical selection of suitable electronic components for this exercise is displayed in Figure 1-2 resting on a prototyping "breadboard."

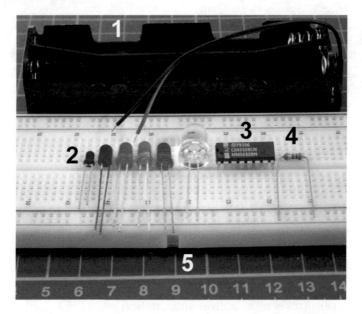

Figure 1-2. *Prototyping Breadboard and Assorted Components*

Item 1 is a plastic battery case able to hold eight AA-size cells to provide a nominal 12 volts. (Eight fresh alkaline cells at 1.5 V each will provide 12 V, while eight nickel metal hydride (NiMH) rechargeable cells at 1.2 V will provide an initial 9.6 V DC power supply. Li AA cells can provide a nominal 3.6 volts each.)

The items beside caption 2 are LEDs. The left-hand red LED is a 3 mm (1/8 in) miniature device, the next four colored diodes are 6 mm (1/4 in) devices, while the right-hand clear device is a 10 mm (3/8 in) white light LED.

Item 3 is a CD4050 non-inverting hex buffer (see the following text). Item 4 is a typical 1/8-watt, current limiting resistor, while item 5 is a 2 in (50 mm) by 6 1/4 in (163 mm) prototyping board. The board has two independent power rails at the top and bottom of the top surface marked with a red (+) and blue (–) line. Each rail power line can accommodate 50 power connections and 50 ground connections. Between the upper and lower power rails are two independent banks of 63 columns of five tie points.

Circuit Schematic: DAQFactory and LabJack Combination

The circuit schematic in Figure 1-3 is used in the first two exercises. The full four-LED circuit is used in Chapter 2 in which the individual power consumptions of the various colored LEDs are monitored. For the first exercise, use only the wiring in the red LED circuit.

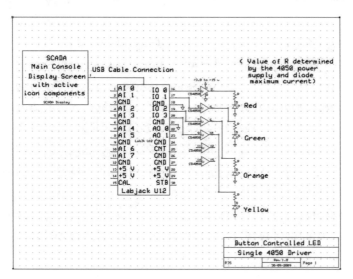

Figure 1-3. Circuit for LED Power Control

Individual switches in the CD4050 chip are monodirectional in that a voltage change applied to the input affects the output but voltage fluctuations at the output do not affect the input pins.

Software

Page Component Required: A Single Button

As discussed in the "Exercise Road Map," detailed notes should always be kept while working with any scientific discipline. For this exercise, the name of the channel to be used to control the HMI, or in this case the LabJack, should be chosen and the software configured to deliver the channel output signal to the first input/output terminal (I/O 0) available on the LabJack terminal board. (See the LabJack U12 or U3-HV user guide.) The details in the DAQFactory and LabJack user guides should be followed, and for this exercise, the author used a channel name of RedLed. The channels to be used in any DAQFactory project should be configured and activated by the Apply button before placing screen components. By defining the channels before creating the screen components, the channel names will appear in the pop-up menu as seen in Figure 1-11. (For use of microcontrollers in place of LabJacks, see Chapter 11, "Experimental Downloading.")

As with all programming, documentation is required. To not document software is poor practice, at best. Before placing and configuring the button, a descriptive text message should be placed on the screen to document what the button does. The text component is created from the right mouse button pop-up menu (RMB-PUM) by selecting the Static option and then the Text option. A window enabling a screen message to be created is displayed.

Figures 1-4, 1-5, and 1-6 depict the selection of a static text screen component, the display of the component properties subwindow, and the active text entry panel.

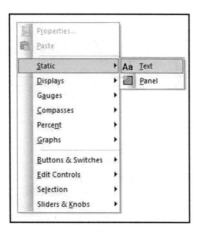

Figure 1-4. *Simple Button Control*

Figure 1-5. *Simple Button Control Properties*

With the message outline frame in place and in the selected mode, a right-click will bring up the menu containing the Properties option. Selecting the Properties entry in the menu will bring up the properties window that will allow the entry of the lettering to be displayed in the text component.

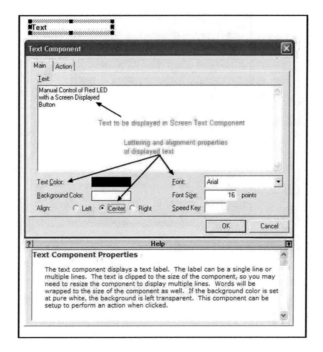

Figure 1-6. *Text Box Configuration*

Having entered the desired lettering into the text box and chosen the alignment, color, font, and size, the main tab can be closed with the OK button to place the text message. The text box as seen in Figure 1-7 may have to be expanded/resized to display the entire message.

Figure 1-7. *Sizing of the Button Icon*

In keeping with the philosophy of constant documentation, it is probably a good time to name the page with the Page Properties box as seen in Figure 1-8. The box is displayed by right-clicking the current page_n designator in the page list and selecting the middle option: Page Properties.

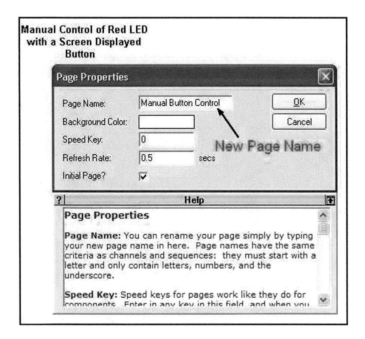

Figure 1-8. *DAQFactory Page Naming Box*

The button component is selected from the RMB-PUM, and with the Ctrl key pressed, the component can be positioned beneath the appropriate text.

Following positioning of the button component on the screen, it can be configured for actual usage by completing the appropriate tabs found in the component properties dialog box. The properties dialog box is invoked by right-clicking the selected icon as depicted in Figure 1-9. To connect the screen displayed button to an action in the experimental environment, the "Do Action" option is selected as seen in Figure 1-9.

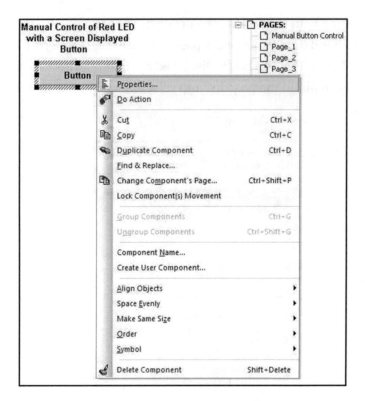

Figure 1-9. *Button Properties Dialog Box*

As can be seen in Figure 1-10, the button component properties window contains two tabs, Main and Action.

The Main tab allows the button to be labeled with the desired font and size of characters and appropriate coloring of lettering, which is centered, in the displayed icon by default. As can be seen in Figures 1-6 and 1-8, a Help screen is displayed below the properties window for a convenient reference while configuring the screen component. The textual content of the Help box can be viewed through the scrolling controls on the side of the Help box.

The button component box is depicted in Figure 1-10.

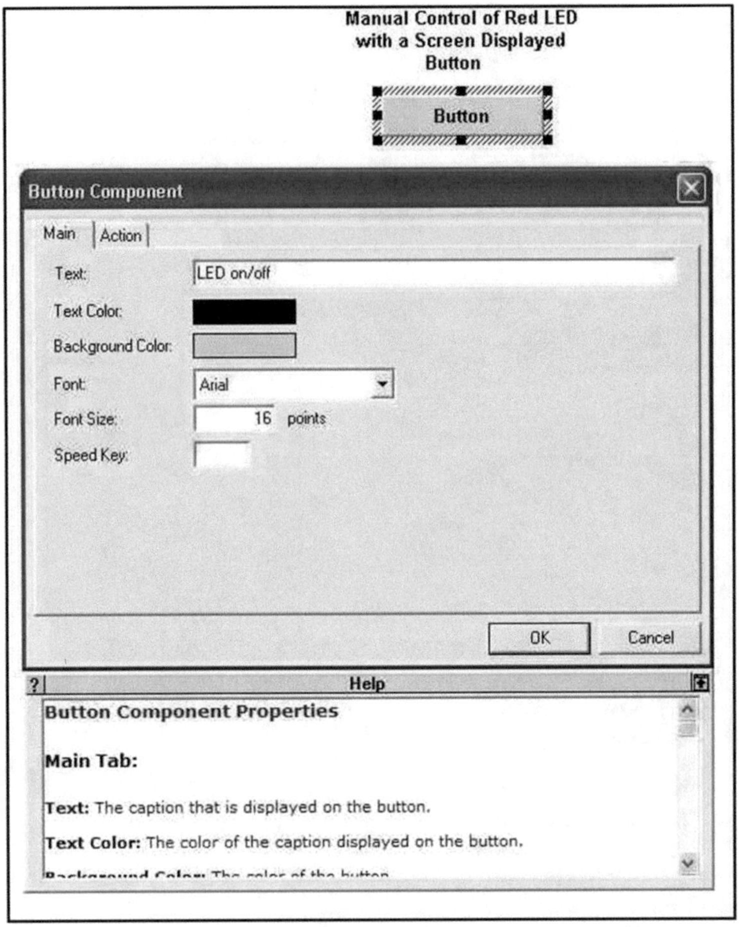

Figure 1-10. *The Main Tab of the Do Action Button Selection*

As the name suggests, the component Action tab configures the action invoked when the button icon is clicked with the mouse cursor. As seen in Figure 1-11, the Action tab brings up a drop-down list of actions or options from which the desired selection can be made. The details of the various entries on the drop-down action list are found in the component Help file attached to the bottom of the window.

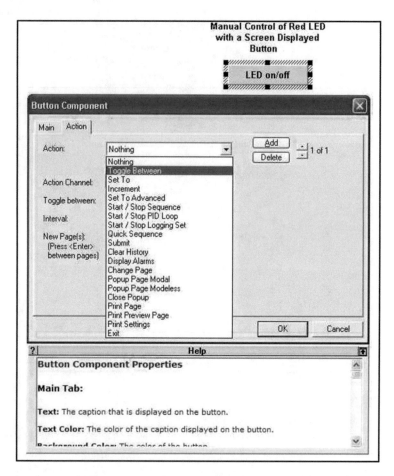

Figure 1-11. *The Action Pop-Up List from the Do Action Selection*

For the manual control of the LED on the breadboard, the Toggle
Between option from the drop-down list is selected. Selection of the Toggle
Between option then requires the completion of several more dialog boxes
that specify exactly what is to be done as depicted in Figure 1-12.

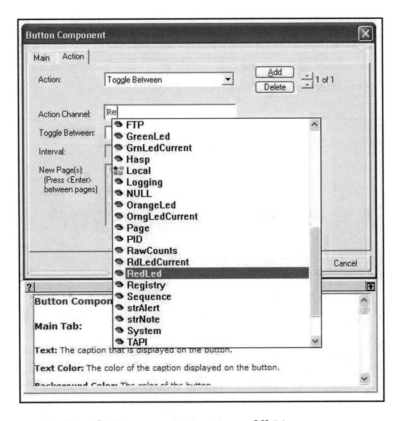

Figure 1-12. *Toggle Between Action Auto-fill List*

When the Toggle Between option has been selected, it is usually a channel that is to be switched between two alternate voltages such as 0 and 5 volts. As noted at the beginning of this software configuration section, the completion and entry of the I/O channel configuration data is now reflected in the RedLed entry in the intelligent pop-up selection list of Figure 1-12. Double-clicking the RedLed channel entry will enter the channel name in the box. Ensure that the name entered into the box is correct and that no extra characters have inadvertently been appended to or deleted from the desired name.

The Action tab also has several other grayed-out options that are activated with various selections from the action list. In this case, there are boxes for the entry of the values to "toggle between" as seen in Figure 1-13 that will appear as axes on the channel's graphical display.

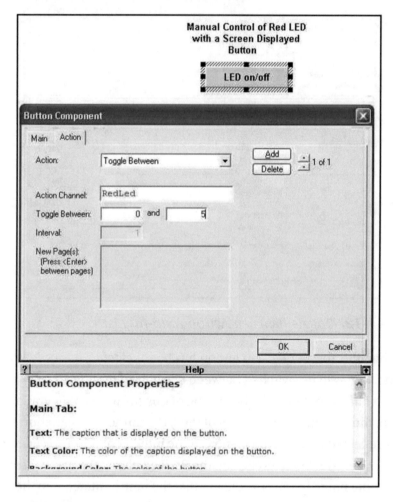

Figure 1-13. *DAQFactory Button Action Screen Completed*

The purpose of this exercise is to directly couple the button to the LED power controller without any need for scripting.

Observations, Testing, and Development

Connect the positive lead of a digital voltmeter to the I/O 0 terminal and the black lead to the GND terminal of the LabJack. Set the meter scale so as to be able to measure 5 volts. Turn the meter on and ensure that the reading is zero. Then click the LED on/off button, and the reading should rise to 5 volts.

If a 5-volt reading does not appear, then begin by verifying the channel name spelling in all components and tables. RedLed is case sensitive and must appear exactly as spelled in all instances of occurrence in the screen components and channel table. Ensure that the "Toggle Between" values are 0 and 5 volts.

When the 5-volt signal is obtained at the LabJack terminals, then the wiring from the terminals to the CD4050 IC chip can be prepared. Insert the CD4050 hex non-inverting buffer chip into the breadboard at a convenient location along the central dividing slot. It is customary to place the chip so as the number 1 pin is in the bottom left-hand corner position when the chip is viewed from the top.

Connect the number 1 pin to the + supply line on the breadboard, the number 8 pin to negative or – supply on the breadboard, and the wire from I/O 0 to pin number 3. Connect the GND terminal on the LabJack to the – supply on the breadboard. With the external power supply connected to the breadboard's + and – lines, connect the voltmeter with the positive lead going to pin 2 of the IC and the negative meter lead going to the negative supply line of the breadboard. Click the LED on/off button, and the meter voltage should rise to a nominal +5 volts.

If a 5-volt signal does not appear on the meter, verify the power supply first and then retrace every wired connection as is indicated in the RedLed schematic in Figure 1-3.

When a nominal 5-volt signal is obtained at pin 2 of the CD4050 buffer and can be cycled on/off with the screen icon, then the power limiting calculation for the red LED to be activated by the control screen's button can be made. Use Ohm's law to calculate the size of the resistor required to limit the current through the red LED chosen for this project to the mid-range of that suggested by the manufacturer. From the data sheet, the bright LED source used by the author's construct was specified for a 30 mA maximum current with a nominal 1.8 voltage drop. An application of Ohm's law indicated a resistance value of 213 Ω would limit the diode current to half of the allowable maximum value specified. Any standard resistor of 220 Ω or higher could protect the LED, and a nominal 470 Ω resistor was available and used in the experimental setup.

It is good practice to calculate the theoretical size of the resistor required to limit the LED current to the maximum amount specified in the diode data sheet, from the nominal voltage of the power supply. Using the data sheet maximum current and supply voltage nominal value generates a resistor value for the LED in use that is adequate to protect the diode. If the next standard value resistor above the "adequate" calculated value is used, the diode will be well lit and have an extra margin of current overload protection that will further extend the service life of the device and aid in minimizing the load drawn from the power supply.

After determining the correct size of the current limiting resistor and then assembling the resistor, diode, and CD4050 buffer to power supply connections, the illumination of the red LED should now be controlled by the button icon on the control screen. (Ensure that the diode is wired with the cathode or short lead going to ground.)

The simple DAQFactory graphical user interface is depicted in Figure 1-14.

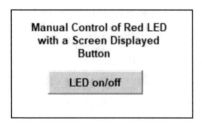

Figure 1-14. *DAQFactory Button for LED Illumination Control*

Discussion

In this exercise, the button has been created with the SCADA software. The logic signal from the state of the button is then transmitted to the LabJack terminal board that in turn controls an IC capable of handling the power required to activate the LED. The LED itself is powered by an external power supply so as the current required to produce the light is not drawn from the PC supply. If the circuitry of the CD4050 hex buffer is examined, it will be evident that a voltage signal is controlling a double CMOS inverter configuration (Figure 1-15).

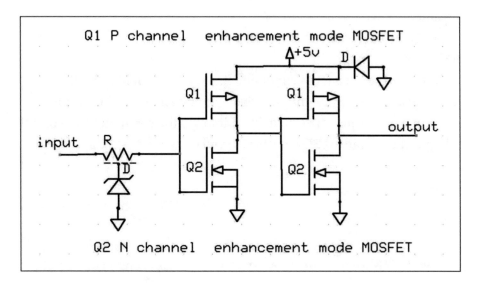

Figure 1-15. *Individual CMOS Buffer Circuit*

As can be seen in the preceding schematic and is discussed in detail in several references[1] on integrated circuit electronics, there are internal complementary metal oxide semiconductor insulated gate devices that virtually stop any DC current flow into the CD4050. The voltage change from the HMI is the control signal that puts virtually no current load on the USB system.

Raspberry Pi, Python, Screen Push Button LED Control

LED illumination from a screen display can be implemented by several methods with the Raspberry Pi (RPi) single-board computer (SBC). Power control can be implemented from the command line of the Pi's Linux operating system, from a mouse click on a button image created on the system screen display with the Python programming language library called easyGUI, with Python's graphical user interface library called tkinter, or with an Arduino microcontroller board interface between the RPi and the LED.

All of the LabJack DAQ devices are compatible with the Linux OS and the Python language.

In this first exercise, the command line methods for illuminating the diode using either the interactive or scripting mode of the Python interpreter will be demonstrated. In addition to the command line control, a simple, dual-button, LED control GUI will be created with the easyGUI library.

---

[1] 1) *Guide to CMOS basics, circuits, & experiments*, Berlin, Howard W. Sams & Co., Inc., ISBN 0-672-21654-X

2) *CMOS Cookbook* 2nd Edn., Lancaster and Berlin, SAMS, ISBN 0 672-22459-3

Implementation of LED control with the Arduino microcontroller interface is introduced in Chapter 4 when its 10-bit analog-to-digital converter (ADC) is required for digitization of analog signals.

Assembly and configuration of the basic Raspberry Pi computer is discussed in texts such as *Practical Raspberry Pi* from Apress books and in up-to-date detail in the online documentation from the Raspberry Pi Foundation.

Experimentation with the RPi GPIO can be done with minimal complexity by connecting the pins of the SBC as defined in Figure 1-16 directly to the breadboard as depicted in Figure 1-17. Ribbon cables are commercially available to connect the bank of dual pins on the RPi SBC to prototyping boards, and if used, the investigator should ensure that the white or red strip on the ribbon cable is connected to the top left-hand pin of the double row of pins on the main board, when viewed from above.

RPi B rvn 1

	Physical	Position	
+3.3 volts	1	2	+5.0 volts
GPIO 0 or I²C SDA	3	4	ncr or +5.0 volts
GPIO 1 or I²C SCL	5	6	Ground
GPIO 4 or Gnral prps clck	7	8	UART transmit (TXD) or GPIO 14
Ground or ncr	9	10	UART receive (RXD) or GPIO 15
GPIO Pin 17	11	12	GPIO Pin 18
GPIO Pin 21	13	14	ncr or Ground
GPIO Pin 22	15	16	GPIO Pin 23
3.3 volts or ncr	17	18	GPIO Pin 24
GPIO 10 or SPI MOSI	19	20	ncr or Ground
GPIO 9 or SPI MISO	21	22	GPIO Pin 25
GPIO 11 or SPI SCLK	23	24	SPI chip select 0 or GPIO 8
Ground or ncr	25	26	SPI chip select 1 or GPIO 7

RPi A/B rvn 2

	Physical	Position	
+3.3 volts	1	2	+5.0 volts
GPIO 2 or I²C SDA	3	4	ncr or +5.0 volts
GPIO 3 or I²C SCL	5	6	Ground
GPIO 4 or Gnral prps clck	7	8	UART transmit (TXD) or GPIO 14
Ground or ncr	9	10	UART receive (RXD) or GPIO 15
GPIO Pin 17	11	12	GPIO Pin 18
GPIO Pin 27	13	14	ncr or Ground
GPIO Pin 22	15	16	GPIO Pin 23
3.3 volts or ncr	17	18	GPIO Pin 24
GPIO 10 or SPI MOSI	19	20	ncr or Ground
GPIO 9 or SPI MISO	21	22	GPIO Pin 25
GPIO 11 or SPI SCLK	23	24	SPI chip select 0 or GPIO 8
Ground or ncr	25	26	SPI chip select 1 or GPIO 7

RPi B+ rvn 2

	Physical	Position	
+3.3 volts	1	2	+5.0 volts
GPIO 2 or I²C SDA	3	4	ncr or +5.0 volts
GPIO 3 or I²C SCL	5	6	Ground
GPIO 4 or Gnral prps clck	7	8	UART transmit (TXD) or GPIO 14
Ground or ncr	9	10	UART receive (RXD) or GPIO 15
GPIO Pin 17	11	12	GPIO Pin 18
GPIO Pin 27	13	14	ncr or Ground
GPIO Pin 22	15	16	GPIO Pin 23
3.3 volts or ncr	17	18	GPIO Pin 24
GPIO 10 or SPI MOSI	19	20	ncr or Ground
GPIO 9 or SPI MISO	21	22	GPIO Pin 25
GPIO 11 or SPI SCLK	23	24	SPI chip select 0 or GPIO 8
Ground or ncr	25	26	SPI chip select 1 or GPIO 7
ID_SD for I2C or ncr	27	28	ncr or ID_SC for I2C
GPIO Pin 5	29	30	Ground
GPIO Pin 6	31	32	GPIO Pin 12
GPIO Pin 13	33	34	Ground
GPIO Pin 19	35	36	GPIO Pin 16
GPIO Pin 26	37	38	GPIO Pin 20
Ground	39	40	GPIO Pin 21

Cautions: 1) the pins are numbered across the array rather than along it.
2) some sources suggest no connections recommended as pin has internal use.
3) do not draw excessive power from the pins check the specifications for the model RPi in use.

Figure 1-16. *GPIO Pin Identification*

Experimental

In Figure 1-17, the long lead on the light emitting diode (LED) is the anode and is connected to the positive supply. LEDs are solid-state devices that only pass current in one direction. The flow of current through the device controls the intensity of illumination, but excessive current can destroy the diode, so a current limiting resistor is used in the circuit.

To ensure communication between Python and the RPi hardware pin array, a library called gpiozero is included in the Raspbian operating software distribution. To create active screen components, a very simplified GUI creation library called easyGUI can be downloaded as detailed in following and used in these introductory exercises.

At the RPi terminal, enter "sudo apt-get install python3-easygui". The 3 is required in order to get the correct library for Python 3 versions.

In Figure 1-17, the connections for an early 26-pin model of the RPi SBC are depicted.

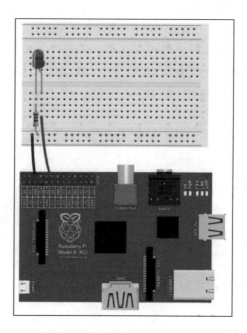

Figure 1-17. *Direct Wiring of GPIO Pins to Prototyping Boards*

As can be seen in Figure 1-17, the anode is connected to a +5-volt pin in the GPIO array through the column of connected pins on the prototyping board. The cathode of the diode is series connected to the current limiting resistor that is grounded. The resistance value is determined from the maximum current specification for the LED device in use.

The Linux operating system of the RPi has a Python programming language interpreter with which the investigator can activate or energize to +5 volts some of the pins on the GPIO bus. The Python commands can be processed either in an interactive mode, processing one line at a time in response to the code entered at the terminal, or as an automatically executed series of Python commands written as a script.

In the interactive mode, we may consider this as the "manual" mode since we are processing one line of code at a time as it is entered from the keyboard. The interactive mode is very useful for setting up and testing the circuitry with the keyboard, and in interactive mode we can turn the LED on and off in the Python shell as needed. When the experimenter uses just the shell and keyboard to turn the LED on and off, there will not be any record of the previous actions of the system.

When the RPi is used with a Python script, explicit print statements can be written into the code to record each action taken, which thus provides a history of the system status.

Observations

The easyGUI library written in Python presents the experimenter with the code required to create a selection of screens containing typical elementary GUI applications. Figure 1-18 is a "Light the LED" action box that has been modified from the Cancel/Continue dialog box example presented in the easyGUI library. Clicking Continue lights the LED and Cancel turns it off. The library code has been modified by the author to record the previous actions or history of the icon usage. The text record is displayed in the Python shell in which the dialog box is running.

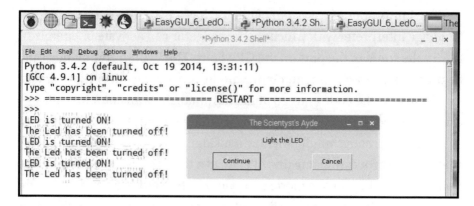

Figure 1-18. *A Simple GUI for LED Control*

The resizing buttons on the Light the LED box work, but the stop program button does not. The two-button dialog box is literally running in a window in the Python shell, and it is the shell stop program button that is effective as seen in Figure 1-19.

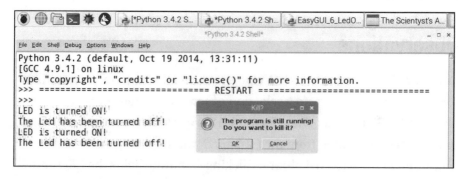

Figure 1-19. *The "Kill" Dialog Box of the Python Shell*

In the code listings at the end of this chapter, there are the manual and GUI-based listings that can be used to activate the LED wired to the GPIO pins.

Discussion

DAQFactory is commercial SCADA finished software. Purchase of this "turnkey" system that "is ready to run straight out of the box" allows the investigator to connect to the system to be controlled and assemble the required GUI from the configurable icons provided on a complex instruction set computing (CISC) device. The Raspberry Pi is a very-low-cost reduced instruction set computing (RISC) device that uses free, open source software that is able to engage in physical computing.

As noted in previous introductions, the RPi represents a very-low-cost entry method to control experimental processes or measurement experiments being made as part of an educational program or an actual scientific research investigation. The RPi can be programmed to implement the management of simple or very complex experimental setups but requires increasing development time commitments from the investigator as the complexity of the experiment being managed increases.

Code Listings

After assembling an LED with the appropriate current limiting resistor (CLR), connect the series wired devices to the GPIO pin 2 and ground, and then enter the code from Listing 1-1 into the Python shell or the interactive terminal.

Listing 1-1. Manual LED Control

```
from gpiozero import LED
grnLed = LED(2)
grnLed.on()
grnLed.off()
```

23

This simple series of code lines will open the gpiozero library and make the LED object available for assignment to GPIO pin 2. The grnLed. on() line sets the GPIO pin 2 to a high or true value and lights the LED. The next line grnLed.off() sets the GPIO pin 2 to low or false and turns the LED off (Listing 1-2).

Listing 1-2. A Button GUI LED Control

```
# Exercise with easyGUI to turn a LED on and off
# an adaptation of the continue or cancel dual
# button message box.
#
from easygui import *
import time
from gpiozero import LED
#
redLed = LED(2)
#
# Use a while loop for continuous activation
while 1:
    msg = "Light the LED"
    title = "The Scientyst's Ayde"
    #
    if ccbox(msg, title):  # show a Turn On/Off dialog box
        print("LED is turned ON!")
        redLed.on()
        # LED power turned on

    else:  #user chose cancel
        print("The Led has been turned off!")
        redLed.off()
        # LED power turned off
```

Summary

–   A basic button icon on a monitor controls an electronic device remote from the host computer.

–   Computer-experiment interfaces can be implemented by configuration in more expensive systems or programmed from basic principles in less expensive component-based systems.

–   In Chapter 2, a more interactive two-way control system will be developed with multiple buttons and an experimental data display.

CHAPTER 2

Power Control, Monitoring, and Creation of Dedicated Graphical User Interfaces

The "SC" in the SCADA acronym stands for supervisory control, while the "DA" is for data acquisition. The purpose of the development of complete software packages such as DAQFactory has been to monitor a real-world electro-mechanical process and supervise or control its operation. This chapter and its exercises expand upon the single button control by creating multiple LED buttons and then monitoring the power consumed by activation of these individual LEDs. The reading of process operating values in response to control system inputs of one or more unit operation activations is thus demonstrated.

The various sizes, methods of construction, intended use, and colors of LEDs result in different voltage drops across their semiconductor junctions as discussed in detail in the "Experimental" section. Each current limiting resistor (CLR) of a fixed nominal value has its own unique resistance that

© Richard J. Smythe 2021
R. J. Smythe, *Arduino in Science*, https://doi.org/10.1007/978-1-4842-6778-3_2

lies within the standard value tolerance for that type of device (i.e., +/- 10, 5, or 1%). When the load resistance variation is combined with the diode voltage drop and the ON resistance of the CD4050 buffer and all are taken into account, it becomes evident that each current flow through the different colored LED circuits will be different.

Table 2-1. *Typical 5 mm LED Parameters*

Diode Color	Typical Voltage(V) Drop	Wavelength (nm)	Current (mA)
Red	1.63–2.03	610–760	30
Green	1.9–4.0	500–570	25
Orange	2.03–2.10	590–610	30
Yellow	2.10–2.18	570–590	30
Blue	2.48–3.7	450–500	30
White	2.48–3.7	450–500	30
Violet	2.76–4.0	400–450	30
Ultraviolet	3.1–4.4	< 400	30

This exercise will measure the individual currents drawn by illumination of the different colored LEDs and provide information on the overall system performance by monitoring the power consumption of the individual operations and the system as a whole.

There are several methods that can be used to measure direct current flow with ammeters, electrometers, and induction or Hall effect devices as presented in many electronics reference texts[1] and in *Arduino*

[1] 1) *Building Scientific Apparatus* 4th Edn., Moore, Davis, and Coplan, Cambridge University Press, ISBN 978-0-521-87858-6 hardback

   2) *The Art of Electronics* 2nd Edn., Horowitz and Hill, Cambridge University Press, ISBN 13 978-0-521-37095-0 hardback

   3) *Practical Electronics for Inventors* 3rd Edn., Scherz and Monk, McGraw Hill, ISBN 978-0-07-177133-7

Measurements in Science. However, at this introductory stage of the
manuscript and for ease of implementation, resistance voltage drop
measurements and Ohm's law calculations will be used to monitor the
current flow through the systems under test.

Experimental

Light emitting diodes (LED) are diodes whose current, voltage, resistance,
and luminosity properties can be better understood when examined with
respect to both Ohm's and Kirchhoff's voltage laws.

Physically LEDs are manufactured in a variety of forms as depicted in
Figure 2-1.

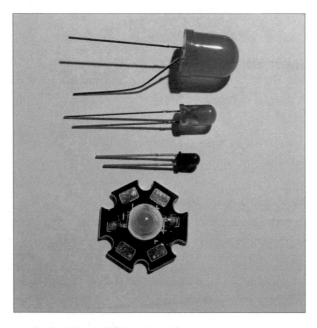

Figure 2-1. *Various Forms of LED*

Depicted in Figure 2-1 are a 10 mm green, a 5 mm blue, and a 3 mm red LED through hole devices. (LEDs are available in flat, bar-shaped, and surface mount configurations such as those visible in any photos of the Arduino or Raspberry Pi circuit boards. For ease of experimental setups with the prototyping boards illustrated in Chapter 1, Figure 1-1, LEDs with two leads are preferred.) The star-shaped disk at the bottom of Figure 2-1 is a 3-watt illumination diode. The top three indicator-type devices can be powered from a computer or a USB device, but the bottom diode designed for lighting or illumination service typically draws enough current to warrant being bolted to a heat sink and hence when in service usually requires a special high-current supply that far exceeds the current capability of a computational device.

LEDs are often classified as indicators or illuminators according to the type of light they produce. Indicators typically create a diffused light from a colored body that is visible from all angles, while illuminators, usually with clear bodies, generate a concentrated beam of light that is most intense longitudinally or directly ahead of the device. LED brightness is measured in millicandelas (mcd) or radiant intensity. A common candle emits about 1 candela.

Tables 2-2 and 2-3 are typical listings of the electrical and optical parameters often found on LED data sheets.

Table 2-2. *Typical LED Electrical Parameters*

ITEMS	Symbol	Absolute Maximum Rating	Unit
Forward Current	I_F	20	mA
Peak Forward Current	I_{FP}	30	mA
Suggested operating current	I_{SU}	16-18	mA
Reverse Voltage (V_R=5V)	I_R	10	uA
Power Dissipation	P_D	105	mW
Operation Temperature	T_{OPR}	40 ~ 85	°C
Storage Temperature	T_{STG}	40 ~ 100	°C
Lead Soldering Temperature	T_{SOL}	Max. 260°C for 3 Sec. Max. (3mm from the base of the expoxy bulb).	

Table 2-3. *Typical LED Optical Parameters*

ITEMS	Symbol	Test condition	Min.	Typ.	Max.	Unit
Forward Voltage	V_F	I_F=20mA	1.8	---	2.2	V
Wavelength (nm) or TC(k)	Δ λ	I_F=20mA	620	---	625	nm
*Luminous intensity	lv	I_F=20mA	150	---	200	mcd

When consulting a data sheet for information, always verify that the
data being retrieved is for the correct package size at hand. A compromise
is always required in selecting the currents to be used in an LED circuit
since the higher the current, the brighter the light and the shorter the
service life of the device. Listings on the data sheet give typical operating
currents, short time maximum currents, and longer service life operating
currents.

Optical properties specified for the diode are also given on the data
sheet that include the frequency or wavelength of the emitted light, the
diode voltage drop, and light output brightness at a given diode current.

To avoid damage to the diodes being used in an experimental
application, a current limiting resistor (CLR) is connected in series with
the LED. The voltage of the source must be high enough to turn the LED
on, and the difference between the source voltage and the diode voltage
can be dropped across a current limiting resistor to regulate the current
flow in the indicator or illumination circuit. (Either Kirchhoff's voltage law
that notes that the total voltage drop around an electrical circuit is zero
or Ohm's law can be used to determine the resistance value required to
regulate the current flow in an LED circuit.)

Theoretical calculations using Ohm's law and the data for a typical
5 mm LED indicate that a 200 Ω resistor should sufficiently limit the
current from the nominal voltage of our power supply. The author's 6 V
AA battery supply and 30 mA bright source diodes suggest that a
6 V/30 mA = 200 Ω resistor should be adequate to protect the diode and

the CD4050 buffer (see Figure 2-2). The nearest larger standard value resistor is 220 Ω, and using 5% tolerance components, we select four pieces for use in this exercise. With a digital volt-ohm meter, we measure the individual values of the four resistors and record the data. For the sake of convenience and simplicity, the resistors are named by LED color. In the author's development work, Red is 221 Ω, Green 219 Ω, Yellow 216 Ω, and Orange 216 Ω. Make sure the individual resistors are identified and their actual numerical resistance values recorded, as these values will be required to calculate the individual load currents.

Hardware

Four bright LEDs of various colors and four measured resistance 220 Ω standard resistors of sufficient wattage rating for the expected currents are used in the development of the exercise. (Values noted are based upon the author's experimental setup using a nominal 6 V supply and 30 mA diodes.)

For this exercise, four of the six gates available on a CD4050 IC buffer chip are used to isolate the LEDs from the USB and draw power from an auxiliary supply.

A flat, rectangular battery pack, capable of holding four AA cells connected in series, provides a nominal 6-volt power supply for the experimental assembly mounted on a prototyping board. (See "Discussion" for more details on the use of batteries as an auxiliary power supply).

Figure 2-2 displays the circuit schematic for this exercise. In order to measure the current flow through the individual LED-resistor series combinations, the analog output and input signal terminals of the LabJack U12 are used.

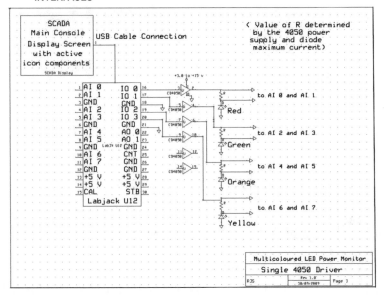

***Figure 2-2.** Circuitry for the Four-LED Display*

Software

A total of eight channels are required. Four are configured as output to
control the power switching of the LEDs, and four channels monitor the
voltage developed across the individual, measured value, load resistors.

The output channels can be labeled as in the previous exercise
as RedLed, GreenLed, and so on. The input channels are labeled as
RedLedCurrent, GreenLedCurrent, and so on. The DAQFactory channel
table for this project exercise is depicted in Figure 2-3.

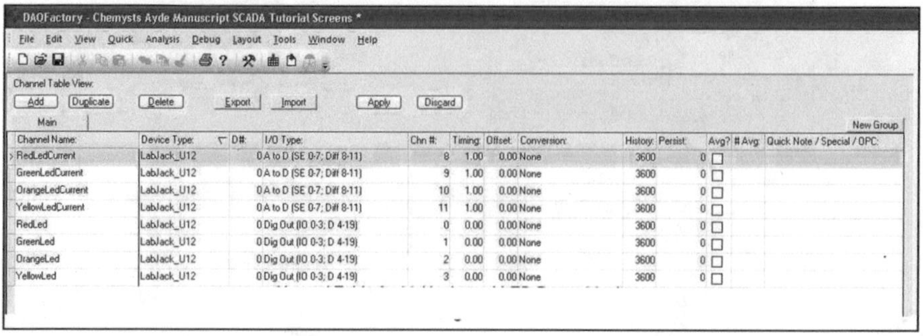

Figure 2-3. *The DAQFactory Channel Table*

Page Components Required

Four buttons, five variable value components (VVCs), and two text displays, as depicted in Figure 2-4, are placed on the screen to form the basic structure of the desired control screen user interface.

(The DAQFactory manual provides the details on creating the screen components, positioning them on the screen, and creating the text labels and messages that identify the different components and the values being entered or displayed. As per the manual, a collection of independent screen components can be grouped together to form a single unit for ease of manipulation on the screen. The individual grouped components can be displayed against a distinctive background color to provide the end user or the operating process controller with a visually comprehensible control screen. Blocking together related components and isolating them with individually colored backgrounds to attract the eye and thus increase ease of use while minimizing the chance of operator errors is good design. The coloring of group backgrounds should be left to the final configuration of a control screen before deployment for actual use in an application as the creation of the background color panel limits access to the individual components in the group and thus creates unnecessary complexity during system development.)

Multiple LED Power Monitoring
Button
Value: 0.000 V
Button
Value: 0.000 V
Button
Value: 0.000 V
Button
Value: 0.000 V
Text
Value: 0.000 V

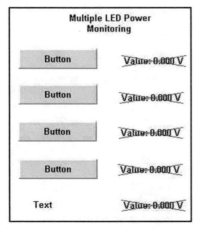

Figure 2-4. *Preliminary Assembly of Desired GUI Components*

Each of the four buttons is labeled according to the color of the LED being activated, and the corresponding variable value components are set to display mA of current. The fifth variable value display can be set to indicate the total current, again in milliamperes, mA.

Figure 2-5 illustrates the power monitoring panel and Figure 2-6 the typical expression for a colored button power draw entry.

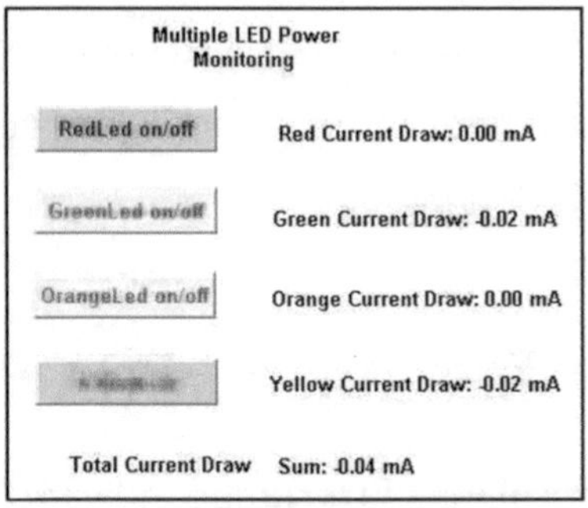

Multiple LED Power Monitoring
RedLed on/off
Red Current Draw: 0.00 mA
GreenLed on/off
Green Current Draw: -0.02 mA
OrangeLed on/off
Orange Current Draw: 0.00 mA
Yellow Current Draw: -0.02 mA
Total Current Draw
Sum: -0.04 mA

Figure 2-5. *Preliminary Coloring of the GUI*

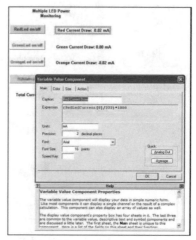

Figure 2-6. *Typical Calculation Expression for the Power
Monitoring GUI*

The variable value expressions use the following calculation:

$$(RedLedCurrent\ [0]/221)*1000$$

where RedLedCurrent [0] is the most recent voltage read across the red diode
current limiting resistor, 221 is the actual DVM measured resistance value
in ohms of the red diode current limiting resistor, and the *1000 multiplier
converts the current from fractional amps to whole numbers of mA.

The expression in the total component display sums all four individual
current expression calculations.

Observations, Testing, and Development

Activation of one or more of the LEDs should indicate the current flowing
through the individual diode and the total current being drawn. The values on
the display screen should update every second, as that is the default value for
the timing entry in the channel table. A more visually effective colored LED
control panel can be created by adding LED symbols to the left of the control

buttons on the panel. The LED symbols can be set to the corresponding colors of the LEDs being activated, and the entire assembly grouped together to form a coherent unit as is illustrated in Figure 2-7. The panel component is used to provide a background for the grouping (see the DAQFactory manual), and an identifying number is displayed on the grouping panel to tie the panel to a set of notes/instructions displayed at the bottom of the main display screen, of which the following panel could be a component.

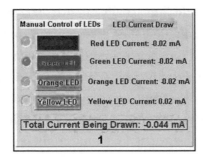

Figure 2-7. *Power Monitoring Graphical User Interface*

A different and perhaps more effective visual display of the power consumption can be achieved by using the DAQFactory linear gauge component as depicted in Figure 2-8.

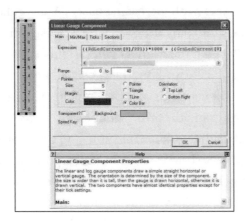

Figure 2-8. *Option of Gauge Addition*

If the linear gauge component is set to display the total current being consumed by summing the four individual colored LED currents, it can be placed alongside the button control panel to display the total current draw from the power supply in a more visually comprehensive format.

Discussion

Fresh AA alkaline batteries are usually rated at 2890 mA · hr per unit. If all four LEDs are illuminated, they draw approximately 30 mA each, which suggests a useful service life, in the author's setup, from the 6-volt four-battery holder, of approximately 100 hours. An estimated 100-hour service life is theoretical in nature, and it must be recognized that the light emitting diode has an approximate 2-volt drop and the resistor a 2-volt drop and the CD4050, the rest of the wiring connections, and the internal resistance of the cells themselves are taking up the remainder of, in the author's case, a nominal 6-volt power supply. At some point in time, well before the estimated 100-hour lifespan, the voltage output of the battery pack will drop to the point that the diode will be too dim to see or will not light at all. The literature indicates that the primary cell alkaline chemistry battery discharges in a somewhat linear manner, losing both voltage and current delivery capacity with increasing usage. A secondary cell chemistry battery such as nickel metal hydride (NiMH) has a significantly lower open circuit voltage (OCV) than the primary cell system (1.2 vs. 1.5 V) and a slightly lower rating of 2500 mAh for the AA size. The secondary cell NiMH chemistry battery however tends to have a much lower rate of voltage loss and instead of failing gradually throughout its discharge history holds the voltage delivered at a relative constant value and then discharges rapidly and completely in a very short time, as its power runs out. Researchers using battery power should understand the properties of the different battery systems available. (Six volts in alkaline AA batteries is obtained from four units, but nominally 6 volts in NiMH requires five rechargeable units.)

It is evident with battery packs that as the load on the power source is increased, the voltage drops and the current supplied to an individual current-consuming load will decrease. Regardless of whether alkaline or NiMH batteries are used as each diode is turned on, the current being delivered to each individual diode drops. The power monitoring panel will show a decrease in the current being drawn by the red LED as the green, orange, and yellow diodes are activated. To minimize the power decrease as load increases in more critical field or laboratory operations, a regulated power supply, battery packs connected in parallel or larger battery formats such as C or D cells, may be necessary to maintain current and voltage levels under experimental load.

The gradually decreasing currents monitored by the panel displays are a real-time indicator of the power being delivered from the battery pack, and the gradual decline can be used to roughly estimate the service life left in the power supply.

In general terms, it can be said that new primary cells or freshly charged secondary cell batteries will exhibit a minimal internal resistance that gradually rises to a maximum value as the cells discharge. Charge monitoring can be done by determining the open circuit voltage (OCV) and the internal resistance of the battery cells themselves. The OCV is measured at no load conditions, but the determination of the internal resistance of the battery pack is a dynamic process requiring the simultaneous recording of both the current drawn and the instantaneous circuit voltage. By recording the simultaneous rates of change of both I and V graphically, the resistance R of the cell can be determined. Plotting of the OCV and internal resistance of the cells can be used to determine the useful life remaining in the battery pack. (See powering experiments in *Arduino Advanced Techniques in Science.*)

Power concerns can be reduced by using a significantly less expensive microcontroller that can be used to develop an experimental interface similar to the fully functional, industrial-grade LabJack DAQ. However, a significant amount of time and effort is required to implement a portion of

the functionality for the task at hand into a microcontroller that is built into
the commercially available HMI devices. In order to implement the power
controlling GUI exercise with a microcontroller, the basic steps involving
the configuration of both the DAQFactory and microcontroller programs
will be presented. (See Chapter 11 for more details.)

As in the previous iteration of this experiment with a LabJack, four
nominal 220 Ω resistors were selected from the lab 5% tolerance supply
and their actual resistance measured with a DVM. For simplicity and
ease of assembly, the known value resistors were mounted directly onto a
prototyping board without the CD4050 buffers as depicted schematically
in Figure 2-9 and pictorially in Figure 2-12.

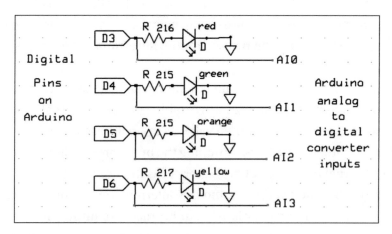

Figure 2-9. *DAQFactory GUI Development for Arduino Control of a Bank of LEDs*

In order for DAQFactory to recognize and communicate with a
microcontroller through the serial communications port, the com port in
use by the microcontroller must be identified. By connecting a USB cable
between the host computer and the microcontroller and launching the
microcontroller integrated development environment (IDE) program,
the port identification can be found on the port: entry of the Tools

menu. Once the port has been identified, confirm connection and board functionality by loading and then running the "Blink" program from the file/examples/01.Basics/Blink menu of the IDE. The onboard LED of the microcontroller should flash at a rate of one "blink" per second, thus confirming the communications link. (The onboard LED is the glowing green dot beside the "RedBoard" logo box as seen in the lower-left corner of the red board depicted in Figure 2-12.)

A common control screen in the DAQFactory program can service either the LJ DAQ or the microcontroller experimental interface. However, the channel configurations seen in Figure 2-3 use the LabJack U12 device for which the driving software has been written. A new device will have to be created in the DAQFactory environment in order to transmit data to a low-level communications port on a microcontroller. A typical low-cost microcontroller is the "RedBoard" Arduino-compatible device seen as item 4 in Figure 1-1 of Chapter 1 and in a wired configuration in Figure 2-12. A DAQFactory com device is created by selecting a port and a protocol. (See Chapter 11, Figures 11-4, 11-5, and 11-6.)

An identifiable device must be created before it can appear in the channel creation table of the DAQFactory program. Selection of the Quick ➤ Device Configuration entry on a DAQFactory page brings up the Device Configuration window that contains a listing of the devices available and a New Serial (RS232/485) / Ethernet (TCP/IP) device entry. (See Figure 11-4, Chapter 11.) To create a new serial device, click the New Serial (RS232/485) / Ethernet (TCP/IP) device entry to highlight it and the Select button in the upper-right corner of the window to bring up the Ethernet / Serial Device configuration window. (See Figure 11-5, Chapter 11.) In the configuration window, enter the new device name. (DAQFactory names must begin with a letter and contain only letters, numbers, or the underscore.) The device in use has been named "ardyRb" as a mnemonic for RedBoard and Arduino. To create the new serial port, click the New Serial button to bring up the Serial Port Configuration window. (See Figure 11-6, Chapter 11.)

The name of the port was partially defined by the inquiry of the Arduino in use for its communications port number that was found to be com port 4, and hence a name such as COM4 would suffice for the new connection name. The serial port number entry into the DAQFactory configuration table must be 4 to correspond with the connected microprocessor's serial port number. (See Chapter 11, Figure 11-6.) The remainder of the Serial Port Configuration window default settings are best accepted as entered, and as the window Save button is clicked, a check box "COM4" should appear in the serial port list of the Ethernet / Serial Device window. A protocol must be assigned to the device being created, and since the flow of data is to be controlled from a DAQFactory sequence or scripting, the NULL protocol is selected. The NULL or nothing protocol allows for the use of low-level communications functions from a sequence. Selection of the protocol and checking the "COM4" box allow the "ardyRb" device to be saved for use where required when the OK button is clicked in the upper right-hand corner of the Ethernet / Serial Device window.

To develop a power monitoring facility with a much simpler microcontroller interfacing device while adhering to the fundamental concept of starting from a simple system and progressing into a more complex one, a single Arduino-powered LED will initially be controlled from a control screen in DAQFactory. The single LED can then be expanded to a bank of four LEDs. The simplest form of button control of an LED is to create two buttons in a DAQFactory control screen as depicted in the upper-left corner of Figure 2-10.

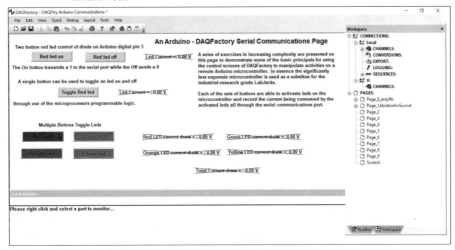

Figure 2-10. *DAQFactory GUI for Control of Arduino LEDs*

DAQFactory is usually running on a PC-based computing platform, while the ATmega328 chip is hosting the Arduino operating system. The programs are able to talk to each other through the serial port software, but only one program at a time can use the serial port. In essence the visual activation of an "on screen icon" in the DAQFactory display initiates a streaming of low-level commands to the serial port. On the other side of the serial port is the ATmega328-controlled Arduino microcontroller essentially running on the C language that can be programmed to process the low-level commands appearing on the serial port.

In Figure 2-10, the top two buttons are the "Red led on" and "Red led off" icons. The two buttons are configured on-screen as explained in Chapter 1, and in the listing of possible actions to be initiated when the "Red led on" button is clicked, as depicted in Figure 1-11 of Chapter 1, the "Quick Sequence" selection is taken. The Quick Sequence selection brings up the window depicted in Figure 2-11.

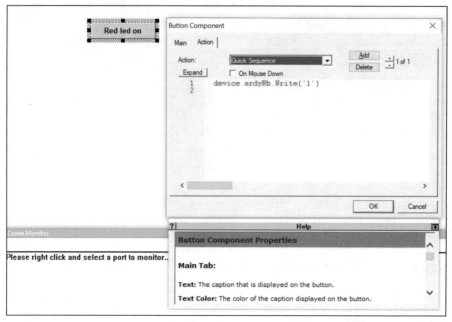

Figure 2-11. *The Quick Sequence window*

A Quick Sequence entry is unique in that it is accessed and executed only when the button to which it is bound is activated. The single line of code in Figure 2-11 is a complete sequence that writes the character 1 to the serial port.

The DAQFactory serial port is connected through hardware and software to the USB that is also connected through hardware and software to the Arduino's C-based operating system. Both of the software systems have facilities for processing low-level communications based on the serial transmission and receiving of characters in the bit and byte formats.

In the simple example of Figures 2-10 and 2-11, an ASCII (American Standard Code for Information Interchange) value of 49 in decimal notation representing the numerical value of 1 is sent to the serial monitor on activation of the "Red led on" button.

Arduino programs are referred to as sketches, and the code for receiving the "1" character on the serial port and switching a digital pin on is in Listing 2-1 (all code listings provided in the "Code Listings" section at the end of the chapter). Examination of Listing 2-1 will reveal that the code will accept a 0, an ASCII code of 48, on the serial port and turn the LED off. The two-button control scheme is simple and uncomplicated and uses a single sketch to manage the two possible LED power levels.

In the second row of the control screen is a single button labeled "Toggle RED led" that switches the LED on when the button is first clicked and off when clicked for the second time. The Arduino sketch in Listing 2-2 contains the logic for the "toggling action" in the form of the flag variable "oofR" that records the status of the LED as either on or off and thus enables the code to switch or alter the present power state of the device.

The set of four colored buttons in the bottom-left corner of the control screen extend the power control capability to four buttons with the Arduino code of Listing 2-3.

Each colored button in the control screen is coupled to a Quick Sequence action that writes an R, G, O, or Y character to the serial monitor. On the Arduino side of the connection, the code compares the new character that arrives on the serial port with a collection of four characters in what is termed a "case" structure. When a match is found, the code associated with the identified "case" is executed. In Listing 2-3, the action involves toggling the colored LED corresponding to the DAQFactory control screen button color on or off.

The control screen in Figure 2-10 contains seven screen icons called variable value components that can be used to provide a visual numerical display or readout of a process value.

The exercise has been set to demonstrate the remote activation of a device and also measure a process variable in the form of the current drawn by the active device. Listings 2-4, 2-5, and 2-6 list the Quick Sequence codes that can be used to pass action initiation requests one way and pass resultant effects back. Listing 2-6 is a shorter Quick Sequence DAQFactory side method for declaring that a current flow has been stopped.

An Arduino microcontroller is equipped with a six-channel, 10-bit analog-to-digital converter (ADC) capable of converting 0–5-volt signals into digital values between 0 and 1023 (2^{10} or 1024). The 5 volts when divided into 1024 units yields 4.8828 millivolts per digital counting unit. As seen in Figure 2-9, each of the four diode voltage drops is measured by the analog inputs of the ADC. On completion of the voltage drop measurement, the calculated diode current is written to the serial port using the Arduino's "Serial.println(iRed);" format that appends the carriage return–line feed (CR-LF) ASCII characters to the diode current value characters sent to the serial port. The \013\010 serve as markers delineating or identifying the end of the characters presenting the numerical values of the measured diode current to the DAQFactory Quick Sequence data parsing logic.

Listings 2-9 and 2-10 are DAQFactory Quick Scripts that are run when one or more colored buttons in the panel of four in the lower-left corner of Figure 2-10 are activated. Each button has a Quick Sequence scripting that clears the serial input buffer and sends an uppercase letter representing the color of the button and corresponding LED to be altered to the DAQFactory entrance or memory location of the serial port. The Arduino microprocessor C code examines the character sent from the DAQFactory control screen and conducts the required actions posting the return data parameters to the serial port. Listings 2-7 and 2-8 are the Arduino codes supporting the DAQFactory action requests. The Quick Sequence initiates a delay after sending the activation request and then begins to process the characters that appear on the serial port.

Listing 2-9 processes only the current being drawn by the active LED, while Listing 2-10 processes both the individual currents being drawn by any active LEDs and the total current drawn by all active LEDs.

These simple systems demonstrate one of the great advantages of SCADA systems in that no error checking or error handling capability is required for serial communications between the two computing platforms. The characters sent and received are fixed in software and only require the activation of the screen icon to achieve the desired activity and measurement. There is minimal action required by the operator of the control screen in that no data entry is required, only the clicking of the correct icon on the control screen. In an electrically noisy industrial or experimental environment, these simple programs may require error checking and error handling capability.

The two-button on/off control panel is as simple as possible, and the operator has two choices that turn the LED on and off. The illumination of any diode mounted on the prototyping board as seen in Figure 2-12 alerts the operator to the status of the system and to which button is active in changing the state of the system.

Figure 2-12.   *The Arduino-Controlled Four-LED Array*

The measurement of the current has been automated, and with additional work in an actual experimental application, the process could be validated to determine the accuracy and reproducibility of the current measurements.

Both the Arduino and DAQFactory programs have extensive facilities to aid in the development of serial communications. Serial communications systems are very simple and widely used in industrial manufacturing and experimental research and development programs. Both of the software systems in use in this exercise have serial port windows that allow the visualization of the data resident on the serial monitor interface and allow the researcher to receive or transmit serial data from or to the host program.

The Arduino serial port is used for numerous applications in addition to serial port communications between programs and can stream data from numerous types of sensors connected to the microcontroller. Details of the various measurements possible are found in *Arduino Measurements in Science*.

In Figure 2-13, the DAQFactory serial port has been expanded to test and monitor actions taking place at the serial port.

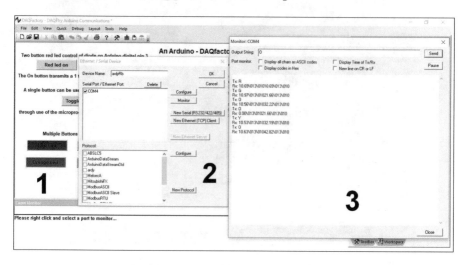

Figure 2-13. *The DAQFactory Serial Port Monitor*

In order to see the DAQFactory serial port monitor in operation, the host computer must be running a microcontroller program compatible with the control screen in use. With the microcontroller program running in the minimized or background configuration, the DAQFactory program containing the control screen can be run in the foreground as labeled 1 in Figure 2-13. From the "Quick" menu, "Device Configuration" is selected, and the Device Configuration window as depicted in Figure 11-4 of Chapter 11 appears. From the entries in the Device Configuration window, the "ardyRb" is selected; and when the Select button in the top right-hand corner of the window is clicked, the "Ethernet / Serial Device" window, panel 2 in Figure 2-13, appears. With the correct name and communications port entered, the "Monitor" button can be activated to bring up the serial port monitor for COM4 labeled as panel 3 in Figure 2-13.

When activated, the serial port monitor for COM4 now controls the data flow to and from the serial port. The two buttons still visible on the underlying control screen in panel 1 are no longer responsive, and only by sending the correct, uppercase first letter of the diode color to the serial port can the corresponding diode on the Arduino array be activated. As can be seen in the activity record in panel 3, the transmission of an R, recorded as "Tx R," is followed by the script Rx 10.69\013\01010.69\013\010. Rx is the "received a transmission" notation, and 10.69 is a numerical sequence appended with the ASCII codes 013, a carriage return, and 010, a line feed. Immediately after the line feed notation is a numerical sequence again appended with the CR-LF pair of printing instructions.

As discussed in the preceding text, the Arduino code has recognized the R and activated the red diode sending back the individual diode current and the total current being drawn with both numerical values followed by the CR-LF combination. If an uppercase O is sent to the port, the expected action occurs; and if the Enter key is used while the uppercase O is still resident in the Send compartment, the Arduino code will toggle the orange diode as seen in panel 3.

As noted previously, the substitution of a very inexpensive microcontroller board for the industrial research-grade interface is a practical exercise in which the significantly increased development time can be used to advantage as a hands-on learning experience.

Power Monitoring and Control with Raspberry Pi

For investigators, experimentalists, or educators who are not familiar with the Raspberry Pi (RPi) educational computer and its use in physical computing through its general-purpose input and output (GPIO) pin array, several texts are available.[2] Current information and software are available online from the Raspberry Pi Foundation that should be reviewed before attempting the following exercises.

Although the Raspberry Pi single-board computer (SBC) originated as a very inexpensive teaching aid, it can be used, with some limitations, as a physical computing platform for SCADA applications. The RPi SBC does not have the capability for analog-to-digital conversions, but several methods exist for working around this voltage measurement limitation. Voltages from experimental sensors can be measured with external ADC chips or a USB connection to an Arduino microcontroller board and by using a Python library with the RPi to measure the time constant of a known value resistor–capacitor series connection. The documentation written for the gpiozero Python library points out that the RPi operating system itself is not completely compatible with the "real-time" requirements of physical computing. It is noted that attempts to use

---

[2] 1) *Raspberry Pi User Guide*, Upton and Halfacree, John Wiley and Sons, ISBN 978-1-11846446-5
2) *Practical Raspberry Pi*, Horan, Apress, ISBN 978-1-4302-4971-9
3) *Learn Raspberry Pi with Linux*, Membrey and Hows, Apress, ISBN 978-1-4302-4821-7

GPIO pins for programmed pulse width modulation (PWM) on devices such as LEDs may suffer from "jittering" as the Pi operating system may be involved with internal processes that detract from or interfere with the timed processing of the pulse widths.

A USB connection between the RPi and an Arduino microcontroller is very similar to the ease of use and assembly demonstrated in the preceding DAQFactory-LabJack exercise. Arduino boards are comparable in cost to the RPi, and the Arduino integrated development environment (IDE) is available as a Linux-compatible download from the Arduino and RPi Foundations. By using the Arduino microcontroller board as an intelligent interface between the RPi and an experimental apparatus or setup, significant reproducible and predictable physical computing can be achieved. However, the implementation of an Arduino microcontroller as a smart I/O peripheral for the RPi involves a significant amount of scripting to interface the two systems that is explored in the next chapter and exercise on scripting.

Of the various options available for measuring voltages and hence calculating current flows with the RPi, the least expensive option is the use of a stand-alone analog-to-digital converter (ADC) such as the Microchip MCP3008 integrated circuit (IC). The IC chip costs approximately $5 (CDN) and is a 10-bit successive approximation register (SAR) device. A 10-bit resolution as used in the LabJack, Arduino, and MCP3008 divides the input voltage into 1024 units for quantification. The IC is connected to the RPi GPIO pins as detailed in Figure 2-14 and uses the Python serial peripheral interface (SPI) protocol implemented with the py-spidev Python library. See raspberrypi.org/documentation/hardware/raspberrypi/spi/README for the RPi setup instructions for implementing the SPI protocol on the GPIO pin array.

Experimental

As noted, an inexpensive voltage measurement capability for the RPi can be implemented with the Microchip Technology MCP3008. The chip is a 16-pin, plastic dual in-line package (PDIP), integrated circuit, 10-bit analog-to-digital converter. The IC has eight input channels that can be used to digitize the voltage at up to eight different points in a circuit with respect to a common ground or measure up to four differential voltage drops between eight points in the circuit. (See Chapters 4, 5, and 6 for digital concepts and 10- or 12-bit ADC details, 10 bit $= 2^{10}$ or 1024 and 12 bit $= 2^{12}$ or 4096.)

Figure 2-14 is a graphical depiction of the connections to be made from the RPi GPIO array to the MCP3008 and a schematic drawing of the four channels that can be used to measure the current flow through the colored diodes.

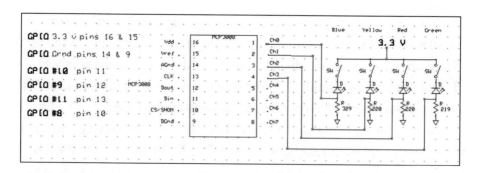

Figure 2-14. *RPi Circuitry for Power Monitoring of LEDs*

To simplify the graphic of Figure 2-14, the connecting wires between the GPIO pins and those on the MCP3008 have not been drawn. The 3.3 V supply of the RPi on the upper-left pin of the GPIO array is connected to pins 16 and 14 on the IC. The remainder of the connections are specified and connected in the same manner.

The Python code for strobing (activating) the ADC chip to conduct
a conversion and then reading and displaying the 10-bit voltage value is
listed in Listing 2-11.

As with all complex experimental systems, the investigator begins
with the simple components testing each and validating its individual
performance as a stand-alone entity. A complex system is assembled by
adding a single component at a time and if possible testing the assembly as
each increment is made until a completed operational apparatus is built.

The early models of the RPi are reported to have been designed to
provide an output current of 3 mA at the 3.3 V logic level, and hence the
entire power draw available was 17 pins × 3 mA = 51 mA in total. Tiny
3 mm indicator LEDs are limited to a maximum current draw of 20 mA
and should be operated in the 16–18 mA range. 5 and 10 mm LEDs draw
currents in the 20–40 mA range and for longer service lives should be
operated at 15–20% below their maximum short-term current handling
capability.

LED emissions are directly proportional to the current flowing through
the diodes. The current recommendations in a data sheet are given
for a device operating at or near its maximum brightness, which is not
always required for experimental work. LED currents of 5–10 mA often
produce ample brightness for experimental work and can be used to avoid
overloading the RPi power connections on the GPIO pins.

To accommodate the limited current available from the RPi GPIO pins,
the circuit of Figure 2-14 can be assembled with readily available 5 mm
LEDs, suitable CLRs, and individual manual power control switches, all
set in the open position during assembly. An array of open switches is
the configuration to be used in the initial testing of the power monitoring
exercise.

Each of the four LEDs in the array should be tested independently,
followed by all of them together, to confirm their illumination when
power is applied from the supply. (See Chapter 1 for the command line
terminal method for manual LED activation.) Once each and all of the

LED diodes have been successfully illuminated, then with the power off, the junction of the diode and its CLR is connected to the appropriate input channel of the ADC. With the ADC correctly wired to the LED array, the connections between the MCP3008 and the RPi GPIO pins can be made, and the Python program can be run. The initial output from the system should indicate no output current for each channel and none for the sum. The simplicity of the system requires a manual operating mode to see the data resulting from the power loading and distribution of the LED lighting system. As each LED is manually switched on and illuminated, the power monitoring program should be run to calculate and display the individual currents drawn and their sum.

By keeping the currents through the LEDs in the 12–16 mA range, the RPi should fully illuminate three of the LEDs easily and be able to illuminate the fourth diode for short periods of time while the power monitoring program collects and displays higher power consumption data. For experiments using more power than is available from the GPIO pins, an auxiliary supply and several CMOS 4050 buffer chips could be used.

Observations

One of the objectives of this exercise is to impart to the investigators using the RPi GPIO pins to provide power to their experimental setup a method to work safely around the limitations of the system.

A typical output in the Python shell from the power monitoring program is depicted in Figure 2-15.

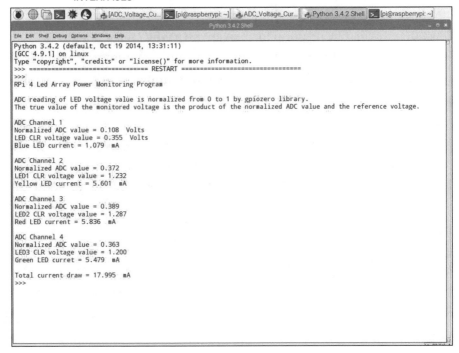

Figure 2-15.   *RPi Display of Power Monitoring Program Output*

Examination of the schematic drawing portion of Figure 2-14 will reveal that the voltage drop across the measured resistance of the current limiting resistor (CLR) is caused by the current flow through the diode-resistor combination. The MCP3008 channels are being used to directly measure the voltage drop across a grounded resistor to indirectly measure the current that is constant throughout the circuit.

Discussion

As an educational computer, the Raspberry Pi is not only able to function in an information processing mode but also as a physical computing platform. However, when used in a physical computing mode, the limitations of the compact, inexpensive system must be recognized.

55

In very simplified terms, the RPi operating system is process driven and
may not immediately respond to an event on a GPIO pin if a higher-
priority process is running in the processor core. Graphics processing is
a very large consumer of computing resources, and hence the RPi should
use the most utilitarian or minimal screen displays as possible when used
in a physical computing mode.

The Raspberry Pi Foundation has written and makes available
several Python libraries that allow the computer to interface with various
hardware devices to extend communication with external devices and
sensors such as the MCP series of analog-to-digital converters.

Code Listings

Listing 2-1. Arduino Code for a Two-Button On and Off Control
Screen

```
// Arduino code for a single led illumination on the red board
// Arduino the pgm waits for an incoming character on com port 4,
// if a 1 the led is turned on if a 0 it is turned off.
const int RedPin = 3;     // red board dig. pin with red led and clr
int incomingByte;       // a variable to hold incoming byte
//
void setup() {
  Serial.begin(9600);         // start the serial port
  pinMode(RedPin, OUTPUT);    // set the pin function
}
void loop() {
  if(Serial.available()> 0) {     // check port for last data byte
  incomingByte = Serial.read();  //
```

```
  if (incomingByte == '1') {      // if is H (ASCII 72), turn
                                         the led on

    digitalWrite(RedPin, HIGH);
  }
  if (incomingByte == '0') {
    digitalWrite(RedPin, LOW);   //if L (ASCII, 76), turn the
                                      led off

  }
  }
}
```

Listing 2-2. Arduino Sketch for Toggling the Red LED on the
Arduino RedBoard from the DAQFactory Single-Button Control
Screen

```
// Toggle an led on/off from one DAQFctry button icon on COM4
// The DAQF QS sends an R to the serial port on com 4. On the
// arduino side the status of the RedLed dp is determined and
// toggled as required.
//
const int RedLedPin = 3;     // red led is on dig pin 3
int oofR = 0;                // power state of red diode
char incomingByte = ' ';     // declare incoming byte
//
void setup() {
  Serial.begin(9600);        // start the serial port
  pinMode(RedLedPin, INPUT); // must initially read the dig. pin
}
```

```
//
void loop() {
  if (Serial.available()) {              // check for incoming data
    char incomingByte = Serial.read();       // read the port
    //Serial.print(incomingByte);            // diagnostic
    if (incomingByte == 'R' && oofR == 0) {  // check flag for
                                             // led status
      pinMode(RedLedPin, OUTPUT);       // set pin for output
      digitalWrite(RedLedPin, HIGH);    // if off turn on
      oofR = 1;                         // set status flag
    }
    else {
      if (incomingByte == 'R' && oofR == 1){ // check flag for
                                             // led status
      pinMode(RedLedPin, OUTPUT);            // set pin mode
      digitalWrite(RedLedPin, LOW);          // turn led off
      oofR = 0;                              // set status flag
      }
    }
  }
}
```

Listing 2-3. Arduino Sketch to Toggle Multiple Colored LEDs from a
DAQFactory Control Screen

```
// Toggle leds on/off from DAQFctry button icons on COM4
// The DAQF QS sends an R, G, O or Y to the serial port on com 4.
// On the arduino side the status of the appropriate led
// dp is determined and toggled as required through a switch
   construct.
//
```

```
const int RedLedPin = 3;          // red led is on dig pin 3
const int GreenLedPin = 4;        // green led on dp 4
const int OrangeLedPin = 5;       // orange led on dp 5
const int YellowLedPin = 6;       // yellow led on d pin 6
//
int oofR = 0;                     // on off flags initialized
int oofG = 0;
int oofO = 0;
int oofY = 0;                     // on off flags initialized
//
char incomingByte = ' ';          // define incoming character
//
void setup() {
 Serial.begin(9600);              // start the serial port
 }
//
void loop()
{
  if (Serial.available())         // check for incoming data
  {
  char incomingByte = Serial.read();  // set char value for
                                      //          switch branching
  Serial.print(incomingByte);     // diagnostic for use in
                                  //           debugging code
  switch(incomingByte)            // branch to desired location/option
  {
  case 'R':                       // Red Led Activation
  if (oofR == 0 ) {               // check status flag
  pinMode(RedLedPin, OUTPUT);     // set pin I/O
```

```
    digitalWrite(RedLedPin, HIGH);              // turn led on
    oofR = 1;                                   // re-set flag
    }
    else {                          // flag is set to 1 so led is on
      pinMode(RedLedPin, OUTPUT);       // set pin mode to output
      digitalWrite(RedLedPin, LOW);     // turn led off
      oofR = 0;                         // re-set flag to off
    }
  break;
  //
  case 'G':                             // Green Led Activation
    if (oofG == 0 ) {                   // check status flag
    pinMode(GreenLedPin, OUTPUT);       // set pin I/O
    digitalWrite(GreenLedPin, HIGH);    // turn led on
    oofG = 1;                           // reset status flag
    }
    else {
      pinMode(GreenLedPin, OUTPUT);
      digitalWrite(GreenLedPin, LOW);
      oofG = 0;
    }
  break;
  //
  case 'O':                             // Orange Led Activation
    if (oofO == 0 ) {
    pinMode(OrangeLedPin, OUTPUT);      // set pin I/O
    digitalWrite(OrangeLedPin, HIGH);
    oofO = 1;
    }
    else {
      pinMode(OrangeLedPin, OUTPUT);
```

```
    digitalWrite(OrangeLedPin, LOW);
    oofO = 0;
  }
break;
case 'Y':                             // Yellow Led Activation
  if (oofY == 0 ) {
  pinMode(YellowLedPin, OUTPUT);      // set pin I/O
  digitalWrite(YellowLedPin, HIGH);
  oofY = 1;
  }
  else {
    pinMode(YellowLedPin, OUTPUT);
    digitalWrite(YellowLedPin, LOW);
    oofY = 0;
  }
break;
  }
  }
  }
```

Listing 2-4. Arduino Sketch to Turn Red LED On or Off and
Measure the Diode Current Draw for Display on the DAQFactory
Control Screen

```
// Arduino code for a single led illumination on the red board
// Arduino the pgm waits for an incoming character on com port 4
// if a 1 the led is turned on
// if a 0 it is turned off.
// A0 is wired to Rd led junction and the Arduino calculates
// the led current and prints the value to the serial port.
```

```
//
const int RedPin = 3;   // red board dig. pin with red led and clr
int incomingByte;       // a variable to hold incoming byte
float iRed = 0;         // the led current through the CLR
//
void setup() {
  Serial.begin(9600);                        // start the serial port
  pinMode(RedPin, OUTPUT);                   // set the pin function
}
void loop() {
  if(Serial.available()> 0) {      // check port for last data byte
  incomingByte = Serial.read();    // read serial port value
  if (incomingByte == '1') {       // if is 1, turn the led on
    digitalWrite(RedPin, HIGH);    // set I/O of pin
  // calculate led current and print to the serial port
  iRed = ((analogRead(A0) * 4.8828 )/216);
  Serial.println(iRed);     // note the line feed indication to
                                 append 013\010
// to the transmitted character to aid in the DAQFactory
  parsing of the incoming code.
  }
  //
  if (incomingByte == '0') {
    digitalWrite(RedPin, LOW);           // if 0, turn the led off
  // calculate led current and print to the serial port
  iRed = ((analogRead(A0) * 4.8828 )/216);  // ensures the LED is off
  Serial.println(iRed);    // \013\010 for DAQFactory parsing code
  }
  }
}
```

Listing 2-5. Quick Sequence Code for On Button

```
device.ardyRb.Purge()     // clear residual data from input buffer
device.ardyRb.Write('1')     // write to serial port
delay(0.1)                   // delay to allow processing
global ldCurrnt              // declare variable to be visible
                                throughout
                             // DAQFactory program
private string datain        // declare datain variable
datain = device.ardyRb.readUntil(13)    // parse data up to
                                           line feed and
                                           carriage return
ldCurrnt = strToDouble(datain)      // convert character to
                                       numeric value
```

Listing 2-6. Quick Sequence Alternate Code for Off Button

```
device.ardyRb.Purge()        // clear old data from the serial
                                port buffer
device.ardyRb.Write('0')     // write a zero to the serial port
                                to switch led off
delay(0.1)                   // allow code to be processed
global ldCurrnt              // declare individual diode
                                current to be global
ldCurrnt = 0                 // set individual diode current to 0
```

Listing 2-7. Arduino Code for Single Button Icon Toggling LED On/
Off with Power Measurement

```
// Toggle an led on/off from one DAQFctry button icon on COM4
// The DAQF QS sends an R to the serial port on com 4. On the
// arduino side the status of the RedLed dp is determined and
// toggled as required.
```

```
//
const int RedLedPin = 3;              // red led is on dig pin 3
int oofR = 0;                         // power state of red diode
char incomingByte = ' ';              // declare incoming byte
float iRed = 0;                       // red led current
//
void setup() {
  Serial.begin(9600);                 // start the serial port
  pinMode(RedLedPin, INPUT);          // must initially read the
                                         dig. pin

}
//
void loop() {
  if (Serial.available()) {            // check for incoming data
    char incomingByte = Serial.read();
    //Serial.print(incomingByte);      // diagnostic for code
                                          de-bugging
    if (incomingByte == 'R' && oofR == 0) {  // check action
                                                required and
                                                status
      pinMode(RedLedPin, OUTPUT);      // set pin I/O mode
      digitalWrite(RedLedPin, HIGH);   // turn diode current on
      iRed = ((analogRead(A0) * 4.8828)/216 );  // calculate
                                                  diode current
      Serial.println(iRed);      // send value to serial port
                                    with LF-CR
      oofR = 1;                   // set status flag to "diode on"
    }
```

```
    else {
      if (incomingByte == 'R' && oofR == 1){
      // alternate action toggle to off
      pinMode(RedLedPin, OUTPUT);         // set pin I/O mode
      digitalWrite(RedLedPin, LOW);       // turn power off
      iRed = 0;                   // set red diode current to 0
      Serial.println(iRed);
      oofR = 0;
      }
    }
  }
}
```

Listing 2-8. Arduino Sketch for a DAQFactory Four-Button Control Screen and Power Consumption Indicators

```
// Toggle leds on/off from DAQFctry button icons on COM4
// The DAQF QS sends an R, G, O or Y to the serial port on com
// 4. On the arduino side the status of the appropriate led dp is
// determined and toggled as required through a switch construct.
//
// power drawn calculations, each led has a CLR and the voltage
// on the junction of the resistor and led is measured and used to
// calculate diode
// current by A0 to A3 respectively. Current calcln only done
// when diode activated.
//
const int RedLedPin = 3;         // red led is on dig pin 3
const int GreenLedPin = 4;       // green led on dp 4
const int OrangeLedPin = 5;      // orange led on dp 5
const int YellowLedPin = 6;      // yellow led on d pin 6
//
```

65

```
int oofR = 0;                          // on off flags initialized
int oofG = 0;
int oofO = 0;
int oofY = 0;                          // on off flags initialized
//
char incomingByte = ' ';               // define incoming character
//
float iRed = 0;                        // red led current in
                                          decimal float format

float iGreen = 0;
float iOrange = 0;
float iYellow = 0;
float itotal = 0;
//
void setup() {
 Serial.begin(9600);                   // start the serial port
 }
//
void loop()
{
  if (Serial.available())              // check for incoming data
  {
  char incomingByte = Serial.read();   // set char value for
                                          switch branching
// Serial.print(incomingByte);         // diagnostic
  switch(incomingByte)                 // branch to desired
                                          location/option
```

```
{
case 'R':                                  // Red Led Activation
if (oofR == 0 ) {
pinMode(RedLedPin, OUTPUT);                // set pin I/O
digitalWrite(RedLedPin, HIGH);             // turn led on
oofR = 1;                                  // set flag
iRed = ((analogRead(A0)* 4.8828)/216);     // calc i when
                                              led on
//Serial.print(analogRead(A0));            // diagnostics
//Serial.print("iRed = ");                 // diagnostics
Serial.println(iRed);                      // add CR-LF
itotal = iRed + iGreen + iOrange + iYellow;
// calculate total power consumption
//Serial.print("itotal = ");               // diagnostics
Serial.println(itotal);                    // add CR-LF
}
else {                          // flag is set to 1 so led is on
  pinMode(RedLedPin, OUTPUT); // set pin mode to output
  digitalWrite(RedLedPin, LOW);            // turn led off
  oofR = 0;                                // re-set flag to off
  iRed = 0;                        // turn iRed contribution to
                                      itotal off
  Serial.println(iRed);          // send data to DAQFtry
  itotal = iRed + iGreen + iOrange + iYellow;
  // calculate total current draw
  //Serial.print("itotal = ");                // diagnostics
  Serial.println(itotal);   // send to serial port with CR-LF
  }
```

```
break;
//
case 'G':                                    // Green Led Activation
  if (oofG == 0 ) {                          // check status flag
  pinMode(GreenLedPin, OUTPUT);              // set pin I/O
  digitalWrite(GreenLedPin, HIGH);           // turn led on
  oofG = 1;                                  // reset status flag
  iGreen = ((analogRead(A1)*4.8828)/215);    // calc diodecurrent
  //Serial.print("iGreen = ");               // diagnostics
  Serial.println(iGreen);                    // send data with CR-LF
  itotal = iRed + iGreen + iOrange + iYellow;
  // calculate total current draw
  //Serial.print("itotal = ");               // diagnostics
  Serial.println(itotal);                    // send with CR-LF
  }
  else {
    pinMode(GreenLedPin, OUTPUT);            // set pin I/O mode
    digitalWrite(GreenLedPin, LOW);          // turn green led off
    oofG = 0;                                // set green status flag
    iGreen = 0;                              // turn green contribution
                                             //   to total off

    Serial.println(iGreen);                  // send green current value
                                             //   with CR-LF

    itotal = iRed + iGreen + iOrange + iYellow;
    // calculate total current draw
    //Serial.print("itotal = ");                     // diagnostic
    Serial.println(itotal);    // send total current with CR-LF
  }
```

```
break;
//
case '0':                                   // Orange Led Activation
  if (oof0 == 0 ) {                         // check status flag
  pinMode(OrangeLedPin, OUTPUT);            // set pin I/O
  digitalWrite(OrangeLedPin, HIGH);         // set pin I/O
  oof0 = 1;                                 // set orange flag to led on
  iOrange = ((analogRead(A2)*4.8828)/215);  // calculate orange
                                            //            led current draw
  //Serial.print("iOrange = ");             // diagnostic
  Serial.println(iOrange);     // send to serial port with CR-LF
  itotal = iRed + iGreen + iOrange + iYellow;
  // calculate total current draw
  //Serial.print("itotal = ");              // diagnostic
  Serial.println(itotal);                   // send total to
                                            //             serial port
                                            //             with CR-LF

  }
  else {                                    // orange led is on
    pinMode(OrangeLedPin, OUTPUT);          // set pin I/O
    digitalWrite(OrangeLedPin, LOW);        // turn orange led off
    oof0 = 0;                               // reset orange status
                                            //          flag to off

    iOrange = 0;                            // turn orange contribution
                                            //          to total off

    Serial.println(iOrange);                // send out orange current
                                            //          with CR-LF
    itotal = iRed + iGreen + iOrange + iYellow;
    // calculate total current draw
    //Serial.print("itotal = ");            // diagnostics
    Serial.println(itotal);  // send out total current draw with CR-LF
```

```
  }
break;
case 'Y':                                // Yellow Led Activation
  if (oofY == 0 ) {                      // led is off
  pinMode(YellowLedPin, OUTPUT);         // set pin I/O
  digitalWrite(YellowLedPin, HIGH);      // turn yellow led on
  oofY = 1;                              // re-set lag to led on
  iYellow = ((analogRead(A3)*4.8828)/217);
  // calculate yellow led current
  //Serial.print("iYellow = ");          // diagnostic
  Serial.println(iYellow);               // yellow led value to
                                         //    serial port with CR-LF
  itotal = iRed + iGreen + iOrange + iYellow;
  // calculate total current draw
  //Serial.print("itotal = ");                        // diagnostic
  Serial.println(itotal);       // send to serial port with CR-LF
  }
  else {                          // yellow led on
    pinMode(YellowLedPin, OUTPUT);  // set pin I/O mode
    digitalWrite(YellowLedPin, LOW);    // turn yellow led off
    oofY = 0;                       // re-set flag to yellow led off
    iYellow = 0;                    // set yellow led current to 0
    Serial.println(iYellow);  // send value to serial port with CR-LF
    itotal = iRed + iGreen + iOrange + iYellow;
    // calculate total current and send with CR-LF
    //Serial.print("itotal = ");                     // diagnostic
    Serial.println(itotal);    // send total current with CR-LF
  }
break;
  }
 }
}
```

Listing 2-9. Toggle Red LED DAQFactory Quick Sequence

```
device.ardyRb.Purge()       // clear serial buffer
device.ardyRb.Write('R')    // initiate repeat activation
delay(0.1)                  // allow code to execute
global ldCurrnt             // declare global variable in
                               DAQFactory code
private string datain    // define local variable in DAQFactory code
datain = device.ardyRb.readUntil(13)  // parse out character
                                         codes for numeric
                                         value
ldCurrnt = strToDouble(datain)        // convert character
                                         codes to numeric value
```

Listing 2-10. Toggle Red LED DAQFactory Quick Sequence with
Diode Power Draw

```
device.ardyRb.Purge()          // clear the serial buffer
device.ardyRb.Write('R')       // send R to serial port for
                                  repeat activation
delay(0.1)                     // allow for code execution
global iRed                    // declare diode current as
                                  global variable
global iTotal                  // declare total current as
                                  global variable
private string datain1         // declare private variable for
                                  1st data value
private string datain2         // declare private variable for
                                  2nd data value
datain1 = device.ardyRb.ReadUntil(13)    // parse out 1st value
datain2 = device.ardyRb.ReadUntil(13)    // parse out 2nd value
```

```
iRed = strToDouble(datain1)          // convert characters to
                                        numerical values

iTotal = strToDouble(datain2)        // and assign to declared
                                        variables
```

Listing 2-11. Python Code for the Raspberry Pi Monitoring the
Power Draw of a Four-LED Array

```
print("RPi 4 Led Array Power Monitoring Program")
print() # a blank line for output screen spacing
print("ADC reading of LED voltage value is normalized from 0 to
1 by gpiozero library.")
print("The true value of the monitored voltage is the product
of the normalized ADC value and the reference voltage.")
print()
# a single normalized value is printed each time the module is run

from gpiozero import MCP3008
# create an object representing the device and assign the input
  channels
ADC_vlu = MCP3008(0)    # the number in brackets is the channel
on the device
ADC_vlu1 = MCP3008(1)
ADC_vlu2 = MCP3008(2)
ADC_vlu3 = MCP3008(3)
#
print("ADC Channel 1")
print('Normalized ADC value = %.3f'%ADC_vlu.value,' Volts')
# the blue LED in the author' circuit
#
# convert object, value into a numerical parameter
ledVltg = float(ADC_vlu.value) * 3.3
print('LED CLR voltage value = %.3f'%ledVltg, ' Volts')
```

```python
# calculate the LED current from Ohms law
blue = (float((ADC_vlu.value) *3.3) / 329) * 1000
print('Blue LED current = %.3f'%blue,' mA')
#
print()
#
print("ADC Channel 2")
print('Normalized ADC value = %.3f'%ADC_vlu1.value)
# the yellow LED in the author's circuit
#
# convert object, value into a numerical parameter
led1Vltg = float(ADC_vlu1.value) * 3.3
print('LED1 CLR voltage value = %.3f'%led1Vltg)
# calculate the LED1 current from Ohms law
yellow = (float((ADC_vlu1.value) *3.3) / 220) * 1000
print('Yellow LED current = %.3f'%yellow,' mA')
#
print()
#
print("ADC Channel 3")
print('Normalized ADC value = %.3f'%ADC_vlu2.value)
# the red LED in the author's circuit
#
# convert object, value into a numerical parameter
led2Vltg = float(ADC_vlu2.value) * 3.3
print('LED2 CLR voltage value = %.3f'%led2Vltg)
# calculate the LED2 current from Ohms law
red = (float((ADC_vlu2.value) *3.3) / 220) * 1000
print('Red LED current = %.3f'%red,' mA')
#
```

```
print()
#
print("ADC Channel 4")
print('Normalized ADC value = %.3f'%ADC_vlu3.value)
# the green LED in the author's circuit
#
# convert object, value into a numerical parameter
led3Vltg = float(ADC_vlu3.value) * 3.3
print('LED3 CLR voltage value = %.3f'%led3Vltg)
# calculate the LED3 current from Ohms law
green = (float((ADC_vlu3.value) *3.3) / 219) * 1000
print('Green LED current = %.3f'%green,' mA')
#
print()
#
ttl_Currnt_drw = blue + yellow + red + green
print('Total current draw = %.3f'%ttl_Currnt_drw, ' mA')
```

Summary

 – An interactive control panel GUI able to activate
    multiple components in an external experiment and
    display data from that experiment is developed.

 – Microcontrollers can be used with robust industrial
    pre-configured SCADA systems or with readily
    available inexpensive components and the appropriate
    programming.

 – In Chapter 3, more detailed scripting and programming
    techniques will be introduced.

CHAPTER 3

Introduction to Scripting

SCADA is an industrial concept in which information about an active process is collected and then used to both monitor and control that operation. Scripting, in both the industrial-scale applications and these scientific measurement experiments, permits the automation of process control or data acquisition. In this chapter, code assembled into small programs called sequences in the DAQFactory (DF) software will be used to control and monitor the LED circuitry assembled on the breadboard in the previous exercises.

The DF user manual indicates that the scripting language syntax used to create sequences is similar to most standard languages such as the variations of C, Python, Visual Basic, Pascal, and others such as Fortran.

The previous notation made with respect to the naming of channels is also applicable to the scripting language used in DF. The language is case sensitive, and thus it is very important to avoid typing errors and spelling mismatches in naming channels, variables, scripts, and pages. It is suggested that the C style of naming or a variation be used as noted in these MySpecialName, My_Special_Name, My_Spcl_Nm, and MySpclNm examples. Choose names that are expressive and meaningful to minimize errors.

It is strongly suggested that documentation in the form of liberal use of comments and indentation of code segments be used, to make the script code legible and easy to follow. The DAQFactory code editor used to create

© Richard J. Smythe 2021
R. J. Smythe, *Arduino in Science*, https://doi.org/10.1007/978-1-4842-6778-3_3

sequences indents when the Tab key is pressed, and a dotted vertical line delineates the code blocks. Other investigators must be able to follow code scripts and reproduce any scientific work.

The mathematical operations available for use in scripted sequences are described in the DAQFactory software manual in the section "Expressions." An expression is a formula that calculates a result from some initial values. Expressions have been used in the variable value screen components in the previous exercise to calculate individual colored LED currents and the total current being drawn.

As in most languages, variables or arrays must be declared with declaration statements, have appropriate names, and have instances created, before use in sequence scripting.

For the majority of researchers, the skills required for creating and running programming or scripting codes are best developed by practice. Virtually all of the popular programming languages in wide use today can be learned through an abundance of online tutorials. The tutorials and language documentation can be reviewed and practiced at a rate that is comfortable for the investigator. The DAQFactory manual has an introductory tutorial and a detailed documentation that should then be kept at hand for reference as the investigator develops a facility for the scripting of DAQFactory sequence code.

Experimental

Once an electro-mechanical system is configured and the hardware validated on a breadboard, do not hesitate to experiment with the scripting code on a fresh new DAQFactory page. Science is experimental in nature, and this manuscript is hopefully an aid to grasping the fundamentals of physical computing and applying them to conduct experimental measurements as quickly as possible.

Hardware

Use the multicolored LED circuitry from the previous exercise as the process operations whose control will be transferred from direct manual screen control to a coded script or sequence.

For the circuit schematic, see Chapter 2, Figure 2-2.

Software

Page Components Required

For the required basic screen configuration, a text message should be placed over a button control. The text content should indicate that the button controls the starting and stopping of a script that produces a short "light show" on the bank of four multicolored LEDs.

In previous exercises using channels, the channels had to have been created and entered into the channel table in order to appear in the pop-up, typing aid listing. The same is true for script sequences that must be named and entered into the sequence summary table. Once named and entered into the summary table, the appropriate sequences can be selected from the listing during button configuration as depicted in Figures 3-1 and 3-2.

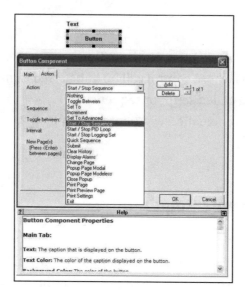

Figure 3-1. *Button Action Tab Entries*

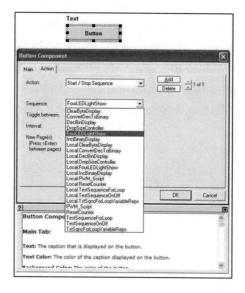

Figure 3-2. *Named Sequence Entry Listing*

Scripting

DAQFactory has a script entry and editing program that assembles the code as depicted in Figure 3-3.

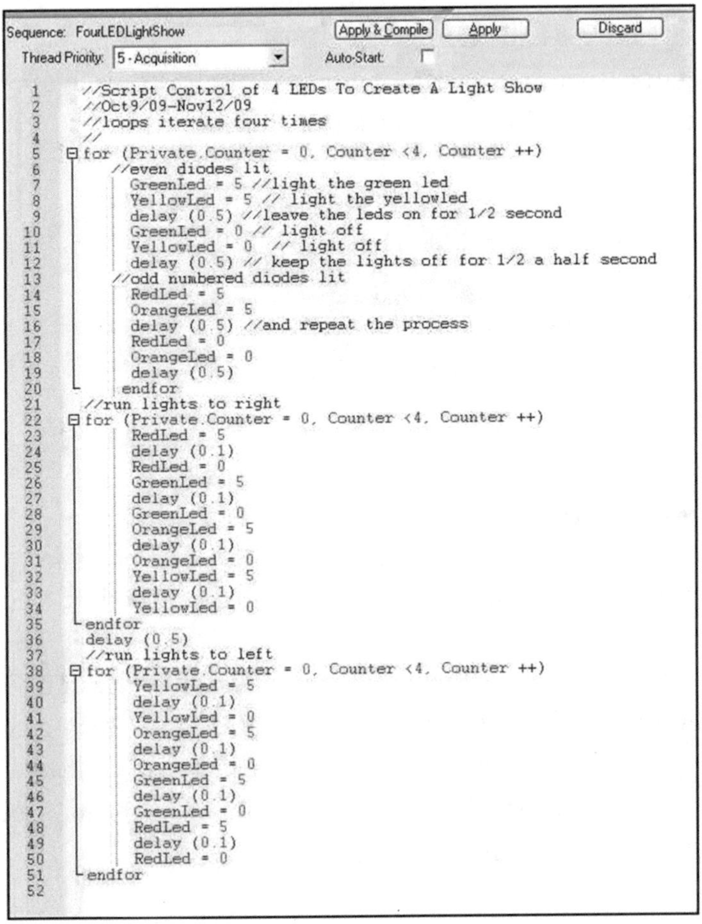


```
//Script Control of 4 LEDs To Create A Light Show
//Oct9/09-Nov12/09
//loops iterate four times
//
for (Private.Counter = 0, Counter <4, Counter ++)
   //even diodes lit
      GreenLed = 5 //light the green led
      YellowLed = 5 // light the yellowled
      delay (0.5) //leave the leds on for 1/2 second
      GreenLed = 0 // light off
      YellowLed = 0  // light off
      delay (0.5) // keep the lights off for 1/2 a half second
   //odd numbered diodes lit
      RedLed = 5
      OrangeLed = 5
      delay (0.5) //and repeat the process
      RedLed = 0
      OrangeLed = 0
      delay (0.5)
   endfor
//run lights to right
for (Private.Counter = 0, Counter <4, Counter ++)
      RedLed = 5
      delay (0.1)
      RedLed = 0
      GreenLed = 5
      delay (0.1)
      GreenLed = 0
      OrangeLed = 5
      delay (0.1)
      OrangeLed = 0
      YellowLed = 5
      delay (0.1)
      YellowLed = 0
endfor
delay (0.5)
//run lights to left
for (Private.Counter = 0, Counter <4, Counter ++)
      YellowLed = 5
      delay (0.1)
      YellowLed = 0
      OrangeLed = 5
      delay (0.1)
      OrangeLed = 0
      GreenLed = 5
      delay (0.1)
      GreenLed = 0
      RedLed = 5
      delay (0.1)
      RedLed = 0
endfor
```

Figure 3-3. *Scripting for the LED Light Show*

The scripting for the light show uses a collection of coded statements that toggle the channel output voltage values for the individual colored LEDs to 5 volts and then reset them to 0 volts. By embedding delay statements in between the light activation lines and encasing blocks of code inside iterative "for loops," a "light show" can be created. The documentation in the code of Figure 3-3 is hopefully self-explanatory. The author's diodes were ordered from the left as red, green, orange, and yellow. Thus, the even diodes of 2 and 4 were green and yellow, while the odd diodes were red and orange.

The Start Display button can be grouped with a descriptive text component to form a panel as shown in Figure 3-4.

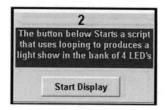

Figure 3-4. *Scripting Activation Button*

Observations

When the Start Display button is activated with a mouse click, a light show occurs on the bank of four LED lights.

When the light show sequence was run on an older desktop computer with a CPU running at 1.48 GHz with 736 MB RAM and a high-resolution graphics card, the power monitoring panel created in the previous exercise was just able to keep up with the light display timing of the half-second delays, while the graphical display was not.

Discussion

This exercise demonstrates the ability of the SCADA software to control the activation of electronic circuits through software programming and the HMI device.

Details in the user manual describe the use of the descriptive text screen component with several others that have the tabbed properties window allowing the setting of certain properties and the selection of an action. The descriptive text component has the ability to display a Running/Stopped message, indicating the status of the selected sequence attached to the screen component.

A scripted sequence of code runs virtually at the clock speed of the computer and hence is much faster than either the screen's ability to display rapid changes, the HMI's speed, or the rate at which human vision is able to follow.

The inability of the graphical power monitor display to keep up with the scripted sequence switching of the LED currents is indicative of the system limitations. The DAQFactory program is a video display–intensive software, and if insufficient time is available for painting the screen, the display lags or does not even update. In marginal cases, as was possible with the older desktop computer, lowering the screen resolution allowed a sluggish screen to perform adequately.

High-speed data transfers are an area of specialty often required in spectroscopy, reaction kinetics, and physics. The current exercises are focused on the development of methods that use time scales measured in seconds and longer. Higher-speed "data streaming" for faster capture rates is dealt with both in the appropriate hardware or software user manuals and in later sections of this manuscript.

DAQFactory Sequences: Arduino LED Array

In Chapter 2, an inexpensive microcontroller board was used in place of a robust industrial-grade interface to respond to a control screen set up in a SCADA system. The low-cost benefit of using the Arduino can be realized in this scripting exercise if the experimenter can devote the time required to rewrite the serial communications code developed to monitor the power draw of the Arduino-mounted LED array to accommodate a scripted light show.

Experimental

The Arduino microcontroller is wired with four different colored diodes as depicted in Chapter 2, Figure 2-9. The Arduino holds the C program of Listing 3-1 that provides the LED illumination required, while the regular or Quick Sequence DAQFactory code in Listing 3-2 of the following programs writes the appropriate characters to the serial port (all code listings provided in the "Code Listings" section at the end of the chapter).

A DAQFactory control panel is set up as depicted in Figure 3-5.

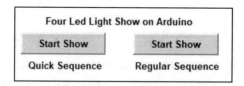

Figure 3-5. *A Dual-Button Scripting Activation Screen*

Although the Quick Sequence code and the regular sequence code are identical, the Quick Sequence code is visible only through the Quick Sequence selection. Regular sequences can be used anywhere in DAQFactory and are visible on all sequence selection listings.

Discussion

The DAQFactory code listing depicted in Figure 3-3 makes use of channels to vary the LabJack output connections between 5 volts and ground. The upper- or lowercase sequence codes sent to the serial port are collected by the Arduino logic and power the digital pin connected to the appropriate LED on or off directly without the use of complex channels.

Raspberry Pi

The RPi uses Python and the gpio and gpiozero Python libraries to communicate with and control directly the individual pins of the GPIO array. The RPi can only set a pin to a high or low voltage for the output mode or read the pin status as high or low in the input mode.

With careful design and care in programming, a "light show" can be assembled to run directly off the GPIO pins without the need for any intermediate hardware. As detailed in Chapter 1, Figure 1-16, there are two versions of the GPIO array: on earlier models, there were 26 pins, while on the newer models, there are 40. The first 26-pin array is common to all models, while newer versions of the RPi have an additional 14 pins as identified in Figure 1-16. In summary the 40-pin array consists of 26 GPIO pins, 2 3.3-volt and 2 5-volt power pins, 8 ground pins, and 2 serial input-output pins, assigned and located as detailed in Table 3-1.

A simple four-LED "light show" program in Python code is in Listing 3-3.

In Chapter 2, the RPi was able to power the four LEDs for short periods of time, while the Python program read the ADC voltages and computed the total power draw from the GPIO array. In this exercise, scripting creates timed sequences of illumination to produce a simple "light show." If more light sources are added to the prototyping board to increase the visual appeal of the display created, the pin outputs should be buffered to avoid the possibility of overloading the current supply capability of the RPi.

A high input impedance buffer chip such as the CD4050 hex non-inverting integrated circuit as used in Chapter 1 can be employed to buffer the GPIO pins to handle many small current loadings, while a chip such as the ULN2803 Darlington transistor array can handle up to 500 mA for each of the eight buffered GPIO pins. (The CMOS 4050 high-impedance buffer chips are $0.50 CDN, while the ULN2803 chips are $2.50 CDN.)

Table 3-1 displays the GPIO pin names and their positions in the 0.1 in (2.45 mm) spacing array on the SBC. (When viewed from the top of the RPi board with the array to the right, the number 1 pins are at the top, while the number 20 pins of the right- and left-hand columns are at the bottom adjacent to the USB connectors.)

Table 3-1. *Assignment and Positioning of the RPi GPIO Pin Array*

GPIO Pin	Location of GPIO Pin in RPi Array	GPIO Pin	Location of GPIO Pin in RPi Array
2	left hand column #2	15	right hand column #5
3	left hand column #3	16	right hand column #18
4	left hand column #4	17	left hand column #6
5	left hand column #15	18	right hand column #6
6	left hand column #16	19	left hand column #18
7	right hand column #13	20	right hand column #19
8	right hand column #12	21	right hand column #20
9	left hand column #11	22	left hand column #8
10	left hand column #10	23	right hand column #8
11	left hand column #12	24	right hand column #9
12	right hand column #16	25	right hand column #11
13	left hand column #17	26	left hand column #19
14	right hand column #4	27	left hand column #27
3.3 volts	left hand column #1	5 volts	right hand column #1
3.3 volts	left hand column #9	5 volts	right hand column #2
Grounds	right hand column #3, #7, #10, #15, #17	Grounds	left hand column #5, #13, #20
I/O pin	left hand column #14	I/O pin	right hand column #14

With a sufficiently powerful auxiliary supply and CMOS or Darlington pair buffering of the RPi pins, scripting should be able to control up to 26 LEDs.

Code Listings

Listings 3-1 through 3-3 provide the complete programs for the chapter.

Listing 3-1. Arduino LED Illumination Code

```
// Arduino code for multiple led illumination on the red board
// Arduino the prgrm waits for an incoming character on com
// port 4 and then processes the data to identify which led is
// to be turned on or off. R, G, O and Y turn the diode ON and
// r, g, o, and y turn the diode OFF.
//
int RedPin = 3;                    // red board dig. pin with red
                                   led and clr
```

```
const int GreenPin = 4;        // red board dig. pin with
                                  green led and clr

const int OrangePin = 5;       // red board dig. pin with red
                                  led and clr

const int YellowPin = 6;       // red board dig. pin with
                                  yellow led and clr
char incomingByte = ' ';       // variable to hold incoming byte
//
void setup() {
  Serial.begin(9600);                  // start the serial port
  pinMode(RedPin, OUTPUT);             // set the pin function
  pinMode(GreenPin, OUTPUT);
  pinMode(OrangePin, OUTPUT);
  pinMode(YellowPin, OUTPUT);
}
void loop() {
  //
  while (Serial.available() == 0)      // wait for a character
  {
                                   // do nothing until data arrives
  }
  if (Serial.available() > 0)              // a char has arrived
  {
    char incomingByte = Serial.read();
      // set character comparison variable to new char
  //Serial.print(incomingByte);                 //diagnostic
  if (incomingByte == 'R' ) {      // R sets the red led
                                      power to high

    // Serial.print("logic OK");   // logic diagnostic
    digitalWrite(RedPin, HIGH);     // turn red led on
    }
```

```
if (incomingByte == 'r' ) {        // turn red led off
  //Serial.print(incomingByte);    // diagnostic
  digitalWrite(RedPin, LOW);       // r sets the red led
                                   //   power to low

}
if (incomingByte == 'G') {         // G sets the green led
                                   //   power to high

  digitalWrite(GreenPin, HIGH);
}
if (incomingByte == 'g') {
  digitalWrite(GreenPin, LOW);     // g sets the green led
                                   //   power to low

}
if (incomingByte == 'O') {         // O sets the orange led
                                   //   power to high

  digitalWrite(OrangePin, HIGH);
}
if (incomingByte == 'o') {
  digitalWrite(OrangePin, LOW);    // o sets the orange led
                                   //   power to low

}
if (incomingByte == 'Y') {         // Y sets the yellow led
                                   //   power to high

  digitalWrite(YellowPin, HIGH);
}
if (incomingByte == 'y') {
  digitalWrite(YellowPin, LOW);    // y sets the yellow led
                                   //   power to low

}
}
}
```

Listing 3-2. DAQFactory Regular Sequence Code for Light Show

```
// Scripted Control of 4 Leds on an Arduino MC for a Simple
// Light Show DAQFactory script uses serial port transmission
// to control MC. Buttons on a DAQFactory control screen
// activate a quick sequence or regular sequence scripting, to
// transmit the led activation codes to the serial port where
// the Arduino resident C code parses the commands and
// activates the appropriate diode.
// Main loop iterates four times. May 21, 2019
//
for (Private.Counter = 0, Counter < 4, Counter ++)
   // even diodes lit
   device.ardyRb.Write('G')            // light the green led
   device.ardyRb.Write('Y')            // light the yellow led
   delay(0.5)               // leave the lights on for 1/2 sec.
   device.ardyRb.Write('g')      // green led off
   device.ardyRb.Write('y')      // yellow led off
   delay(0.5)               // keep lights off for 1/2 sec
   // odd numbered diodes lit
   device.ardyRb.Write('R')              // red on
   device.ardyRb.Write('O')              // orange on
   delay(0.5)                            // time delay
   device.ardyRb.Write('r')              // red off
   device.ardyRb.Write('o')              // orange off
   delay(0.5)                            // time delay
endfor
// run lights to right
for (Private.Counter = 0, Counter < 4, Counter ++)
   device.ardyRb.Write('R')              // red on
```

```
    delay(0.1)                          // on for 1/10 sec
    device.ardyRb.Write('r')            // red off
    device.ardyRb.Write('G')            // green on
    delay(0.1)                          // on for 1/10 sec
    device.ardyRb.Write('g')            // green off
    device.ardyRb.Write('O')            // orange on
    delay(0.1)                          // on for 1/10 sec
    device.ardyRb.Write('o')            // orange off
    device.ardyRb.Write('Y')            // yellow on
    delay(0.1)                          // on for 1/10 sec
    device.ardyRb.Write('y')            // yellow off
endfor
//
delay (0.5)
// run lights to left
for (Private.Counter = 0, Counter < 4,Counter ++)
    device.ardyRb.Write('Y')                // yellow on
    delay(0.1)                              // on for 1/10 sec
    device.ardyRb.Write('y')                // yellow off
    device.ardyRb.Write('O')                // orange on
    delay(0.1)                              // on for 1/10 sec
    device.ardyRb.Write('o')                // orange off
    device.ardyRb.Write('G')                // green on
    delay(0.1)                              // on for 1/10 sec
    device.ardyRb.Write('g')                // green off
    device.ardyRb.Write('R')                // red on
    delay(0.1)                              // on for 1/10 sec
    device.ardyRb.Write('r')                // red off
    endfor
```

Listing 3-3. Raspberry Pi Scripted "Light Show"

```
# Led "Light Show" Ex. 3 Scripting on Raspberry Pi
# Pins are numbered sequentially from the top down in the right
# and left columns for ease of assignment and counting when
# wiring jumpers
from gpiozero import LED
from time import sleep
# Define and assign the leds
redLed = LED(2) # left column pin 2
grnLed = LED(3) # left column pin 3
orngLed = LED(4) # left column pin 4
yelLed = LED(5) # left column pin 15
# repeat code for flashing 4 times
for i in range(4):
    redLed.on()
    grnLed.on()
    orngLed.on()
    yelLed.on()
    sleep(1)
    redLed.off()
    grnLed.off()
    orngLed.off()
    yelLed.off()
    sleep(1)
# reoeat code for streaming to left 4 times
for i in range(4):
    redLed.on()
    sleep(0.1)
    redLed.off()
```

```
    grnLed.on()
    sleep(0.1)
    grnLed.off()
    orngLed.on()
    sleep(0.1)
    orngLed.off()
    yelLed.on()
    sleep(0.1)
    yelLed.off()
# repeat code for streaming to the right 4 times
for i in range(4):
    yelLed.on()
    sleep(0.1)
    yelLed.off()
    orngLed.on()
    sleep(0.1)
    orngLed.off()
    grnLed.on()
    sleep(0.1)
    grnLed.off()
    redLed.on()
    sleep(0.1)
    redLed.off()
# repeat code for alternate pair flashing 4 times
for i in range(4):
    redLed.on()
    orngLed.on()
    sleep(1)
    redLed.off()
    orngLed.off()
    grnLed.on()
```

```
yelLed.on()
sleep(1)
grnLed.off()
yelLed.off()
```

Summary

- Commercial SCADA software has a scripting facility to augment the built-in control functions and enable communication with remote processes or experimental setups.

- SCADA systems assembled from inexpensive readily available components require more detailed program development in the programming languages of the computing platforms in use.

- Scripting or programming techniques will be further developed in Chapter 4 when the host screen is used to enter and display data.

CHAPTER 4

Data Entry from the Screen

A control system must include the capability of entering data from the screen, to be able to modify or vary the operation of a sequence or process. In this chapter, numerical values entered from the keyboard are used to modify scripted sequences of programming code that oscillate LEDs on and off for a predetermined number of cycles. In addition, two options are created for the modes of power control in which the illumination for the diode cycles from full on to off and the diode output intensity is incrementally stepped from off to full brightness to create a "fade" or "fading" effect. LED brightness is determined by the current through the device. The maximum current through the LED is set by the current limiting resistor (CLR) placed in series with the diode, power source, and ground. The current through the LED can be regulated by varying the voltage of the supply. However, diode intensity control by voltage variation can only be effective above the voltage level required for conduction in the device, typically 1.8–3 volts.

In this chapter, a DAQFactory sequence code that increments the power applied to the diode in a fixed number of voltage increments is created with a screen confirmation of the entered data value. This exercise also demonstrates the ability of the software to appear to run two sequences simultaneously in what is often termed a "threaded" application.

© Richard J. Smythe 2021
R. J. Smythe, *Arduino in Science*, https://doi.org/10.1007/978-1-4842-6778-3_4

The various control and monitoring options are then grouped together in a simple graphical user interface (GUI) data entry, process control panel.

Diode intensity is more efficiently controlled with a technique known as pulse width modulation (PWM). In a PWM control operation, full power is applied to the load being driven as a series of square wave voltage pulses whose time width is altered in a controlled manner or modulated with respect to increasing or decreasing time period. Both the frequency of the square wave power source and the pulse width of the power application can be numerically controlled or modulated from screen input values. (Greater details on the application and implementation of PWM are part of Chapter 7.)

An alternative screen data entry exercise using a much less expensive microcontroller has been developed. The microcontroller exercise is being presented as with the previous exercises with a minimum of explanation of the more complex code required to implement the exercise. Details of microcontroller usage are introduced later in the manuscript at which point some of the advantages and deficiencies of these relatively inexpensive devices can be fully appreciated.

Hardware

The red LED electronic circuit wired for the previous exercises as indicated in Chapter 1, Figure 1-3, is to be used for a portion of this exercise; and a green LED is wired to the first analog output channel (AO 0) on the LabJack terminal board. The AO 0 signal is wired into the base of a 2N3904 transistor, in accordance with the schematic in Figure 4-1.

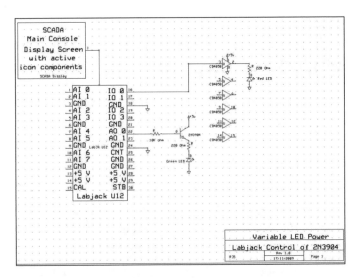

Figure 4-1. *Prototype Circuit for DAQFactory Control Screen with Data Entry Facility*

The collector and emitter of the transistor are connected so as the base voltage controls the size of current from the +5 V supply to the red LED with its current limiting resistor. Recall that transistors are current control devices. The size of the base current entering the transistor is determined by the voltage applied to the series resistor in the base circuit. The applied voltage is set by the script-controlled AO 0 output of the LabJack HMI.

If the circuit depicted in Figure 4-1 is modified, the experimenter should ensure that the current limiting resistor does not allow currents larger than that specified as a maximum for the diode in use to flow in the circuit.

Software

Page Components Required

The DAQFactory data entry panel as seen in Figure 4-5 consists of a total of eight lines composed of four text components, two edit boxes for data entry, two buttons configured to start sequences, and two descriptive text components.

In order to assemble the control panel, the previous techniques used to create, position, and configure screen components can be used, and where necessary, the DAQFactory user manual can be referenced to place and configure the new screen icons used in this exercise.

The following list identifies the page components that make up the finished control panel as depicted in Figure 4-5:

1) A text message is used to identify the panel/grouping and its function (top line, yellow background, black lettering; text and background colors selected from boxes in the component configuration window; see Chapter 1, Figure 1-6).

2) An edit box is configured (see Figures 4-2 and 4-3) and labeled to identify and receive the data to be entered into the panel. The "Flash led repeats" is the number of times to flash the red LED in Figure 4-1 in an on and off manner. The variable in DAQFactory holding the flash number index is defined as flsh_Rpts and is declared as a global variable in an auto-start sequence (Listing 4-1; all code listings provided in the "Code Listings" section at the end of the chapter). In order for the correct variable names to automatically appear in the drop-down list as seen in Figure 4-2 with the

"cycles" entry being highlighted, the variable names must be declared as global with a short sequence that is automatically run when the page is loaded (see Figure 3-1 in Chapter 3). Line 2 in the panel is configured entirely from the Caption box and the checking of the "Set on Set Button press" check box as seen in Figure 4-3. The "Set button caption" is entered into the appropriate box to appear on the button in the second line of the panel. When configuring and editing the edit box components, make sure the cursor tip is within the edit box active area and that the Ctrl key is pressed prior to clicking the left mouse button that will then highlight the edit box itself with the thick hatched border seen in Figure 4-4. With the edit box highlighted, the right mouse button can be clicked to bring up the properties dialog boxes of Figures 4-2 and 4-3. The values entered into the edit box are then placed into the channels or variables as required.

3) A second edit box is created to receive a variable numeric value that will cycle the intensity or brightness of the green LED in Figure 4-1 from off to full brightness and back to off. The variable holding the number of fade cycles is declared as fd_Rpts in the same auto-start sequence as the flash index.

4) In the fourth line of the panel, a static text beneath the data entry boxes identifies the variable entered. For enhanced contrast, the black text is written against a green background. (See options in Chapter 1, Figure 1-6).

5) A descriptive text component forms the fifth line of the panel and is used to confirm, visually, the value entered in the edit box that has been set as the value of the scripting variable "flsh_Rpts" used by the scripting code. Figure 4-6 illustrates the properties window of the descriptive text component. A descriptive text component needs a caption, an expression, and a comparison table. Entries into the comparison table are made with a numerical value in the left column and a text string to the right. The Add and Delete buttons are used to get the desired table assembled. Once assembled and configured, if 0 is entered into the edit box on clicking the Enter button, the descriptive text component looks up the value of the variable flsh_Rpts and prints the corresponding entry in the text column that is "no value entered." Entering a 4 in the edit box will cause the message "four times" to be printed after the caption "Flash repeats:" In essence, the comparison table has a numerical value range for the variable at hand and a corresponding text message to display when the variable falls within a defined range.

6) The sixth line consists of a descriptive text to the left and a push button to the right. An appropriately labeled button is used to initiate the "n" repeats of the script-controlled, on/off flashing of the red diode. In Figure 4-5, the DAQFactory control screen is configured to run the regular sequence code listed in Listing 4-2. The power to the LED is controlled by the RedLed channel whose output can be found on the LabJack I/O 0 pin.

7) In the seventh line of the control panel is a second descriptive text component configured to report the number of times to repeat the fade in/fade out oscillation of the green LED.

8) A descriptive text and a second button make up the eighth and last row of the control panel. The button controls a pair of sequences, the first of which is the red LED flashing sequence, while the second, in Listing 4-3, is the fade in/fade out code for the green LED. In Figure 4-7, the Action tab for the button component is displayed. Pulling down the edit box list of actions will reveal a long list of single choices. If more than one action is desired on the button click, then the Add/Delete up/down arrows can be used to add actions to be invoked when the button is clicked. In this demonstration exercise, the flash and fade sequences are run simultaneously.

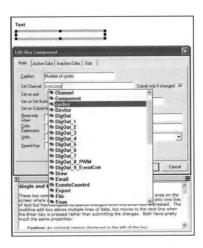

Figure 4-2. *Edit Box Main Tab to Set a Channel or a variable value*

99

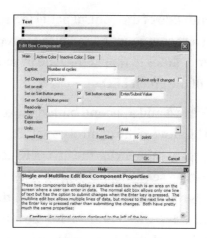

Figure 4-3. *Edit Box Main Tab Completed*

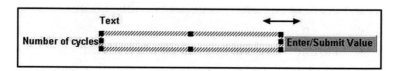

Figure 4-4. *Edit Box Ready for Sizing*

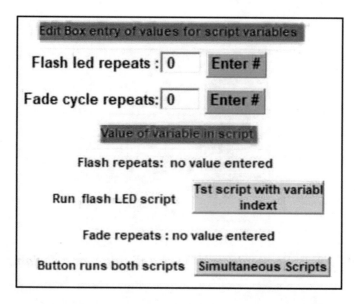

Figure 4-5. *Control Panel to Vary LED Illumination Repetitions*

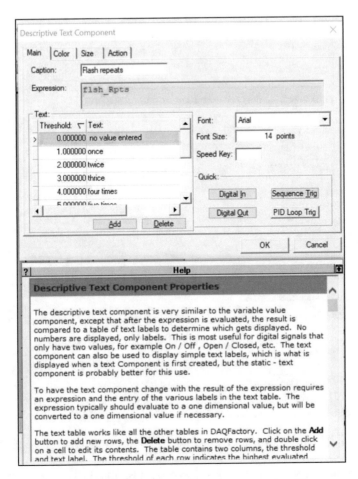

Figure 4-6. *Configuration Panel for the Descriptive Text Component*

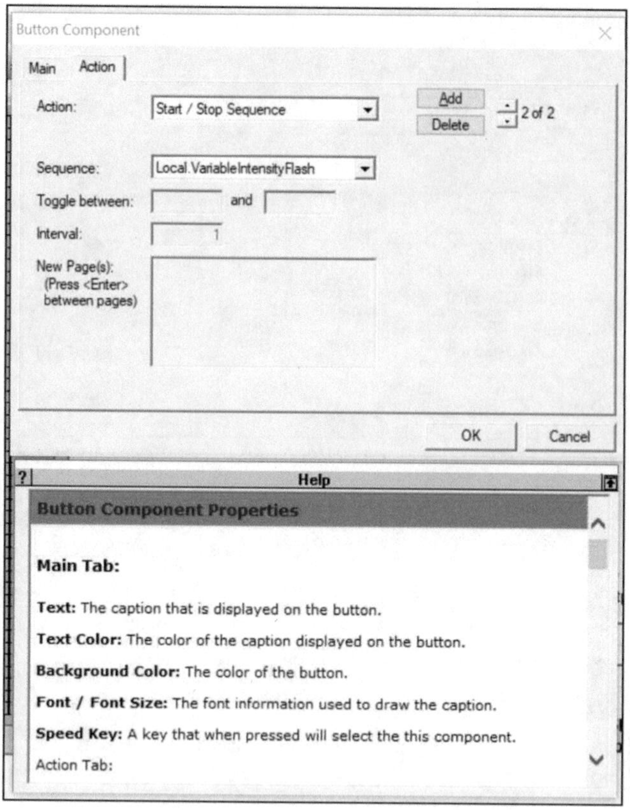

Figure 4-7. *Button Component Multiple Action Selection Panel*

For visual clarity, panel components can be used to create a background for the various groups of active screen components making up a specific operation control screen. A bold numeral positioned at the base of the panel can be used to associate an entry in a table of notes and instructions on the main control screen.

Scripting

Listing 4-1 is an important procedure to employ when screen components are used to alter the contents of variables. The sequences for flashing and fading the red and green LEDs are detailed in Listings 4-2 and 4-3, while the 27-step process for varying the green LED voltage between the minimum turn-on voltage and power supply maximum is to be found in Listing 4-4. Listing 4-3 varies the green diode illumination by calling the AnalogUp() and AnalogDwn() functions to step the diode through the incremental voltage levels as required in the fade in/fade out effect. The sequence is for a low to high transition, and a second routine is written for high to low transition to enable the system to both increase and decrease the LED brightness in 1.3 seconds.

Observations

The on-off cycle of the red diode is definitive in that the light is at full brightness or it is off. The stepping of the voltage or current applied to the base of the 2N3904 in a series of increments produces a "noisy" increase and decrease in the illumination of the semiconductor. (See "Discussion.")

The descriptive text component application is a very simple illustration of the usage of the icon but does provide an overview of how the comparison table is assembled and operates.

Data entry into the variable loop indexing is a simple illustration of the technique, and the dual initiation of the two different scripts from a single button illustrates the ability of the DAQFactory programming to demonstrate "threading" in which two programs appear to execute simultaneously. (Threading is an advanced programming topic that if required for an experimental control can be studied in detail from the literature of Python programming.)

Discussion

As can be seen in the code for the script to switch the power on and off to the red LED, the variable "flsh_Rpts" is declared as a global entity. When the script has been typed and the "Apply & Compile" button clicked successfully, the global variable "flsh_Rpts" appears in the pop-up typing aid listing of channels, variables, and sequence scripts.

A transistor is an amplifier of current.[1] Any signals that are created by the DAQFactory software and are ultimately expressed as a voltage level impressed upon the AO 0 terminal of the LabJack will contain noise. The noise, riding on top of the impressed DC signal levels created by the DAQFactory script, is augmented by the 10 kΩ resistor protecting the transistor base from excessive current. The noise on the signal that is impressed upon the base of the 2N3904 is amplified by the transistor's gain or amplification factor h_{fe}, typically a value between 35 and 100, to generate the easily visible flicker and irregular transitions of the fade in or out.

Although a PNP transistor has been used in the exercise, an NPN could be used with the changes illustrated in Figure 4-8 (2N3904 and 2N2222 are suitable NPN devices).

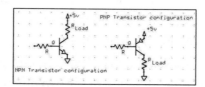

Figure 4-8. *NPN and PNP Power Control*

The scripting code for the on/off diode switching is contained in a loop whose index is declared as a global-type variable, the value of which is set from the screen edit box. The same code can be used with two functions

---

[1] *Electronics Cookbook*, Monk, O'Reilly Media Inc., ISBN 978-1-49195340-2

labeled AnalogUp() and AnalogDwn() that are called in place of the assignment statements setting the analog output channel AO 0 to either 5 volts or 0 in the simple on/off cycling. The functions stepping the intensity of illumination up and down by voltage adjustment are very simplistic approaches to altering the power delivered to the green diode. There are probably numerous more elegant code sequences that can be written to control the illumination intensity. (Note: Analog up and analog down will change function if PNP and NPN transistors are interchanged.)

U12 LabJacks can be configured for PWM outputs to provide smooth power control applications as opposed to the coarse demonstration method used in this exercise. Newer data acquisition and interfacing devices are usually equipped with built-in PWM facilities as presented in Chapter 7.

Screen Entry of Data with the Arduino Microcontroller

A screen entry of data can also take the form of a series of numerical control values generated from a control panel in DAQFactory. Numerical values from a grouping of DAQFactory icons forming a control screen on the host computer can be passed to a microcontroller through the serial port to convert the entered data into process variations or experimental control actions. Data must pass through the serial port portal between the two different computing systems at the low-level bit and byte or on/off communication level. Although the on/off recognition capability is organized in both systems as ASCII (American Standard Code for Information Interchange) characters, the information must be turned into numerical integer or numerical floating-point values for mathematical operations or alphabetic characters for identification purposes.

As has been presented in previous exercises, an Arduino microcontroller can be controlled from a serial port. In addition to the much lower cost of the microcontroller board, the microcontroller has many updated features such as programmable hardware timers that can be used to vary the time width of 5 V electrical pulses to implement pulse width modulation. (See Chapter 7 for details.)

An Arduino normally has 14 digital I/O pins, of which 6 can provide PWM power control.

Connecting the SCADA software to the Arduino microcontroller through the serial port limits the electronics to processing one signal at a time. Regardless of how many data streams are multiplexed or mixed before being transmitted to the serial port and then parsed back out into their individual streams on the microcontroller side, only one bit at a time passes through the serial connection.

Greater details on the serial connection and its use are presented in Chapter 11.

Experimental

To implement the use of the Arduino microcontroller instead of the LabJack U12 to demonstrate the control screen entry of numerical values for controlling and receiving data for display from the microprocessor, the digital pin and ADC inputs depicted in Chapter 2, Figure 2-9, can be used.

In all DAQFactory-Arduino programming, only one program or the other can be in control of the serial port. The author's normal practice is to develop the Arduino code required for the task at hand and then test the code by launching the Arduino's serial monitor and sending into the microcontroller code the character string that will be sent by the DAQFactory control screen. Once the correct Arduino response has been confirmed, the serial port on the Arduino is closed, and the Arduino IDE window is minimized to run in the background. Once the Arduino code to receive the correct DAQFactory character string to invoke the action required is running in the background, the DAQFactory program containing the page with the control screen to be placed into service can be launched to begin the control session. In this exercise, the DAQFactory screens seen in the figures shown are resident in the SCADA software that has access to and control of the serial port through which characters can be sent to initiate the desired action from the devices connected to the Arduino I/O connections.

An initial DAQFactory screen as depicted in Figure 4-9 was created to begin the progressive development of serial communications.

The Red led on and Red led off buttons are coupled to the Quick Sequence code of Listing 4-5 that transmits a 1 or 0 to the serial port where the Arduino code of Listing 4-6 activates/inactivates the red LED as required. The Arduino code also reads the voltage drop across the measured, known value current limiting resistor and sends the current data back to the serial port where the DAQFactory Quick Sequence code parses out the current data for display on the control screen.

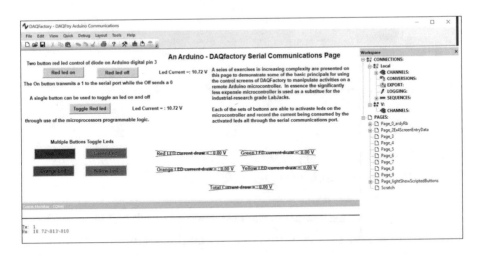

Figure 4-9. *DAQFactory Control Screen for Directing Actions on an Arduino Microcontroller Board*

The second button in the upper-left corner of the DAQFactory control screen is coupled to a second Quick Sequence that activates a more complex and more efficient toggling of the red LED on the Arduino board. The programs of Listings 4-7 and 4-8 are the Quick Sequence code and Arduino code that manage the toggling effect.

Figure 4-10 depicts the DAQFactory control screen display obtained when the green and orange LEDs on the Arduino board have been activated by the corresponding buttons on the DAQFactory control screen. The transmission history of the serial port action on the COM4 monitor is recorded in the bottom left of the figure frame. Listings 4-9 and 4-10 control the colored buttons of the control panel.

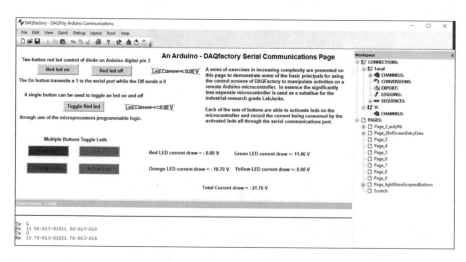

Figure 4-10. *DAQFactory Control Screen for Directing Multiple Actions on an Arduino Microcontroller Board*

Listings 4-9 and 4-10 contain the DAQFactory quick sequence code activated by clicking on a coloured button and the responding Arduino code for the control screen coloured buttons and variable value readouts visible in Figure 4-10.

In Figure 4-5, the DAQFactory screen data entry panel has been developed using the LabJack devices and an auto-start sequence to declare the variables required to hold the loop indexing values to be entered. The auto-start sequence in DAQFactory is also activated when the page holding the data entry panel is loaded for use with the Arduino microcontroller. All of the features discussed with respect to DAQFactory previously are active with the microcontroller except for the threading demonstration button. (See "Discussion.")

The "Tst script with variable index" button is coupled to the Quick Sequence program as shown in Listing 4-11. The Quick Sequence relies on a "for loop," executed "flsh_Rpts" times to send an on/off or "1"/"0" serial port transmission to the Arduino running the code listed in Listing 4-6 to power the red diode on or off. Alternately, Listings 4-12, 4-13, and 4-14 can be used to operate the Arduino's PWM functionality to both fade and flash the orange diode on the microcontroller board. (See "Discussion.")

Observations

When the screen data entry uses the edit box screen components with the LabJack, it is possible to enter two different values into the flash and fade edit boxes, and when the bottom button "Simultaneous Scripts" is activated, the flash and fade actions on the two diodes both run together. (See "Discussion.")

The remainder of both the LabJack and Arduino screens and functions work as expected.

Discussion

In addition to the DAQFactory scripting language, Python is a programming language that is able to accommodate "threading." The details and applications of threading are much more advanced topics than can be examined in this introductory work, and for more information, the literature of Python can be consulted.

Examination of the Arduino code in Listing 4-8 will reveal that the logic for determining the status of the red LED has been written, for simplicity, entirely into the microcontroller system. In the event that the microcontroller were in a remote location and the operator of the DAQFactory control screen needed to know the status of the red LED or the device attached to the digital pin, a flag could be passed back to the control screen through the serial port along with the current drawn data.

The experimenter must take care when using the digital and PWM pins on the Arduino as only 6 of the 14 digital I/O pins support PWM (i.e., Arduino pins 3, 5, 6, 9, 10, and 11 are PWM capable.)

When working with the DAQFactory serial port, the experimenter must manually add a line feed ASCII marker to the end of each transmission if it is to be used by Arduino code to mark the end of character transmission. The Arduino serial monitor has a selection box in the lower right-hand corner of the field of view to select the desired line endings for the terminal session at hand.

The PWM activation code using the 0–255 integral power level can be used with both the fade and flash modes of LED activation by calculating the timing and power requirements in the DAQFactory sequence scripting and only transmitting the power activation commands as and when required.

Raspberry Pi: Screen Entry of Data

Data entry in the Python language used by the RPi is accomplished with the input statement. An input statement in Python takes a string value argument that may then need to be converted into the appropriate numerical value as an integer or float. A typical screen entry code is as follows (# marks a comment line):

```
input_str = input("Enter the desired input characters", )
variable = int(input_str)    # can only be used for non-floating
                               point conversion of numbers
variable = float(input_str) # can only be used for floating
                              point numeric strings
```

Control of LEDs with the Python language can use a basic library called RPi.GPIO or a more advanced capability library known as gpiozero. The documentation for both libraries is available online.

Because the GPIO array is a digital input/output system, voltage control is not easily implemented without resorting to PWM and capacitor smoothing. (PWM is introduced in Chapter 7.)

A simple exercise demonstrating the screen entry of data with Python and the RPi can be created by blinking an LED with a flash length set from a screen-entered value for a set number of repeats, also set by screen entry. The Python program in Listing 4-15 produces the output of Figure 4-11 and flashes the nominal LED as recorded.

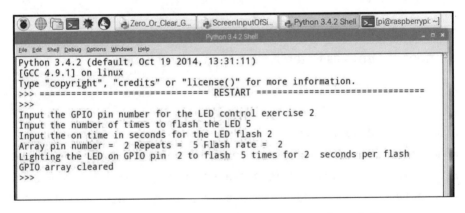

Figure 4-11. *Output from Python Screen Entry of Data Program*

Occasionally, when switching on the power for the RPi when peripherals are attached to the GPIO array, some of the array pins may be in a high or powered state. Two utility programs able to re-zero or turn off the active pins are presented in Listing 4-16. One utility makes use of the channel list function, and the second uses a Python loop to process the individual pins of the GPIO array.

Code Listings

Listing 4-1. DAQFactory Auto-start Sequence Code to Declare Variables

```
// Auto declare variables is a sequence that runs when the Main
// Screen page is run. Two variables are declared globally,
// flsh_Rpts and fd_Rpts representing the number of times to
// flash the red led and fade the green.
//
global flsh_Rpts
//
global fd_Rpts
```

Listing 4-2. DAQFactory Code to Flash the Red LED a Variable Number of Times as Entered from the Control Screen

```
// Sequence Name --: TstSqncForLoopVariableReps
//Screen Entry of Alph-Numeric Values
//Oct9/09 and Nov. 13/09
//A screen Edit Box accepts entered values as a variable called
//flsh_Rps. The variable is declared as a global type with an
//auto-run sequence and is used as the loop counter value to
//vary the number of times the loop iterates.
//
global flsh_Rpts
//
```

```
for (Private.Counter = 0, Counter < flsh_Rpts, Counter ++)
   //
   RedLed = 5
   delay(0.5)
   RedLed = 0
   delay(0.5)
   //
endfor
```

Listing 4-3. DAQFactory Code to Fade In and Out the Green LED Brightness

```
//Variable Intensity Flash varies the voltage of the
//AO 0 channel to raise and lower the intensity of the
//green LED
//Nov. 16/09
//
global fd_Rpts
AnalogOut = 0
for (Private.Counter = 0, Counter < fd_Rpts, Counter ++)
AnalogUp ()
AnalogDwn ()
endfor
AnalogOut = 0
```

Listing 4-4. DAQFactory Regular Sequence for LED Illumination Intensity Variation

```
//Analog Voltage is raised from 2.4 volts to 5.0
// in steps of 0.2v with a delay of 0.05 sec
// between increments. Rvn. Jan4/10
AnalogOut = 2.2
```

```
delay (0.05)
AnalogOut = 2.4
delay (0.05)
AnalogOut = 2.6
delay (0.05)
AnalogOut = 2.8
delay (0.05)
AnalogOut = 3.0
delay (0.05)
AnalogOut = 3.2
delay (0.05)
AnalogOut = 3.4
delay (0.05)
AnalogOut = 3.6
delay (0.05)
AnalogOut = 3.8
delay (0.05)
AnalogOut = 4.0
delay (0.05)
AnalogOut = 4.2
delay (0.05)
AnalogOut = 4.4
delay (0.05)
AnalogOut = 4.6
delay (0.05)
AnalogOut = 4.8
delay (0.05)
AnalogOut = 5.0
return()
```

Listing 4-5. DAQFactory Quick Sequence to Turn the Red LED On from the Button and Read the LED Current

```
device.ardyRb.Purge()
device.ardyRb.Write('1')
delay(0.1)
global ldCurrnt
private string datain
datain = device.ardyRb.readUntil(13)
ldCurrnt = strToDouble(datain)
```

Listing 4-6. Arduino Code for DAQFactory Code of Listing 4-5

```
// Arduino code for a single led illumination on the red board
// Arduino the pgm waits for an incoming character on com
// port 4 if a 1 the led is turned on if a 0 it is turned off.
// A0 is wired to Rd led junction and the Arduino calculates
// the led current and prints the value to the serial port.
//
const int RedPin = 3;        // red board dig. pin with red led
                             and clr
int incomingByte;            // a variable to hold incoming byte
float iRed = 0;              // the led current through the CLR
//
void setup() {
  Serial.begin(9600);              // start the serial port
  pinMode(RedPin, OUTPUT);         // set the pin function
}
void loop() {
  if(Serial.available()> 0) {      // check port for last
                                   data byte
```

```
incomingByte = Serial.read();    //
if (incomingByte == '1') {        // if is 1, turn the led on
   digitalWrite(RedPin, HIGH);
// calculate led current and print to the serial port
iRed = ((analogRead(A0) * 4.8828 )/216);
Serial.println(iRed);
}
//
if (incomingByte == '0') {
   digitalWrite(RedPin, LOW);         // if 0, turn the led off
// calculate led current and print to the serial port
iRed = ((analogRead(A0) * 4.8828 )/216);  // ensures the LED
                                                     is off
Serial.println(iRed);
}
}
}
```

Listing 4-7. DAQFactory Quick Sequence Code to Toggle Red LED
and Read the Power Consumption

```
device.ardyRb.Purge()
device.ardyRb.Write('R')
delay(0.1)
global ldCurrnt
private string datain
datain = device.ardyRb.readUntil(13)
ldCurrnt = strToDouble(datain)
```

Listing 4-8. Arduino Code for Receiving the DAQFactory Control
Screen Button Request to Toggle Red LED Illumination

```
// Toggle an led on/off from one DAQFctry button icon on COM4
// The DAQF QS sends an R to the serial port on com 4. On the
// arduino side the status of the RedLed digpin is determined
// and toggled as required. Led current calculated and written to
// Ser prt where DAQFtry parses out floating point current value.
//
const int RedLedPin = 3;      // red led is on dig pin 3
int oofR = 0;                 // power state of red diode
char incomingByte = ' ';      // declare incoming byte
float iRed = 0;               // red led current
//
void setup() {
  Serial.begin(9600);         // start the serial port
  pinMode(RedLedPin, INPUT);  // must initially read the dig. pin
}
//
void loop() {
  if (Serial.available()) {          // check for incoming data
    char incomingByte = Serial.read();
    //Serial.print(incomingByte);             // diagnostic
    if (incomingByte == 'R' && oofR == 0) {
      pinMode(RedLedPin, OUTPUT);
      digitalWrite(RedLedPin, HIGH);
      iRed = ((analogRead(A0) * 4.8828)/216 );
      Serial.println(iRed);
      oofR = 1;
    }
```

```
   else {
     if (incomingByte == 'R' && oofR == 1){
     pinMode(RedLedPin, OUTPUT);
     digitalWrite(RedLedPin, LOW);
     iRed = 0;
     Serial.println(iRed);
     oofR = 0;
     }
   }
  }
}
```

Listing 4-9. DAQFactory Quick Sequence Code for Multiple-Button Control of Arduino LEDs

```
device.ardyRb.Purge()
device.ardyRb.Write('R')
delay(0.1)
global iRed
global iTotal
private string datain1
private string datain2
datain1 = device.ardyRb.ReadUntil(13)
datain2 = device.ardyRb.ReadUntil(13)
iRed = strToDouble(datain1)
iTotal = strToDouble(datain2)
```

Listing 4-10. Arduino Code Supporting DAQFactory Multiple-Button Colored Diode Selection with Power Consumption

```
// Toggle leds on/off from DAQFctry button icons on COM4
// The DAQF QS sends an R, G, O or Y to the serial port on com
// 4. On the arduino side the status of the appropriate led
// digpin is determined and toggled as required through a
// switch construct.
//
// power drawn calculations, each led has a CLR and the voltage
// on the junction of the resistor and led is measured and used
// to calculate diode current by A0 to A3 respectively. Current
// calcln only done when diode activated.
//
const int RedLedPin = 3;          // red led is on dig pin 3
const int GreenLedPin = 4;        // green led on dp 4
const int OrangeLedPin = 5;       // orange led on dp 5
const int YellowLedPin = 6;       // yellow led on d pin 6
//
int oofR = 0;                     // on off flags initialized
int oofG = 0;
int oofO = 0;
int oofY = 0;                     // on off flags initialized
//
char incomingByte = ' ';          // define incoming character
//
float iRed = 0;                   // red led current in
                                  //    decimal float format

float iGreen = 0;
float iOrange = 0;
```

```
float iYellow = 0;
float itotal = 0;
//
void setup() {
 Serial.begin(9600);                     // start the serial port
 }
//
void loop()
{
  if (Serial.available())                // check for incoming data
  {
  char incomingByte = Serial.read();   // set char value for
                                         //    switch branching
// Serial.print(incomingByte);           // diagnostic
  switch(incomingByte)                   // branch to desired
                                         //    location/option

  {
  case 'R':                              // Red Led Activation
  if (oofR == 0 ) {
  pinMode(RedLedPin, OUTPUT);            // set pin I/O
  digitalWrite(RedLedPin, HIGH);         // turn led on
  oofR = 1;                              // set flag
  iRed = ((analogRead(A0)* 4.8828)/216); // calc i when led on
  //Serial.print(analogRead(A0));        // diagnostics
  //Serial.print("iRed = ");             // diagnostics
  Serial.println(iRed);                      // add CR-LF
  itotal = iRed + iGreen + iOrange + iYellow;
       // calculate total power consumption
  //Serial.print("itotal = ");                // diagnostics
  Serial.println(itotal);                    // add CR-LF
  }
```

```
  else {                             // flag is set to 1 so led is on
    pinMode(RedLedPin, OUTPUT);        // set pin mode to output
    digitalWrite(RedLedPin, LOW);      // turn led off
    oofR = 0;                          // re-set flag to off
    iRed = 0;                       // turn iRed current
                                    contribution to itotal off
    Serial.println(iRed);             // send data to DAQFtry
    itotal = iRed + iGreen + iOrange + iYellow;
       // calculate total current draw
    //Serial.print("itotal = ");     // diagnostics
    Serial.println(itotal);   // send to serial port with CR-LF
    }
break;
//
case 'G':                           // Green Led Activation
  if (oofG == 0 ) {                 // check status flag
  pinMode(GreenLedPin, OUTPUT);     // set pin I/O
  digitalWrite(GreenLedPin, HIGH);  // turn led on
  oofG = 1;                         // reset status flag
  iGreen = ((analogRead(A1)*4.8828)/215); // calc diodecurrent
  //Serial.print("iGreen = ");            // diagnostics
  Serial.println(iGreen);           // send data with CR-LF
  itotal = iRed + iGreen + iOrange + iYellow;
     // calculate total current draw
  //Serial.print("itotal = ");            // diagnostics
  Serial.println(itotal);                 // send with CR-LF
  }
  else {
    pinMode(GreenLedPin, OUTPUT);     // set pin I/O mode
    digitalWrite(GreenLedPin, LOW);   // turn green led off
    oofG = 0;                         // set green status flag
```

```
      iGreen = 0;    // turn green contribution to total current off
      Serial.println(iGreen);    // send green current value
                                         with CR-LF
      itotal = iRed + iGreen + iOrange + iYellow;
         // calculate total current draw
      //Serial.print("itotal = ");           // diagnostic
      Serial.println(itotal);    // send total current with CR-LF
   }
break;
//
case '0':                           // Orange Led Activation
   if (oof0 == 0 ) {                // check status flag
   pinMode(OrangeLedPin, OUTPUT);       // set pin I/O
   digitalWrite(OrangeLedPin, HIGH);    // set pin I/O
   oof0 = 1;                        // set orange flag to led on
   iOrange = ((analogRead(A2)*4.8828)/215);
           // calculate orange led current draw
   //Serial.print("iOrange = ");              // diagnostic
   Serial.println(iOrange);    // send to serial port with CR-LF
   itotal = iRed + iGreen + iOrange + iYellow;
        // calculate total current draw
   //Serial.print("itotal = ");               // diagnostic
   Serial.println(itotal);         // send total current to
                                       serial port with CR-LF

   }
   else {                           // orange led is on
     pinMode(OrangeLedPin, OUTPUT);       // set pin I/O
     digitalWrite(OrangeLedPin, LOW);    // turn orange led off
     oof0 = 0;                     // reset orange status flag to off
     iOrange = 0;                  // turn orange contribution to
                                       total off
```

```
      Serial.println(iOrange);   // send out orange current with
                                         CR-LF
      itotal = iRed + iGreen + iOrange + iYellow;
         // calculate total current draw
      //Serial.print("itotal = ");        // diagnostics
      Serial.println(itotal);   // send out total current draw
                                      with CR-LF

   }
break;
case 'Y':                               // Yellow Led Activation
   if (oofY == 0 ) {                    // led is off
   pinMode(YellowLedPin, OUTPUT);       // set pin I/O
   digitalWrite(YellowLedPin, HIGH);    // turn yellow led on
   oofY = 1;                            // re-set lag to led on
   iYellow = ((analogRead(A3)*4.8828)/217);
            // calculate yellow led current
   //Serial.print("iYellow = ");                 // diagnostic
   Serial.println(iYellow);        // yellow led current value
                                      to serial port wth CR-LF
   itotal = iRed + iGreen + iOrange + iYellow;
      // calculate total current draw
   //Serial.print("itotal = ");                  // diagnostic
   Serial.println(itotal);     // send to serial port with CR-LF
   }
   else {                               // yellow led on
     pinMode(YellowLedPin, OUTPUT);     // set pin I/O mode
     digitalWrite(YellowLedPin, LOW);   // turn yellow led off
     oofY = 0;                          // re-set flag to
                                          yellow led off

     iYellow = 0;               // set yellow led current to 0
```

123

```
   Serial.println(iYellow);      // send value to serial port
                                      with CR-LF
   itotal = iRed + iGreen + iOrange + iYellow;
      // calculate total current and send wth CR-LF
   //Serial.print("itotal = ");     // diagnostic
   Serial.println(itotal);     // send total current with CR-LF
  }
break;
  }
 }
}
```

Listing 4-11. DAQFactory Quick Sequence for Flashing the Arduino-Mounted LED for the Number of Cycles Requested Through the Screen Data Entry Edit Box

```
for (Private.Counter = 0, Counter < flsh_Rpts, Counter ++)
   device.ardyRb.Write('1')
   delay(0.5)
   device.ardyRb.Write('0')
   delay(0.5)
   endfor.
```

Listing 4-12. DAQFactory Regular Sequence Code for Fading the Green LED on the Arduino Board

```
// Green Led on Arduino pin 5 to be cycled from full power to
// off from a DAQFctry script using the serial port and the
// edit box entry of the requested number of repeats, fd_Rpts.
// Start illumination decrease cycle
```

```
device.ardyRb.Write("255" + Chr(10))
delay(0.25)
device.ardyRb.Write("192" + Chr(10))
delay(0.25)
device.ardyRb.Write("128" + Chr(10))
delay(0.25)
device.ardyRb.Write("96" + Chr(10))
delay(0.25)
device.ardyRb.Write("64" + Chr(10))
delay(0.25)
device.ardyRb.Write("48" + Chr(10))
delay(0.25)
device.ardyRb.Write("32" + Chr(10))
delay(0.25)
device.ardyRb.Write("24" + Chr(10))
delay(0.25)
device.ardyRb.Write("16" + Chr(10))
delay(0.25)
device.ardyRb.Write("12" + Chr(10))
delay(0.25)
device.ardyRb.Write("8" + Chr(10))
delay(0.25)
device.ardyRb.Write("6" + Chr(10))
delay(0.25)
device.ardyRb.Write("4" + Chr(10))
delay(0.25)
device.ardyRb.Write("3" + Chr(10))
delay(0.25)
device.ardyRb.Write("2" + Chr(10))
delay(0.25)
device.ardyRb.Write("0" + Chr(10))
```

Listing 4-13. DAQFactory Regular Sequence to Use the "flsh_Rpts" Screen-Entered Loop Index Counter

```
// Orng led flashed on/off with 255 and 0 PWM Arduino power
level applications
global flsh_Rpts
//
for (Private.Counter = 0, Counter < flsh_Rpts, Counter ++)
//
device.ardyRb.Write("255" + Chr(10))      // turn led full on
delay (0.5)                               // delay 1/2 sec
device.ardyRb.Write("0" + Chr(10))        // turn led off
delay(0.5)                                // delay 1/2 sec
endfor
```

Listing 4-14. Arduino Code to Accept Digits from 0 to 255 to Be Used as PWM Power Application Requests

```
   /* DAQFtry ardyRb PWM Led Control through serial port
Quick Sequence control of Orange led fade with arduino PWM
Arduino PWM requires a 0 - 255 integer to set the PWM DC.
This pgm uses the string to int function to convert a digit
based number into an integer to set the PMW value.
*/
String inString =   " ";
byte pinOut = 5;                   // dig pin for orange led
int pwr_Vlu = 0;
//
void setup() {
  Serial.begin(9600);             // start serial port
  pinMode(pinOut, OUTPUT);        // set output pin
}
```

```
//
void loop() {
  while (Serial.available() > 0) {
  int inChar = Serial.read();
  if (isDigit(inChar)) {
  // cnvrt incoming byte to char and add to strng
  inString += (char)inChar;
  }
  // if nuline convert accumulated to integer
  if (inChar == '\n') {
    pwr_Vlu = (inString.toInt());
    Serial.print(pwr_Vlu);
    //int twotimes = pwr_Vlu * 2;
    //Serial.print(twotimes);
    pinMode(pinOut, OUTPUT);
    analogWrite(pinOut, pwr_Vlu);
    // clear the string for new input
    inString = " ";
  }
 }
}
```

Listing 4-15. Python Data Input from the Host Computer Screen

```
# Input of data from the control screen
#
import RPi.GPIO as GPIO
import time
# set the pin identity mode
GPIO.setmode(GPIO.BCM)
GPIO.setwarnings(False)
```

```
# Reset the array pins to off/false/0
chan_list = (2, 3, 4, 5, 6, 7, 8, 9, 10, 11, 12, 13, 14, 15,
16, 17, 18, 19, 20)
GPIO.setup(chan_list, GPIO.OUT)
GPIO.output(chan_list, GPIO.LOW)
#
# Enter the number of the GPIO array pin connected to the LED
to be activated
input_str = input("Input the GPIO pin number for the LED
control exercise " , )
arry_pn_no = int(input_str)
#
# Input the number of times to repeat the flashing of the LED
input_str = input("Input the number of times to flash the LED ", )
rpts = int(input_str)
#
# Input the number of times to flash the LED in a second
input_str = input("Input the on time in seconds for the LED flash ", )
flsh_rt = int(input_str)
print("Array pin number = ",arry_pn_no, "Repeats = ", rpts,
"Flash rate = ", flsh_rt)
#
print("Lighting the LED on GPIO pin ", arry_pn_no, "to flash ",
rpts, "times for", flsh_rt, " seconds per flash")
#
for i in range(1, rpts + 1):
    GPIO.output(arry_pn_no, GPIO.HIGH)
    time.sleep(flsh_rt)
    GPIO.output(arry_pn_no, GPIO.LOW)
    time.sleep(flsh_rt)
```

```
# Clear the GPIO array
Print("GPIO array cleared")
GPIO.cleanup()
```

Listing 4-16. Python Code to Reset the GPIO Array

```
# Clear, Turn Off or Reset the RPi GPIO array
#
import RPi.GPIO as GPIO
# set the pin identity mode
GPIO.setmode(GPIO.BCM)
GPIO.setwarnings(False)
# Reset the array pins to off/false/0
chan_list = (2, 3, 4, 5, 6, 7, 8, 9, 10, 11, 12, 13, 14, 15,
16, 17, 18, 19, 20)
GPIO.setup(chan_list, GPIO.OUT)
GPIO.output(chan_list, GPIO.LOW)
```

Summary

- Scripting is required in the commercial SCADA system to enter the process variables required to initialize and control the process at hand from the configured host screen GUI control panel.

- Screen-entered process or experimental variables can also be entered into SCADA systems assembled with less expensive components and computing platforms.

CHAPTER 5

Digital Signal Concepts and Digital Signal Outputs

Most of the sensors used in making biological, chemical, or physical measurements create a continuously variable analog electrical output, while computers and large-scale integrated circuits use high or low electrical energy levels to represent binary digital signals that they can process. Supervisory control and data acquisition programs must often function as bidirectional analog-to-digital electronic signal converters. This chapter will begin to develop the use of binary numbering and digital electronics, utilizing the standard 0- and +5-volt signal levels as the representations of binary ones and zeros. In many surface mount technology (SMT) devices, the logic levels are 0 and 3.3 V, and the SMT integrated circuits are often damaged by inadvertent application of 5 V signals.

The LabJack U12, human-machine interface (HMI) user manual indicates that 20 digital signal lines, capable of being set to either receive or output a 5 V electrical signal, are provided on the U12 device. Four lines are available through the I/O 0–I/O 3 connections on the main screw terminal strips on the LabJack, while the remaining 16 are available at the DB-25 connector on the top end of the case. The user guide also advises the experimenter that the four I/O lines on the main terminal connectors

© Richard J. Smythe 2021
R. J. Smythe, *Arduino in Science*, https://doi.org/10.1007/978-1-4842-6778-3_5

are protected by internal, current limiting resistors, while those on the DB-25 connector are equipped with jumper pins to bypass the 1.5 kΩ protection resistors when required.

The DB-25 lines can be physically accessed by several methods. A cable and circuit board with connection terminals for the individual lines is available from the LabJack manufacturer. A DB-25 connector with solder terminals can be purchased from most electronics suppliers. An inexpensive interface can be created from an old DB-25 printer cable with the incompatible end connector removed and the individual wire ends tinned to be inserted into a digital prototyping breadboard. (See Chapter 1, Figure 1-1, items 1 and 3, and HMI U12 in Figure 5-1.)

To reinforce a note of caution concerning the hardware used, recall that the LabJack manufacturer–supplied board for the DB-25 connection contains a pre-installed load limiting resistor, while DB-25 connectors purchased separately from local suppliers or fabricated with cables cannibalized from old printers do not. The philosophy of using an independently powered, buffered connection such as the CMOS CD4050 hex non-inverting buffer chip between the field experiment and the HMI eliminates concerns regarding transient damage to the HMI hardware.

Experimental

This exercise will use the same screen-controlled LED illumination procedure, as has been used in previous exercises, but expanded here to 8 bits, to demonstrate basic digital signal concepts.

Hardware

The CB25 terminal board (item 2, $39 USD) from LabJack Corporation includes the DB-25 cable (item 3) to connect the additional terminal digital I/O lines of the U12 interface to the LED array on the prototyping board (item 1).

Item 4 in Figure 5-1 is the USB connection to the host computer displaying the DAQFactory control panel depicted in Figure 5-3. The DB-25 cable connecting the LabJack DB-25 connector at the top of the device provides access to 16 digital I/O lines from which the first 8 can be used for this exercise.

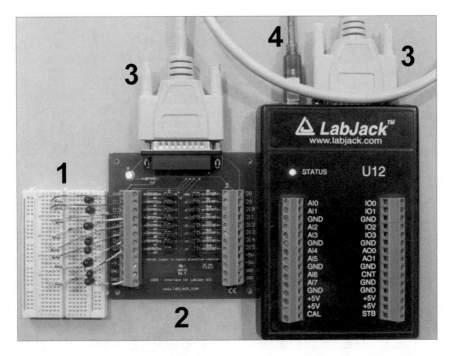

Figure 5-1. *LabJack U12, CB25 Terminal Board, and 8-Bit LED Array*

If additional hardware protection is required because of a transient-prone power supply, the eight digital signal lines can use two CD4050 hex buffer/isolation chips and eight LEDs and current limiting resistors as depicted in Figure 5-2.

The components at hand should be assembled in accordance with the following circuit schematic. The author assembled an initial prototype from an old DB-25 printer cable and plugged the isolated and identified D0–D7 digital I/O lines from the U12 directly into a prototyping board to activate the CLR LED array bits.

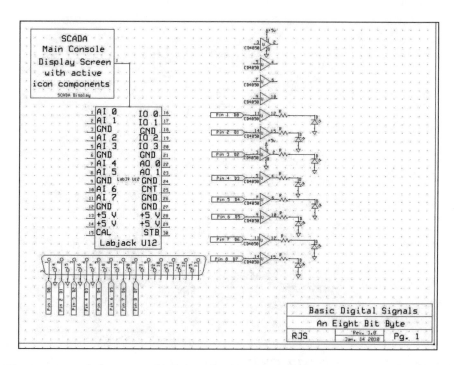

Figure 5-2. *Schematic for 8-Bit Byte LED Display*

Software

Create an eight-button panel with each button labeled as illustrated in Figure 5-3. This exercise demonstrates the configuration of the individual digital line connections between a field experiment using an 8-bit byte and the main SCADA screen.

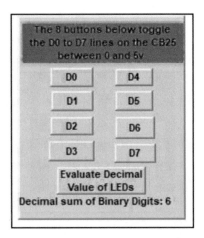

Figure 5-3. *8-Bit Byte LED Display Control Panel*

Each button created is labeled, connected to its channel, and then set to toggle between 0 and 5 volts as previously done in Chapter 1, Figures 1-9 through 1-11. Pressing the Ctrl key and clicking the left mouse button simultaneously allows the experimenter to draw a box around a collection of individual screen components that can be formed into a group with a selection in the Edit drop-down menu. The mouse, Ctrl key, and Edit menu can be used to group and ungroup components as required in assembling a larger more complex GUI screen.

The investigator should also not attempt to alter components on a background panel. Components should be arranged and configured as required, grouped, and then backed by a background panel if desired by using the Ctrl key and the Order entry in the Layout menu.

The DAQFactory sequence program that calculates the decimal sum of the illuminated bits is shown in Listing 5-1.

The buttons representing the 8 bits are linked to the "Toggle Between" selection in the button component Action tab as seen in Figure 1-10, for each of the DigOut_n channels.

Observations

When the diodes, DAQFactory, and the screen are configured properly, clicking any one of the buttons will either light up or turn off the corresponding diode in the 8-bit bank of diodes that represents a byte of digital data.

Figure 5-3 depicts the panel display after the Evaluate button was clicked while the D1 ($2^1 = 2$) and D2 ($2^2 = 4$) LEDs were illuminated. To clear the Decimal sum display, turn all the diodes off and click the Evaluate button.

Discussion

The overall philosophy of not powering experimental setups from the HMI device or the computer power supply is particularly relevant in using the un-protected digital I/O lines of the LabJack interface. As discussed in the Chapter 1 exercise, the CD4050 buffers provide a virtual zero-current or "voltage-only" sensing circuit, in which current flow into or out of the digital line is virtually zero because of the very high resistance of the CMOS gate of the buffering IC chip.

This exercise demonstrates the fundamental basis of digital numerical representation in being able to visually represent any base ten value between 0 and 255 in binary format. The byte LEDs from the right represent 2^0 or 1, 2^1 or 2, 2^2 or 4, 2^3 or 8, and so on up to 2^7 or 128. The decimal value of 3 is thus represented by manually illuminating the LEDs in the 1 and 2 or rightmost pair of diodes as 00000011 representing 2^0 and 2^1. Zero is represented by no LEDs being lit, and 255 is represented when all the LEDs are illuminated.

In keeping with proper experimental development procedures for the assembly of a larger more complex field experiment for data collection, confirm that all 8 bits are being controlled by the buttons before proceeding to the next exercise that makes use of the 8-bit and larger LED banks.

The 8-bit byte can be used to represent the numerical values up to 255, and each additional LED added to the array will approximately double the numerical range able to be displayed by the bank of lights, when the appropriate software adjustments are made. A 10-bit system can represent 1024 values, while a 12-bit system can show 4096 numerical values.

The importance of understanding the binary and decimal numerical domains becomes evident in dealing with analog-to-digital conversions. A large number of electro-mechanical sensors are analog signal generators that are incompatible with digital numerical processing systems, and their analog output needs to be digitized before the beneficiation available from digital signal processing (DSP) can be realized.

DAQFactory Digital Output Exercise with a Microcontroller LED Demonstration Array

Experimental

The DAQFactory SCADA software panel depicted in Figure 5-3 can, with some modification, be coupled to an Arduino microcontroller to provide an inexpensive display. An 8-bit, single-byte, binary, LED illumination display of numerical values can be implemented with the circuit of Figure 5-4 and the Arduino code of Listing 5-3.

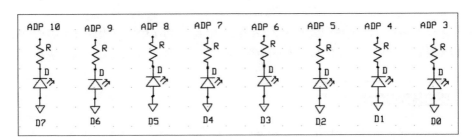

Figure 5-4. *The Connections for an 8-Bit Byte, LED Illumination Bitwise Numerical Display on a Microcontroller*

In Figure 5-4 the nominal Arduino digital pins (ADPs 3–10) would be jumper wire connected to a prototyping board with a 220 Ω current limiting resistor for a typical 10 mm LED, to represent the individual bits of the byte display.

Observations

A typical clicking of the D0, D2, D4, and D6 buttons that represents 1 + 4 + 16 + 64 or 85 is depicted in Figure 5-5.

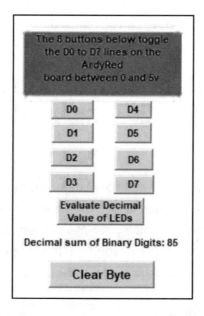

Figure 5-5. *The DAQFactory 8-Bit Byte Keypad for a Microcontroller LED Illumination Bitwise Display*

Discussion

An implementation of the digital visualization exercise in which a microcontroller is used to illuminate the appropriate diodes only needs to create a code to activate the correct diode through the serial port.

On the DAQFactory side, a Quick Sequence code similar to that in Listing 5-2 can be used and adapted for each individual D0–D7 button action. The code sets the weighted inclusion flag variable of DigOut_n for the digital summing program (Listing 5-1) and sends the required diode number as a numerical value equal to the digital pin number to which the diode and its CLR are connected on the Arduino.

The DAQFactory control panels of Figures 5-3 and 5-5 differ in that the extra button labeled "Clear Byte" sends a numerical value of "12" to the microcontroller that in turn triggers code to return all the digital pins to a low state, thus turning all the diodes on the Arduino off. The button activates a DAQFactory Quick Sequence that resets all the number buttons on the control panel in addition to transmitting the "12" to the microcontroller as detailed in Listing 5-5.

Raspberry Pi

An 8-bit binary display representation can be configured in Python with the first eight pins of the RPi's GPIO array. Listing 5-4 provides the code to illuminate an LED binary display and effect a conversion of the illuminated LEDs into an equivalent decimal numerical value. Figure 5-6 illustrates the output from the Python program that has used the tkinter library to create the GUI depicted.

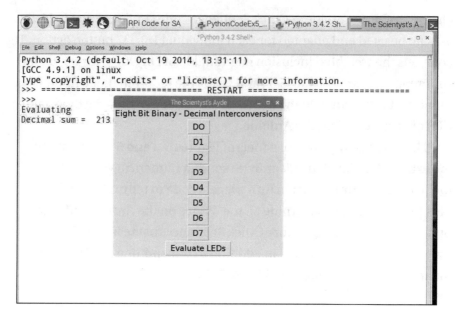

Figure 5-6. *Program Output and 8-Bit Byte LED Display Control Panel*

Figure 5-6 displays the output resulting from clicking the Evaluate LEDs button with the LEDs representing 1, 4, 16, 64, and 128 illuminated in the 8-bit binary LED display.

When assembling the 8-bit LED display on a breadboard, use 330 or 470 Ω current limiting resistors to restrict the current draw from the RPi power supply or use an auxiliary supply and buffer the array outputs.

Control of the panel display is managed by using the "Run Module F5" selection from the Run menu in the "new file" creation. The Python program opens in the interactive interpreter mode, and by selecting the new file option, a new file is created from which the 8-bit LED display program can be located, loaded, and run via the "Run Module F5" selection in the Run menu.

The GUI of Figure 5-6 will appear, and any LEDs illuminated by stray values imposed on the GPIO pins as the RPi starts up are reset to 0 by the internal loop in Listing 5-4. The GUI buttons can then be used to light up the desired bit LEDs in the array. Clicking the "Evaluate LEDs" button will switch to the interactive Python display mode and print "Evaluating" and "Decimal sum =" with the decimal value of the sum of the values represented by the chosen illuminated binary bits.

To reset the program, use the cancel button (X) in the upper right-hand corner of the interactive display and select Yes/OK in the pop-up dialog box to return to the program code listing to rerun the demonstration.

Code Listings

Listing 5-1. DAQFactory Sequence Code to Sum Active Binary Digit Values

```
DAQFactory Sequence Code for dcml_sum
// dcml_sum sums the binary values of the diodes illuminated
global dcml_sum = 0
//
// Examine each of the 8 bits represented by the buttons on the
// digital input panel
// DO button action toggles the DigOut channel between value 0 or 1
if (DigOut == 1)
   dcml_sum = dcml_sum + 1 // if the channel is active 2⁰ = 1
                              is added to dcml_sum
   endif
if (DigOut_1 == 1) // Activation of D1  toggles the channel
                    between 0 and 1
   dcml_sum = dcml_sum + 2 // if the channel is active 2¹ = 2
                              is added to dcml_sum
   endif
```

```
if (DigOut_2 == 1) // Activation of D2 toggles the channel
                      between 0 and 1
   dcml_sum = dcml_sum + 4 // if the channel is active 2² = 4
                               is added to dcml_sum
   endif
if (DigOut_3 == 1)
   dcml_sum = dcml_sum + 8 // if the channel is active 2³ = 8
                               is added to dcml_sum
   endif
if (DigOut_4 == 1)
   dcml_sum = dcml_sum + 16 // if the channel is active 2⁴ = 16
                               is added to dcml_sum
   endif
if (DigOut_5 == 1)
   dcml_sum = dcml_sum + 32 // if the channel is active 2⁵ = 32
                               is added to dcml_sum
   endif
if (DigOut_6 == 1)
   dcml_sum = dcml_sum + 64 // if the channel is active 2⁶ = 64
                               is added to dcml_sum
   endif
if (DigOut_7 == 1)
   dcml_sum = dcml_sum + 128 // if the channel is active
                          2⁷ = 128 is added to dcml_sum
   endif
```

Listing 5-2. DAQFactory Quick Sequence Code for a
Microcontroller LED Byte Display

```
// activation code for D0
global DigOut
device.ardyRb.Write('3' + Chr(10))   // light 1's digit
DigOut = 1                            // add 1 to sum
```

Listing 5-3. Arduino Code for 8-Bit Binary Byte Display

```
// DAQFactory - Arduino LED Illuminated Digital Bits in Byte
// Register DAQFtry screen bttns D0 to D7 light LEDs in digital
// array. Total value of illuminated bits calculated and
// register cleared with buttons. DAQFtr uses scripting to
// evaluate digital bits and serial port transmissions to
// illuminate LEDs after selection by case statement.
//
// digital pins in use 3,4,5,6,7,8,9, and 10
int pv_one = 3;
int pv_two = 4;
int pv_four = 5;
int pv_eight = 6;
int pv_steen = 7;
int pv_threetwo = 8;
int pv_sixfour = 9;
int pv_onetwoeight = 10;
int diod_num;
String inString = "";
//
void setup() {
  Serial.begin(9600);
//
}
//
void loop() {
  while (Serial.available() > 0 ){     // read serial input
   int inChar = Serial.read();
     if(isDigit(inChar)){
       // cnvrt incoming byte to char and add to string
       inString += (char)inChar;
     }
```

```
    // if nuline convert accmlated to integer
    if (inChar == '\n') {
diod_num = (inString.toInt());
      Serial.println(diod_num);
      inString = "";
      }
  }
    switch(diod_num)
    {
case 3:
pinMode(pv_one, OUTPUT);              // units value 2 exp 0
digitalWrite(pv_one, HIGH);
Serial.println("Ones");
break;
//
case 4:
pinMode(pv_two, OUTPUT);              // 2 exp 1 = 2
digitalWrite(pv_two, HIGH);
break;
//
case 5:
pinMode(pv_four, OUTPUT);             // 2 exp 2 = 4
digitalWrite(pv_four, HIGH);
break;
//
case 6:
pinMode(pv_eight, OUTPUT);            // 2 exp 3 = 8
digitalWrite(pv_eight, HIGH);
break;
//
```

```
case 7:
pinMode(pv_steen, OUTPUT);              // 2 exp 4 = 16
digitalWrite(pv_steen, HIGH);
break;
//
case 8:
pinMode(pv_threetwo, OUTPUT);           // 2 exp 5 = 32
digitalWrite(pv_threetwo, HIGH);
break;
//
case 9:
pinMode(pv_sixfour, OUTPUT);            // 2 exp 6 = 64
digitalWrite(pv_sixfour, HIGH);
break;
//
case 10:
pinMode(pv_onetwoeight, OUTPUT);        // 2 exp 7 = 128
digitalWrite(pv_onetwoeight, HIGH);
break;
//
case 12:            // special case to clear array
pinMode(pv_one, OUTPUT);
digitalWrite(pv_one, LOW);
//
pinMode(pv_two, OUTPUT);
digitalWrite(pv_two, LOW);
//
  pinMode(pv_four, OUTPUT);
digitalWrite(pv_four, LOW);
//
```

```
pinMode(pv_eight, OUTPUT);
digitalWrite(pv_eight, LOW);
//
pinMode(pv_steen, OUTPUT);
digitalWrite(pv_steen, LOW);
//
pinMode(pv_threetwo, OUTPUT);
digitalWrite(pv_threetwo, LOW);
//
pinMode(pv_sixfour, OUTPUT);
digitalWrite(pv_sixfour, LOW);
//
pinMode(pv_onetwoeight, OUTPUT);
digitalWrite(pv_onetwoeight, LOW);
break;
    }
}
```

Listing 5-4. Raspberry Pi Python Code for an 8-Bit Binary LED Display

```
# Event handlers join a widget to a type of event and a desired
# resulting action. Command is the method used to detect mouse
# "<Button-1>" events (clicks on the left mouse button) When a
# button is left clicked with the mouse, the self.buttonClick()
# method is invoked to initiate a LED illumination by setting
# the pin to high.
#
import tkinter           # lower case t for current python
                                installation
import RPi.GPIO as GPIO
from time import *
#
```

```python
# the array of LEDs representing the 8 bit binary number must
# be cleared or re-set to low
GPIO.setmode(GPIO.BCM)
GPIO.setwarnings(False)
for i in range(2, 18):
    GPIO.setup(i, GPIO.OUT)
    GPIO.output(i, GPIO.LOW)
#
# define the myWindow class in which to create the GUI window
class myWindow:
    def __init__(self):

        self.mw = tkinter.Tk()
        self.mw.title("The Scientyst's Ayde")
        self.mw.option_add("*font",("Arial", 15, "normal"))
        self.mw.geometry("+250+200")
# GUI function title
        self.lab_1 = tkinter.Label(self.mw, text = "Eight Bit
        Binary - Decimal Interconversions")
        self.lab_1.pack()  # place button widget/image mid window
#
# add eight buttons to the ui
        self.btn_0 = tkinter.Button(self.mw, text = "D0",
        command = self.btn_0_OnClick)
        self.btn_0.pack()
        self.btn_1 = tkinter.Button(self.mw, text = "D1",
        command = self.btn_1_OnClick)
        self.btn_1.pack()
        self.btn_2 = tkinter.Button(self.mw, text = "D2",
        command = self.btn_2_OnClick)
        self.btn_2.pack()
```

```
        self.btn_3 = tkinter.Button(self.mw, text = "D3",
        command = self.btn_3_OnClick)
        self.btn_3.pack()
        self.btn_4 = tkinter.Button(self.mw, text = "D4",
        command = self.btn_4_OnClick)
        self.btn_4.pack()
        self.btn_5 = tkinter.Button(self.mw, text = "D5",
        command = self.btn_5_OnClick)
        self.btn_5.pack()
        self.btn_6 = tkinter.Button(self.mw, text = "D6",
        command = self.btn_6_OnClick)
        self.btn_6.pack()
        self.btn_7 = tkinter.Button(self.mw, text = "D7",
        command = self.btn_7_OnClick)
        self.btn_7.pack()
# Create the evaluation button
        self.btn_8 = tkinter.Button(self.mw, text = "Evaluate
        LEDs", command = self.btn_8_OnClick)
        self.btn_8.pack()
#

        self.mw.mainloop()
#

    def btn_0_OnClick(self): # specify action desired on
    button click
        GPIO.output(2, GPIO.HIGH)
#

    def btn_1_OnClick(self):
        GPIO.output(3, GPIO.HIGH)
#
```

```
    def btn_2_OnClick(self):
        GPIO.output(4, GPIO.HIGH)
#
    def btn_3_OnClick(self):
        GPIO.output(5, GPIO.HIGH)
#
    def btn_4_OnClick(self):
        GPIO.output(6, GPIO.HIGH)
#
    def btn_5_OnClick(self):
        GPIO.output(7, GPIO.HIGH)
#
    def btn_6_OnClick(self):
        GPIO.output(8, GPIO.HIGH)
#
    def btn_7_OnClick(self):
        GPIO.output(9, GPIO.HIGH)
#
    def btn_8_OnClick(self):
        print("Evaluating") # advise of action occurring
        dcml_sum = 0 # define and initialize summing variable
        if (GPIO.input(2)) == True:
        # test array bit status and add appropriate value to sum
            dcml_sum = dcml_sum + 1
        if (GPIO.input(3)) == True:
            dcml_sum = dcml_sum + 2
        if (GPIO.input(4)) == True:
            dcml_sum = dcml_sum + 4
        if (GPIO.input(5)) == True:
            dcml_sum = dcml_sum + 8
```

```
        if (GPIO.input(6)) == True:
            dcml_sum = dcml_sum + 16
        if (GPIO.input(7)) == True:
            dcml_sum = dcml_sum + 32
        if (GPIO.input(8)) == True:
            dcml_sum = dcml_sum + 64
        if (GPIO.input(9)) == True:
            dcml_sum = dcml_sum + 128
#
        print("Decimal sum = ", dcml_sum) # display result.
#
#
if __name__ == "__main__":
    app = myWindow()
```

Listing 5-5. DAQFactory Regular Sequence to Clear Byte Display

```
//ClearByteDisplay
//Nov.14/09
//This sequence just re-zeros the 8 bit byte display
//
DigOut = 0
DigOut_1 = 0
DigOut_2 = 0
DigOut_3 = 0
DigOut_4 = 0
DigOut_5 = 0
DigOut_6 = 0
DigOut_7 = 0
```

Summary

– The concepts of digital numerical values consisting of bits and bytes are visually illustrated.

– Digital visual demonstrations are created with commercial and low-cost SCADA systems.

– Digital numerical concepts have been presented in preparation for Chapter 6 discussing analog and digital conversions.

CHAPTER 6

Analog or Digital Conversions for Input and Output

In the previous chapter, the ability to activate the individual elements of an 8-bit or binary byte LED display and see the decimal numerical equivalent of the number represented by the illuminated diodes was developed. The display in DAQFactory software was visualized with LabJack hardware. In this exercise, a series of DAQFactory sequences, activated by screen buttons and a data entry edit box, display the binary equivalent of the decimal value entered into the edit box.

In this exercise, a decimal value under 255 is entered into the edit box on the main control screen in a grouped panel of components that control the conversion and display options as labeled on the individual buttons. As can be seen in Figure 6-2, the panel contains up and down functions to adjust binary values and an LED display clear function. The actual numerical conversion is done with a scripted sequence invoking a standard numerical analysis base conversion algorithm. The sequence is in Listing 6-1 of the chapter code listings.

In this and the previous exercise, numerical values have been converted between two different base numbering systems consisting of 2^n and 10^n. The numbering systems are of different bases and produce different sequences of digits for the representations of the same number of

© Richard J. Smythe 2021
R. J. Smythe, *Arduino in Science*, https://doi.org/10.1007/978-1-4842-6778-3_6

units or items that are at hand. Changing the type and number of required digits that represent the same number of whole units in either of the two bases is an exercise in mathematics that always yields whole numbers.

Conversions between analog and digital electrical signal values often do not yield exact equivalent results. In theory, an analog signal varies smoothly and continuously as it changes from one value to another. An electronic, digital representation of analog values must divide the range of analog signal variation into a finite number of intervals equal to the number of binary base bits available in the digital display. An 8-bit binary, digital display can represent the decimal numbers between 0 and 255. If we wish to represent an electrical signal that may vary from 0 to 5 volts with the previously developed 8-bit digital light display, then each of the 256 binary digits available must represent $5.0/256 = 0.0195$ V or approximately 19.5 mV.

If the number of LEDs in the binary array is increased from eight to ten, then the 10-bit LED display can represent 2^{10} or 1024 decimal numerical values. A 10-bit array is able to divide a 5.0 V signal into $5.0/1024 = 0.004882812$ volts or approximately 4.88 mV.

A similar expansion of the array to 12 bits allows for the representation of a 5.0 V signal of approximately 1.22 mV per bit.

Often the number of bits available is called the converter or conversion resolution.

Experiments that require conversions between analog and digital formats must be designed and assembled carefully to compensate for the errors introduced by these inexact transformations.

An excellent reference work that covers the history of the development of analog-digital conversions is available as a hardcopy book or as a downloadable series of pdf chapters from Analog Devices (Walt Kester, *Analog-Digital Conversion*, Analog Devices, 2004, ISBN 0-916550-27-3). Two excellent tutorials are available from Analog Devices as MT-015 and MT-016 that explain the fundamentals of digital-to-analog conversion (DAC) and more advanced topics with a host of references for further study. (See "Discussion.")

In a digital representation, the rightmost bit is referred to as the least significant bit (LSB), while the leftmost bit is the most significant bit (MSB). (The exponential power to which the base is raised increases as the digit's position to the left increases.)

Numerous analog-to-digital converter (ADC) integrated circuit devices are available for the transformation of electronic signals. There are several conversion mechanisms in use today such as level or flash converters, successive approximation registers, sigma-delta converters, and other processes whose advantages and limitations are discussed in detail in the electronics literature.[1] (See also Analog Devices referred to previously.) Resistance voltage divider circuits that are used to reduce an electrical signal voltage level can also be used to divide a voltage level into n divisions in accordance with the circuits A–D in Figure 6-1. The increasingly complex circuits from A to D are also known as Kelvin dividers and date from the mid-1800s.

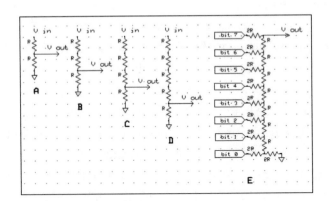

Figure 6-1. *ADC and DAC Resistance Networks*

---

[1] 1) *Building Scientific Apparatus* 4th Edn., Moore, Davis and Coplan, Cambridge University Press, ISBN 978-0-521-87858-6 hardback

2) *The Art of Electronics* 2nd Edn., Horowitz and Hill, Cambridge University Press, ISBN -13 978 -0-521-37095-0 hardback

3) *Practical Electronics for Inventors* 3rd Edn., Scherz and Monk, McGraw Hill, ISBN 978-0-07-177133-7

In circuit A of Figure 6-1, if the resistors are of equal value, the divider circuit halves the input voltage, as $V_{out} = V_{in} * (R/R + R)$.

In circuit B of Figure 6-1, the output voltage is one-third of the input as $V_{out} = V_{in} * (R/R + R + R)$. A series of four and five equal-valued resistors as seen in circuits C and D reduces the voltage division to a fourth and fifth of the input voltage, respectively.

In general, it can be seen that n series resistors between the input voltage and ground will provide a series of junctions. With input voltage n, the voltage drop for each resistor is 1/n that of the input voltage. A string of series resistors and voltage reduction junctions is the electro-mechanical basis behind the "flash" type of analog-to-digital converter, integrated circuits.

Conversion of a digital signal into an analog, in essence, reverses the ADC process. As with a binary, 8-bit ADC having the ability to divide the input into 256 discrete voltage levels, the reverse process of a binary, 8-bit, digital-to-analog conversion (DAC) also provides 2^8 or 256 discrete output voltage levels. The DAC does not produce a true analog signal but creates a stepped voltage approximation of the analog waveform.

An efficient conversion architecture known as an R-2R "ladder" network has been developed that uses only the two resistance values of the eponymous R and 2R. As can be seen from circuit E in Figure 6-1, bit 0 is at the lowest voltage with respect to ground, while bit 7 is at the highest voltage. The significance or "weight" of the bit values increases from least to most significant as the position in the resistance stack increases.

Signal conversions between the analog and digital formats can be realized with relatively inexpensive IC devices such as the single-channel, 8-bit ADC0804 or the eight-channel, 10-bit MCP3008. The ADC0804 can be used with a 5-volt battery pack, to drive an eight-LED display directly and provide a simple, inexpensive ADC demonstration. (An ADC0804 chip costs $6 CDN.)

In addition to the 8-bit LED array, the ease with which an analog signal can be monitored with the LabJack HMI series of devices and DAQFactory software is demonstrated with +/–10-volt input limitations for 10-bit analog-to-digital converters in the U12 series and 3.6-volt input voltage limits with 12-bit converters in the U3 devices. (See Chapter 1, Figure 1-1, item 1. Most surface mount technology (SMT) integrated circuitry operates at 3.5 volts.)

Measurements of larger voltage ranges than those specified by the manufacturer of the ADC device at hand can be realized by using a simple resistance voltage divider to reduce the experimental range to one acceptable to the converter. (See Figure 6-1.) The investigator then has the option of using a correction factor in the mathematical formula entered into the expression box of the variable value configuration window seen in Figure 2-6 of Chapter 2 and Figures 6-10 and 6-11, to display the present value of the experimental voltage. A second variable value display could be added to the GUI being configured to monitor both the experimental and reduced voltages being applied to the ADC input if desired by the researcher as in Figures 6-11 and 6-12.

Digital-to-Analog Conversions

As has been pointed out in the "Exercise Road Map" and previously, the digital-to-analog conversion (DAC) does not and cannot reproduce a truly analog electronic signal. The generated "analog" signal is broken into a fixed number of discrete digital values on DAC, and the analog signal generated from the discrete number of digital values is a stepped waveform similar in shape to the original smooth and continuous analog signal.

There are two basic methods for converting digital signals into analog outputs. One method uses binary, weighted, resistance values, in which the individual digital, bit signals are applied to resistors whose resistance ratio is proportional to the binary power series. Constructing this type of DAC frequently requires nonstandard resistance values. The other method for DAC is much easier to implement and is depicted in circuit

E of Figure 6-1. The R-2R ladder generates an output signal consisting of the sum of the digital inputs in the body of the ladder. There are several advantages to the second method in the need for only two resistance values. The ladder is scalable to the required number of digits, and the output impedance is always constant and equal to the lesser resistance value used in the ladder circuit.

Experimental: LabJack-DAQFactory Decimal-to-Binary Conversions

Hardware

The button-controlled, buffered, 8-bit byte LED display, assembled and tested in the previous chapter's exercise, will serve as the individual bit display or output register for the converted decimal value.

Software

1) A panel grouping consisting of the components depicted is assembled on the main screen.

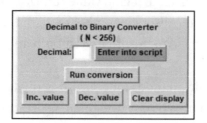

Figure 6-2. *DAQFactory Panel for a Decimal-to-Binary Number Converter*

The panel has been configured from two text components appearing as the top two lines of the panel. An edit box component receives the numerical value to be processed and enters the value into the required variable. The fourth line button component activates the conversion sequence, and the bottom row of buttons performs the actions appearing on their captions.

2) Required scripting

The grouped "Decimal to Binary Converter" panel of Figure 6-2 requires four scripts to activate the converter bit display, increase the binary display by one, decrease the value by one, convert the entered decimal number and then display the binary value, and clear the display.

The individual sequence codes are provided in Listings 6-1 through 6-4 at the end of the chapter.

Analog-to-Digital Conversions

To demonstrate the ease with which an analog-to-digital conversion can be implemented with DAQFactory software and the LabJack HMI, an ADC panel as depicted in Figure 6-3 is configured. The panel consists of three components, a text entry as a heading, a variable value readout displaying the channel[0] or present value of the channel of interest, and the gray panel background.

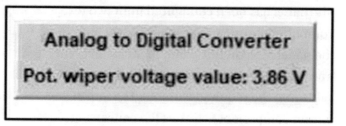

Figure 6-3. An ADC Panel

The circuitry for the analog-to-digital conversion is as depicted in Figure 6-4 in which the ends of the potentiometer are wired between +5 V and ground terminals on the U12 and the wiper is connected to the AI 0, analog input zero, screw terminal.

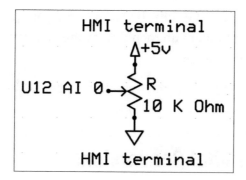

Figure 6-4. An Adjustable Analog Signal Source

As noted previously, an ADC can be used to follow a voltage fluctuation beyond the safe operating limits for the ADC electronics, by using a resistance-based voltage divider to lower the signal strength applied to the converter. A reduced voltage V_{out} can be calculated from the following divider equation:

$$V_{out} = V_{in} * (R_1/(R_1 + R_2))$$

where R_1 and R_2 are the individual resistance values of a series pair of resistors connected between V_{in} and ground and V_{out} is the voltage observed between the junction of R_1 with R_2 and ground. (See circuit A in Figure 6-1.)

A less expensive but more complex to implement ADC LED array illumination binary display can be assembled with the well-established ADC0804 chip from Texas Instruments. (A 57-page pdf documentation is available from www.ti.com/lit/ds/symlink/adc0804-n.pdf.)

The pdf data sheet notes the following:

- No interfacing logic required, operates as a complete stand-alone device with a 135 ns access time, differential voltage inputs, MOS and TTL voltage level compatible, able to use a 2.5-volt reference, an on-chip clock, 0–5-volt input range with a 5-volt supply, no zero adjust required, standard 20-pin DIP package, and a 100 us conversion time

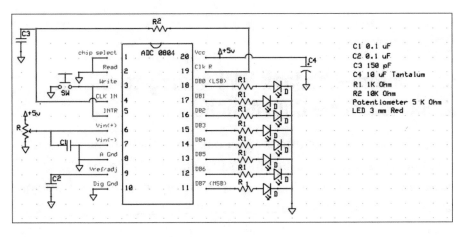

Figure 6-5. *An 8-Bit LED ADC Display*

Figure 6-5 depicts the circuitry that has been used by the author to develop an ADC hardware demonstration using the Texas Instruments ADC0804 8-bit successive approximation analog-to-digital converter. For implementation on a prototyping board, the author used 3 mm red LEDs and 1 KΩ current limiting resistors as a display, a four–AA cell nickel metal hydride battery pack for power, and a connection to the wiper lead of a 5 kΩ potentiometer connected between the nominal 5-volt supply and ground similar to the circuit depicted in Figure 6-4. The wiper voltage provided the varying analog voltage signal for conversion into a digital format to drive the binary LEDs as the shaft on the potentiometer was rotated.

The digital grounds depicted in Figure 6-5 were all brought to a common connection that was then grounded to the negative side of the power supply. An on/off switch was included in the author's implementation of the circuit on the prototyping board but was not needed to initiate the circuit action as when power was applied to the system, the conversions began immediately. The voltage to be converted was applied to pin 6 of the IC.

Observations

DAQFactory–LabJack HMI Analog-to-Digital Numerical Base Conversions

Entry of a decimal value into the edit box and a click on the Enter into script button should light the diodes that correspond to the digital value of the base ten number entered. Entry of the numerical value of say 25 should illuminate the units of the 2^0 (1's), 2^3 (8's, i.e., $2 \times 2 \times 2$), and 2^4 (16's, i.e., $2 \times 2 \times 2 \times 2$) diodes to display the binary equivalent of 25 (i.e., $1 + 8 + 16$).

Clicking either the increase or decrease button should increase or decrease the binary value displayed by one and the clear button should clear the display.

Analog-to-Digital Electronic Signal Conversions

Connecting a nominal 5 V signal across the ends of a 10 kΩ potentiometer should, in theory, if there are no mechanical limitations or discontinuities, give rise to a smoothly varying, analog wiper voltage, ranging between 0 and 5 volts.

A 10-bit ADC as installed in the U12 is theoretically able to divide a 5 V analog signal into 1024 units of 0.0048828 volts or 4.883 mV. A variable value display was configured to read the voltage on the wiper of a 10 KΩ potentiometer wired as depicted in Figure 6-4. As the potentiometer shaft was rotated, the values from 0.010 V to 4.219 V were displayed on the DAQFactory GUI screen when the variable value display was set to display data on the AO 0, analog output zero, channel to three decimal places. The lower voltage value display fluctuated from 0.005 to 0.020, while the upper value display fluctuated from 4.209 to 4.365.

ADC0804: 8-Bit Binary LED Display

Figure 6-6 is a photo of a battery-powered working example of the circuit in Figure 6-5, assembled on a breadboard for visual demonstration of ADC. Careful examination of the diodes in the upper right-hand portion of the field of view will indicate that the 4-, 8-, and 64-bit indicators are lit, indicating a total value of 76. The voltage source is the wiper lead of the 5 KΩ potentiometer visible at the bottom center of the field of view.

When power was applied to the circuit of Figure 6-5, the individual LEDs representing the binary equivalent of the digitized wiper voltage potential lit up immediately. Rotating the shaft of the potentiometer from one extreme position to the other displayed a diode illumination sequence in which the binary numbers either increased from 0 to 255 or the reverse. By slowly rotating the shaft, an individual count could be followed in the binary display. As noted previously, when fully charged, the battery pack produces a nominal 5 V that is applied to the two ends of the potentiometer.

163

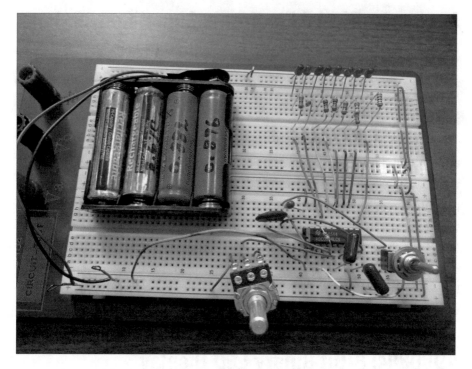

Figure 6-6. *Photo of the 8-Bit LED ADC Display*

A correlation between the applied voltage and the binary display was established by measuring and then comparing the actual voltage applied to the input pin #6 with the binary value displayed by the illuminated diodes of the 8-bit display array.

Examination of both the tabulated data of Figure 6-7 and the ADC0804 data sheet reveals that there is not a 1:1 correspondence between the applied voltage and the digital value produced since an applied voltage of 5.25 generates an output of only 253. The ADC discrepancy can be corrected as explained in the IC data sheet by using the reference voltage input pin, pin #9. (See "Discussion.")

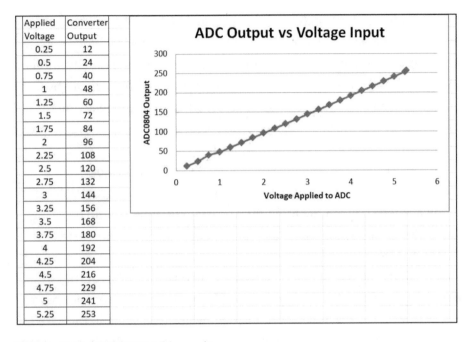

Applied Voltage	Converter Output
0.25	12
0.5	24
0.75	40
1	48
1.25	60
1.5	72
1.75	84
2	96
2.25	108
2.5	120
2.75	132
3	144
3.25	156
3.5	168
3.75	180
4	192
4.25	204
4.5	216
4.75	229
5	241
5.25	253

Figure 6-7. *ADC0804 Linearity*

Discussion

An excellent aid for understanding the concepts of ADC and DAC is found in Figure 1.1 of Chapter 1 of the Analog Devices publication *Analog-Digital Conversions*, at www.analog.com/media/en/training-seminars/design-handbooks/Data-Conversion-Handbook/Chapter1.pdf. The figure is captioned "Early 18th Century Binary Weighted Water Metering System" and contains a series of side and top views of a water metering system implemented in Istanbul, Turkey, in the nineteenth century. The diagrams document the implementation of a DAC in terms of a gravity-powered, hydraulic water distribution and "weighted average" metering system.

Interconversions between analog electronic signal values and digital numerical representations are seldom exact equivalents. Traditional ADCs such as the ADC0804 use a parallel output of eight signal lines, each of which is a representative of a power of 2. The parallel output lends itself to the assembly of the battery-powered visual LED display of Figure 6-6. Newer technology, however, as used in the LabJack devices, does not use a "parallel" output configuration for ADC but relies on the much simpler to implement serial data outputs. Serial data output protocols can be fast enough to monitor many types of sensors, but high-speed instruments often require the use of parallel converters to keep up with data generation rates.

Care must always be exercised in applying voltage dividers in that the ratio of the resistance values chosen must reduce the signal voltage to the desired level but the individual resistance values should be as low as possible to allow sufficient current to pass to drive the "downstream" device or ADC.

An ADC that produces a digital number consisting of an output of parallel signals to drive the logic of the "downstream" devices such as microprocessors, seven-segment LED numeric displays, or, in the case of this primary exercise, an 8-bit binary LED display is usually limited in the current output that it can safely deliver. In some high–current demand displays, it may be necessary to buffer the ADC outputs.

There is a substantial difference in the time and effort required to implement the ADC and DAC demonstrations between the LabJack HMI with DAQFactory software and the assembly of the ADC0804 8-bit LED display or the interfacing of the display to the RPi.

The ADC0804 is a single-channel device that requires the input of one varying voltage source scaled to a 0–5-volt range. The IC has a reference voltage pin #9 that can be used to adjust the step size of the 255 digit levels available. The default setting is 19.5 mV per digital increment so as the entire input span of 5 V will generate a 0–255 binary numerical output. (Further information on using the step size adjustment is contained in the Texas Instruments data sheet for the ADC0804.) A clock is needed to run the conversion logic, and for simplicity, the internal clock is used that requires a series-connected resistor and capacitor (RC) network. The desired RC combination is connected between Clock IN and Clock R pins (pins #4 and #19). The RC time constant ultimately determines how often the IC samples the voltage on pin #6 to generate a conversion at the output pins.

In addition to the clock and input wiring, the ADC0804 demonstration exercise requires a 5 V power supply and eight LEDS and their current limiting resistors to operate.

As noted in previous exercises, the researcher should, where possible, test each component as the system is assembled. Each LED and current limiting resistor can be tested by applying 5 V to the end of the resistor that will be connected to the ADC0804.

In the creation of the code for the buttons, the ability to make use of previously written scripts as functions is demonstrated. As noted in the previous exercise, larger-valued numerical conversions would require the addition of the appropriate number of digital output lines, channels, and diodes and modification of the scripting code.

An 8-bit byte provides a resolution of one part in 2^8 or one part in 256. The Decimal to Binary Converter panel of Figure 6-2 contains the increase and decrease buttons that represent single-digit resolution. If an experimental setup may produce a varying DC signal that can range from 0 to 10 volts, then the 8-bit conversion is able to resolve $10/256 = 0.0390625$ or 39.1 mV. An increase of two more bits in the LED display bank and the corresponding changes of software would allow a 10 V signal range to be spread over 1024 binary digits providing an approximate division of one part in 1024 or millivolt sensitivity or resolution. Increasing the digital capability to 12 bits will provide a sensitivity or resolution of one part in 4096 or 0.0244% (244 ppm, parts per million).

A GUI digital display does not convey any additional information about the value of the voltage being monitored other than its present value. Unless there is a distinct trend of the digital value steadily increasing or decreasing, there is no additional information that can be derived from a numerical digital display of a monitored variable value. However, in many cases where a production process or experimental measurement is being monitored and the constancy of process variables or measurement results is the main goal of the SCADA system, a different form of data presentation such as a timed recording may be of greater value.

Analog-to-Digital Conversions with Microcontrollers

As has been presented in the previous five exercises, much more compact, less expensive, SMT devices able to interface between the DAQFactory SCADA software and experimental sensors or process management hardware have become available in the form of microcontrollers. (See Chapter 9.)

Arduino microcontrollers are readily available, easy-to-use compact devices that have a built-in 10-bit, successive approximation, SMT analog-to-digital converter with six input channels. The ADC chip is capable of converting an input voltage to a digital number in 25 cycles of its 16 MHz clock (approx. 400 microseconds per conversion).

A microcontroller such as the Arduino is a serially oriented device, and in order to pass information back and forth between the DAQFactory control screen and the microcontroller LED array, both the control screen and controller must read from and write to the serial port as in previous exercises.

Serial communications are based upon the ASCII bit patterns of 1 and 0 that allow the transmission of both numerical and alphabetic control characters such as line feeds and carriage returns. Although the ADC hardware can generate single- or multiple-digit integer bit counts, there must be a certain amount of character recognition and interpretation logic software on each side of the serial port in order to create a working communications system.

Experimental

Implementation of the decimal-to-binary display with a serial connection between the DAQFactory control panel and the Arduino-controlled binary array can begin with the creation of the DAQFactory panel depicted in Figure 6-8.

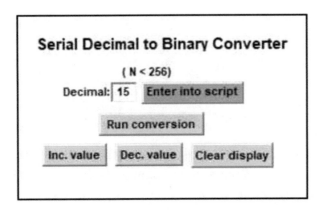

Figure 6-8. *A DAQFactory Control Panel for Serial Control of an Arduino Binary LED Display*

A text component, an edit box, and four buttons have been used in Figure 6-8.

A Figure 6-9 illustrates the edit box configuration window that provides space for creating the box caption and selecting various options and actions.

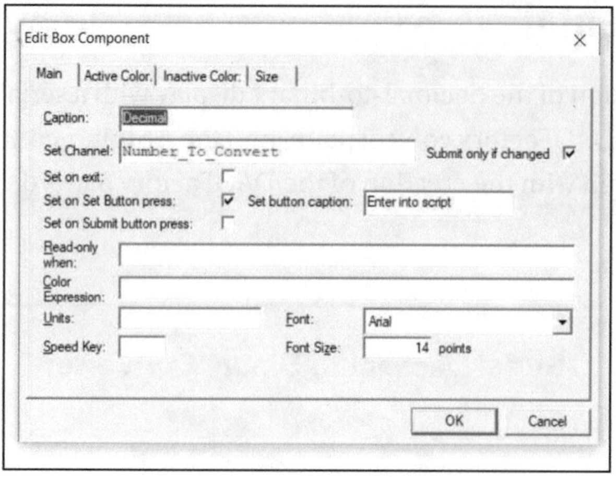

Figure 6-9. *The Edit Box Configuration Window*

The supporting DAQFactory scripting and Arduino sketch codes for implementing the serial panel connection to the microcontroller are provided in Listings 6-5 through 6-9 at the end of the chapter.

In order to use the ADC on a microcontroller board as a serially connected sensor reading device, a pair of variable value display components grouped as a panel on a DAQFactory screen can be configured as in Figure 6-10. Using the channel features of the SCADA software, the integer counts from the ADC and a calculated voltage value corresponding to the counted value can simultaneously be displayed. (Only a cursory introduction to the more involved setup required to provide a data flow between the two systems is being presented here. Greater detail is provided in Chapter 11.)

Two variable value displays are placed on a DAQFactory page as seen in Figure 6-10.

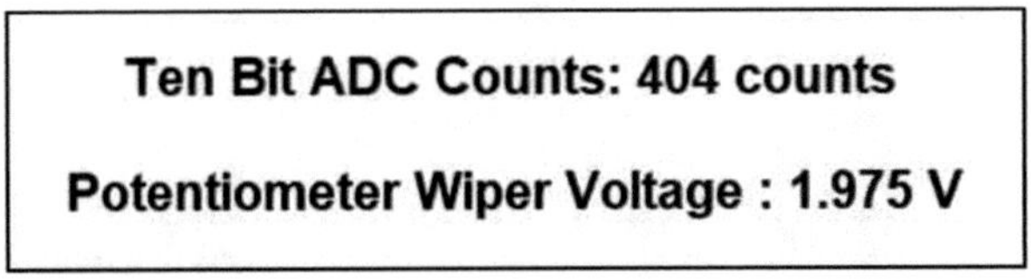

> **Ten Bit ADC Counts: 404 counts**
>
> **Potentiometer Wiper Voltage : 1.975 V**

Figure 6-10. *A Variable Value Component Display for Integer ADC Counts and a Calculated ADC Voltage*

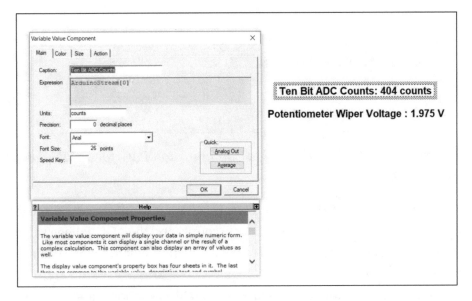

Figure 6-11. *The Variable Value Configuration Page for the Serially Transmitted Integer ADC Count*

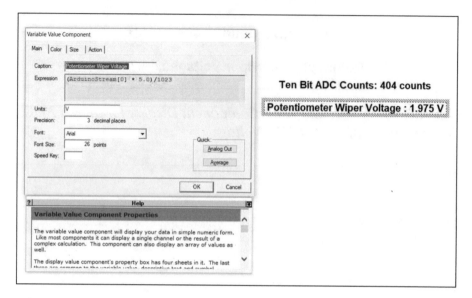

Figure 6-12. *The Variable Value Configuration Page for a Calculated ADC Voltage*

Figures 6-11 and 6-12 display the configuration windows for the integer ADC count display that displays the raw counts and the ADC voltage value display that uses an expression to calculate the immediate voltage value from the ADC.

Figure 6-13 documents the sequence of tables, windows, and entries followed to establish serial microcontroller–SCADA software communications.

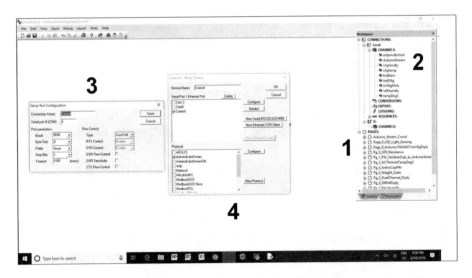

Figure 6-13. *A Configuration Sequence for Implementation of DAQFactory Serial Communication*

Figure 6-13 presents a captioned outline summary of the major procedural actions required to read the serial "data stream" from the microcontroller ADC to the DAQFactory display components. (See Chapter 11 for details.) Item 1 marks the page listing for the DAQFactory program in use on which the panel of Figure 6-10 is assembled from the desired components. Item 2 indicates the channel listing in which the ArduinoStream channel was created by the author to receive the ADC data streamed out from the microcontroller to the serial port (see also Figure 2-3). Items 3 and 4 are the Serial Port Configuration window and the serial device naming and configuration window that are examined in detail in Chapter 11 (see Figures 11-5, 11-6, and 11-7).

To install and use the code in Listing 6-10, click Quick ➤ Device Configuration and select the appropriate device that in the author's demonstration case is Comm4. In the Ethernet/Serial Device window, find the required device and check the adjacent box (Comm4 in figures) and then click the protocol configure button to bring up the I/O Types and

Functions window. Select the "On Receive" function and then copy and paste the code of Listing 6-10 into the space. (See Figure 11-7 in Chapter 11.)

To provide a variable signal simulation for this exercise demonstration, the ends of a potentiometer can be connected between the +5 V supply and ground of the microcontroller and the wiper lead connected to the A0 input of the Arduino ADC. (See the similar circuit diagram of Figure 6-4 for use with the LabJack HMI.)

In keeping with the philosophy of building a complex system from multiple tested and functioning components, we can begin by loading and launching the microcontroller sketch code from Listing 6-11. Once the sketch is running, the Arduino serial monitor can be opened from the Tools menu, and the stream of ADC counts should be visible on the left of the serial monitor field of view. With the data stream generation confirmed, the serial monitor is closed, and the microcontroller IDE is minimized.

The DAQFactory program containing the variable value panel is launched, and if all has been configured properly, the screen components of Figure 6-10 should be active responding to both system noise and any repositioning of the potentiometer wiper control shaft.

Observations

A stream of numbers on the left-hand side of the field of view of the serial monitor window of the microcontroller IDE with values between 0 and 1024 should be seen after launching the microcontroller sketch for ADC reading and serial printing to the port in use.

With the microcontroller running in the background, a complete rotation of the potentiometer shaft on the microcontroller prototyping board changes the integer display from 0 to 1024 and 0 to 5.000 volts on the voltage as has been defined by the setting in the configuration windows of Figures 6-11 and 6-12.

Discussion

Diagnostics for Nonresponsive Displays

In the event that the variable value panel is not responding to the incoming data stream, expand the channel table and confirm that data is being captured by the channel as depicted in Figure 6-14.

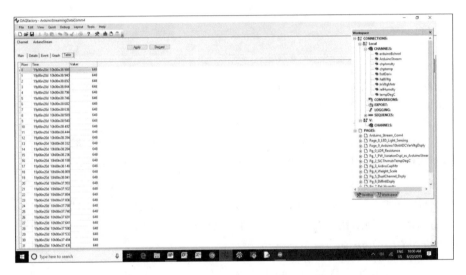

***Figure 6-14.** An Active Channel Timestamped Data Listing*

If the channel is not receiving the ADC data, then the serial port monitor for the DAQFactory program can be accessed to confirm that the data is arriving at the display program's serial port. The serial port monitor is accessed through the Quick ➤ Device Configuration menu and device selection listing panel to get to the Ethernet/Serial Device window as seen in item 4 of Figure 6-13. Clicking the Monitor button immediately below the Configure button will bring up the DAQFactory serial monitor as depicted in Figure 6-15.

Figure 6-15.   *The DAQFactory Serial Monitor Display of Data Passing Through the Port in Use*

In the event that the data is arriving at the DAQFactory serial port but is not being transferred to the proper channel, the port serial protocol can be examined by ensuring that the proper protocol has been selected in the Protocol list and that the correct parsing code (Listing 6-10) has been entered into the "On Receive" I/O Types and Functions entry of the Protocol Configuration window.[2]

System Development and Programming

Although the microcontroller approach to establishing a SCADA-experiment serial connection is significantly less expensive than using the commercially available DAQ systems, the experimental development time and effort required is significant, and the system lacks the robustness found in the commercial products.

---

[2] https://www.azeotech.com/dl/serialguide.pdf

Analog and Digital Conversions for Input and Output with Raspberry Pi

With the available power limitations previously noted, LED visualizations of electronic digital numbering can be created with the RPi and its general-purpose input/output pin array. Numeric conversions between the binary and decimal systems together with ADC can be demonstrated with the two Python libraries available from the Raspberry Pi Foundation. The RPi.GPIO library permits low-level access to the 40-pin array, while the gpiozero library code provides access to numerous hardware devices. The documentation for each library is available from the RPi Foundation website, and the differences between the two library releases will be further developed in the next few exercises.

Binary-Decimal Conversions

As a supplement to the RPi programming and hardware usage introduced in the previous exercises, a 12-bit decimal-to-binary conversion LED visual display has been assembled for the initial portions of this exercise. The code for the converter is in Listing 6-12 at the end of the chapter, and the output from a conversion is depicted in Figure 6-16.

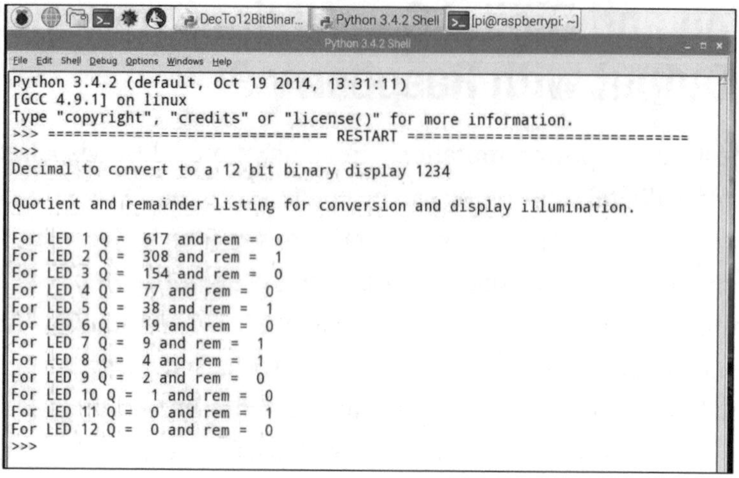


```
Python 3.4.2 (default, Oct 19 2014, 13:31:11)
[GCC 4.9.1] on linux
Type "copyright", "credits" or "license()" for more information.
>>> ================================ RESTART ================================
>>>
Decimal to convert to a 12 bit binary display 1234

Quotient and remainder listing for conversion and display illumination.

For LED 1 Q =  617 and rem =  0
For LED 2 Q =  308 and rem =  1
For LED 3 Q =  154 and rem =  0
For LED 4 Q =  77 and rem =  0
For LED 5 Q =  38 and rem =  1
For LED 6 Q =  19 and rem =  0
For LED 7 Q =  9 and rem =  1
For LED 8 Q =  4 and rem =  1
For LED 9 Q =  2 and rem =  0
For LED 10 Q =  1 and rem =  0
For LED 11 Q =  0 and rem =  1
For LED 12 Q =  0 and rem =  0
>>>
```

Figure 6-16. *A RPi 12-Bit Binary Display of a Decimal Value*

The bank of 12 LEDs is assembled and tested to provide a visual output for several Python and ADC programs. A decimal-to-binary numerical converter, a 10-bit ADC, and a 12-bit ADC can all share the same hardware to provide a graphic visual display of the various outputs from these similar types of programs.

ADC with Raspberry Pi

As noted in previous exercises, the RPi requires external components to digitize analog signals, and the MCP3008 and MCP3201 ICs have been selected by the RPI Foundation as suitable devices for 10- and 12-bit digital conversions. The ICs communicate with the RPi through the serial peripheral interface (SPI) serial protocol. The ADC data is streamed out in a continuous series of bits to the RPi that receives and interprets the 10-digit converted value. The MCP3008 output can be formatted as a floating-point, normalized value from 0 to 1.0 that is proportional to the difference between the sampled voltage and the voltage applied to the reference pin or as an integer value from 1 to 1024. When the ADC chip is referenced to the RPi's 3.3-volt voltage supply, the normalized output must be multiplied by the nominal applied or, for accuracy, the VOM-measured reference voltage to get the actual voltage sampled. A conversion of the integer output of the MCP3008 to the sampled voltage value involves dividing the output value by 1024 and multiplying by the reference value voltage.

The floating-point normalized value representing the analog conversion is not easily amenable to illuminating a 10-bit binary LED visual display. A digital integer output is much easier to interface to a binary LED display.

Experimental

In order to use code of Listings 6-12 and 6-13 for decimal to 10- or 12-bit binary LED visual display and the MCP chips as listed in this exercise, the RPi must be configured to use the serial peripheral interface (SPI) protocol as depicted in Figures 6-21 and 6-22.

A continuously variable voltage from the wiper of a 10 kΩ potentiometer biased between the 3.3 V and ground of the RPi GPIO array was used to create a test voltage for an MCP3008 ADC integrated circuit. The RPi reads the serial output from the IC, interprets the streamed data, and generates the scaled 10-bit integer output that is subsequently used to activate the ten-element LED display.

Figure 6-17 is a semi-schematic of the circuitry used to implement the display. A wiper voltage is applied to the IC that converts the signal from the analog to the digital format and streams the data out in a serial peripheral interface (SPI) form to the RPi GPIO pins. The RPi receives the streamed data, interprets the converted data, and parses the integer output to drive the appropriate diode representation of the converted wiper voltage signal.

Figure 6-17 has been drawn with the Raspberry Pi GPIO pin connections that control and receive data from the IC on the left and the RPi GPIO diode array connections on the right.

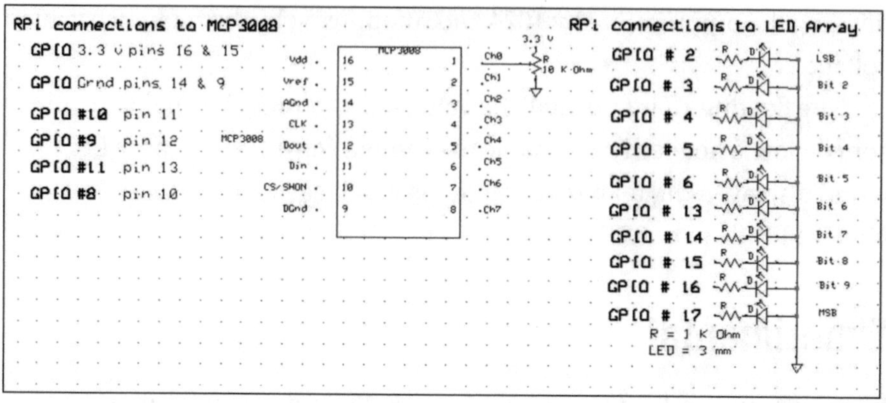

Figure 6-17. *RPi-MCP3008 Circuit for 10-Bit Binary LED Display of Potentiometer Wiper Voltage*

Figure 6-18 illustrates the screen output from the RPi during a simulated experimental setup in which the diagnostic print statements have been inserted into the code to validate the operation of the system. The potentiometer wiper has been rotated to generate a digital output as near to the sequence 123 as possible.

Observations

Figure 6-18 illustrates the continuous output from the Python code that parses the digitized, converted, wiper voltage value to drive the individual elements of the 10-bit LED binary representation of the output value. A closer examination of the output and the actual code being processed will confirm that only when the remainder variable "rem" has a positive or high value does the program print a diagnostic output. Rotation of the potentiometer shaft from one extreme to the other will vary the display from 1 or 0 to 1023. As can be seen in the variation in the data of Figure 6-18, the system has a certain amount of noise included in the wiper output value.

Figure 6-19 depicts the RPi GPIO array interfaced to a 12-bit LED display on a prototyping breadboard. The illuminated diodes correspond to the binary bit pattern of 2 + 4 + 8 + 16 + 32 or decimal 62.

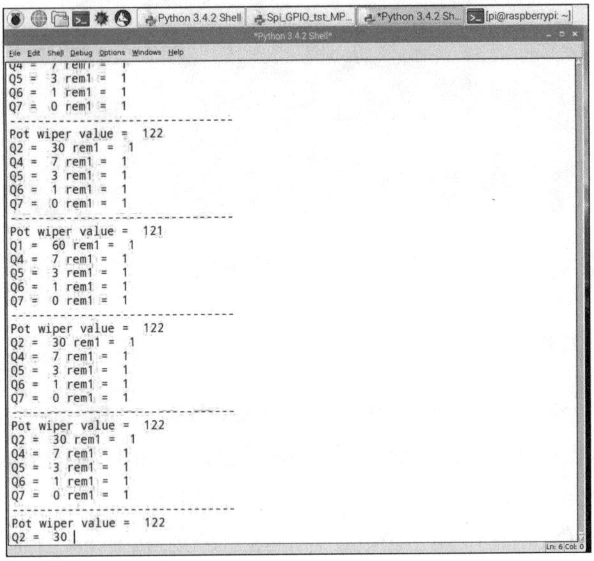

Figure 6-18. *RPi Screen Output During ADC*

Figure 6-19. *A 12-Bit Binary LED Display of Decimal Value 62*

Discussion

Figure 6-19 depicts a bank of 12 3 mm LEDs that can be used in a 10- or 12-bit conversion demonstration. An MCP3201 is a 12-bit conversion IC that can alternately be set up as a binary visualization display. Small 3 mm diodes and 1 kΩ current limiting resistors are being used to minimize the current drawn from the computer with the large number of LEDs in the visual displays.

The figures and photos of the RPi circuits, programming, and wiring are reflective of the complexity required to use the very inexpensive system. As can be seen in the photo of Figure 6-19, the investigator needs to take care in routing jumper wire connections of the RPi GPIO lines and those required to control the conversion functions of the MCP3008 or MCP3201. The RPi GPIO line connections required to activate the 10- or 12-bit binary LED display of the pin array output can be tested during assembly with Listing 6-14. As each pin name appears on the interactive screen, the corresponding LED connected to the nominal pin should illuminate for 3 seconds. Figure 6-20 depicts the test program output display for pin and LED testing.

Listing 6-15 can be used to reset the GPIO array voltage values to zero.

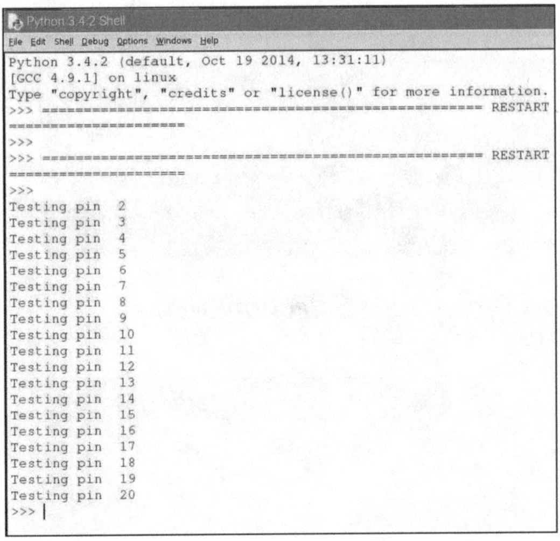

Figure 6-20. *The LED Array Testing Output*

Parallel ADC integrated circuitry as demonstrated with the preceding ADC0804 has been replaced, to a certain extent, by numerous serial communications protocols. Serial communication over a long distance using two or a small number of wires is far more practical than having to use 8, 10, 12, or more parallel wires to transmit high-frequency, digital, data bits. Shielding to prevent "cross talk," physical size, and expense are just some of the problems to be encountered in high-speed data transmission over closely spaced, parallel lines.

A model 3 Raspberry Pi can be configured to use one of several serial communications systems. Figures 6-21 and 6-22 display access to the Preferences ➤ configuration window that allows the implementation of the desired protocol.

Figure 6-21. *RPi Preferences Selection Menu*

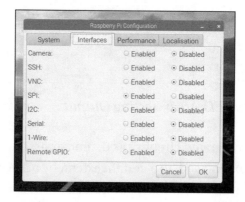

Figure 6-22. *Interfaces Selection Window*

Selection of the serial peripheral interface (SPI) protocol allows the RPi to communicate with devices that "stream out" data in a continuous flow of high and low bit pulses. An ADC is just such a data streaming device. SPI protocols work on a master-slave concept in which either three or four electrical connections form an electronic bus between the master and a single slave or several slave devices. A clock synchronizes the transfer of data. The four lines in an SPI configuration are master out slave in (MOSI), master in slave out (MISO), the clock line (SCLK), and the chip slave select (CSS).

SPI can become difficult to implement if there are a number of slaves, and a second popular protocol is the inter-integrated circuit (I^2C or I2C) protocol. I2C is a two-wire implementation, has slower fixed speeds, uses addressable locations, consumes more power than SPI, and has less noise. I2C is the only protocol that confirms the transmission of the data.

In Figure 6-22, there is a third communications interface called Serial that implements the universal asynchronous receiver and transmission (UART) protocol. An asynchronous communication operates between two devices only, without an external clock, but uses agreed-upon data transmission and receive rates at both ends. Each end of the two-wire bus has an IC that translates between parallel and serial data flows. In the UART transmission, a defined format specifies the beginning and end of the data with start and stop markers. The Serial protocol is used extensively in microprocessor communications.

For further details on the three protocols, see *Practical Electronics for Inventors.*[3]

Code Listings

Listing 6-1. DAQFactory–LabJack U12 Decimal-to-Binary Sequence Codes

```
//Decimal to Binary Conversion
//Oct 14-16, Nov 14/2009
//Program Algorithm
//8 LEDs are connected to the  digital output channels DO (#4)
// to D7 (#11) on the DB25 output of the LabJack. Each line is
// buffered/driven with a 4050 buffer.
```

---

[3] *Practical Electronics for Inventors* 3rd Edn., Schertz and Monk, McGraw Hill, ISBN 978-0-07-177133-7

```
//An EDIT box accepts the Number_To_Convert and the modulo of
// the value with respect to base 2 is determined for each bit
// of a byte. The bit values are then displayed on the LEDs
//A for loop executes 8 times to evaluate each bit of the
//binary digit
// On the control screen the researcher has the option to
// increase/decrease the conversion value and clear the byte
// register.
//
// Declarations
//
global Number_To_Convert
//Preserve original decimal value entered from the control screen
global Orgnl_N_To_Cnvrt = Number_To_Convert
//
Private Converted_Number[0] = 0
Private Converted_Number[1] = 0
Private Converted_Number[2] = 0
Private Converted_Number[3] = 0
Private Converted_Number[4] = 0
Private Converted_Number[5] = 0
Private Converted_Number[6] = 0
Private Converted_Number[7] = 0
//
//
for ( Private.Counter = 0, Counter < 8, Counter++)
     Converted_Number[Counter] = Number_To_Convert %2
     Number_To_Convert = Number_To_Convert/2
     Number_To_Convert = Floor(Number_To_Convert)
   endfor
```

```
//
   if (Converted_Number[0] == 1)
//
      DigOut = 1
   endif
//
   if (Converted_Number[1] == 1)
//
      DigOut_1 = 1
   endif
//
   if (Converted_Number[2] == 1)
//
      DigOut_2 = 1
   endif
//
   if (Converted_Number[3] == 1)
//
      DigOut_3 = 1
   endif
//
   if (Converted_Number[4] == 1)
//
      DigOut_4 = 1
   endif
//
   if (Converted_Number[5] == 1)
//
      DigOut_5 = 1
   endif
```

```
//
   if (Converted_Number[6] == 1)
//
      DigOut_6 = 1
   endif
//
   if (Converted_Number[7] == 1)
//
      DigOut_7 = 1
   Endif
```

Listing 6-2. DAQFactory Script Code to Increase the Converted Value

```
//IncBinDisplay
//Nov.14/09
//This sequence increases the screen entered global variable
//Number_To_Convert that was converted and displayed in
//sequence ConvertDecToBinary. The value of the original
//variable was iteratively reduced to zero by the conversion code
//but was preserved in the global variable Orgnl_N_To_Cnvrt.
//The preserved number is augmented in value and passed back
   through the original sequence.
//
global Orgnl_N_To_Cnvrt
//
//any residual values on the byte register are cleared
ClearByteDisplay()
//
// the original value is augmented
```

```
Number_to_Convert = Orgnl_N_To_Cnvrt + 1
//
//the augmented value is converted and displayed
ConvertDecToBinary()
```

Listing 6-3. DAQFactory Script Code to Decrease the Converted Value

```
//DecBinDisplay
//Nov.14/09
//This sequence decreases the screen entered global variable
//Number_To_Convert that was converted and displayed in
//sequence ConvertDecToBinary and runs the decreased value back
//through the original sequence.
//In the original conversion sequence the Edit Box value,
//variable, Number_To_Convert is iteratively divided by two till
//it vanishes so the entered number is saved in Orgnl_N_To_Cnvrt
//
global Orgnl_N_To_Cnvrt
//clear the register of any residual data
ClearByteDisplay()
//re-initialize the working variable to the desired value to be
converted
Number_to_Convert = Orgnl_N_To_Cnvrt - 1
//convert and display the bit pattern
ConvertDecToBinary()
```

Listing 6-4. DAQFactory Script Code to Clear Display

```
//ClearByteDisplay
//Nov.14/09
//This sequence just re-zeros the 8 bit byte display
//
```

```
DigOut = 0
DigOut_1 = 0
DigOut_2 = 0
DigOut_3 = 0
DigOut_4 = 0
DigOut_5 = 0
DigOut_6 = 0
DigOut_7 = 0
```

Listing 6-5. DAQFactory Code for Decimal-to-Binary Conversion via Serial Connection

```
//Decimal to Binary Conversion
//Oct 14-16, Nov 14/2009, serial port display Jun7/19
//Program Algorithm
//8 LEDs are connected to the  digital output channels D0 (#4)
//to D7 (#11) on the DB25 output of the LabJack. Each line is
//buffered/driven with a 4050 buffer.
//An EDIT box accepts the Number_To_Convert and the modulo of
// the value with respect to base 2 is determined for each bit
// of a byte. The bit values are then displayed on the LEDs. In
// this version a quick sequence writes the number of the
// digital pin on the Arduino connected to the diode to be
// illuminated on the serial port.
//A for loop executes 8 times to evaluate each bit of the
//binary digit
// On the control screen the researcher has the option to
// increase/decrease the conversion value and clear the byte
// register.
//
// Declarations
//
```

```
global Number_To_Convert
//Preserve original decimal value entered from the control screen
global Orgnl_N_To_Cnvrt = Number_To_Convert
//
global Converted_Number[0] = 0
global Converted_Number[1] = 0
global Converted_Number[2] = 0
global Converted_Number[3] = 0
global Converted_Number[4] = 0
global Converted_Number[5] = 0
global Converted_Number[6] = 0
global Converted_Number[7] = 0
//
//
//
//
for ( Private.Counter = 0, Counter < 8, Counter++)
      Converted_Number[Counter] = Number_To_Convert %2
      Number_To_Convert = Number_To_Convert/2
      Number_To_Convert = Floor(Number_To_Convert)
   endfor
//
   if (Converted_Number[0] == 1)
//
//      DigOut = 1
device.ardyRb.Write('3' + Chr(10))
   endif
//
   if (Converted_Number[1] == 1)
//
```

```
//        DigOut_1 = 1
device.ardyRb.Write('4' + Chr(10))
   endif
//
   if (Converted_Number[2] == 1)
//
//        DigOut_2 = 1
device.ardyRb.Write('5' + Chr(10))
   endif
//
   if (Converted_Number[3] == 1)
//
//        DigOut_3 = 1
device.ardyRb.Write('6' + Chr(10))
   endif
//
   if (Converted_Number[4] == 1)
//
//        DigOut_4 = 1
device.ardyRb.Write('7' + Chr(10))
   endif
//
   if (Converted_Number[5] == 1)
//
//        DigOut_5 = 1
device.ardyRb.Write('8' + Chr(10))
   endif
//
   if (Converted_Number[6] == 1)
//
```

```
//        DigOut_6 = 1
device.ardyRb.Write('9' + Chr(10))
   endif
//
   if (Converted_Number[7] == 1)
//
//        DigOut_7 = 1
device.ardyRb.Write('a' + Chr(10))
   endif
```

Listing 6-6. DAQFactory Sequence Code for Increasing the
Converted Value

```
//IncBinDisplay
//Nov.14/09
//This sequence increases the screen entered global variable
//Number_To_Convert that was converted and displayed in sequence
//ConvertDecToBinary. The value of the original variable was
//iteratively reduced to zero by the conversion code but was
//preserved in the global variable Orgnl_N_To_Cnvrt.
//The preserved number is augmented in value and passed back
//through the original sequence.
//
global Orgnl_N_To_Cnvrt
//
//any residual values on the byte register are cleared
ClearByteDisplay()
//
// the original value is augmented
Number_to_Convert = Orgnl_N_To_Cnvrt + 1
//
//the augmented value is converted and displayed
DecimalToBinaryCnvrsnRvn1()
```

Listing 6-7. DAQFactory Sequence Code for Decreasing the
Converted Value

```
//DecBinDisplay
//Nov.14/09
//This sequence decreases the screen entered global variable
//Number_To_Convert that was converted and displayed in
//sequence ConvertDecToBinary and runs the decreased value back
//through the original sequence.
//In the original conversion sequence the Edit Box value,
//variable, Number_To_Convert is iteratively divided by two till
//it vanishes so the entered number is saved in Orgnl_N_To_Cnvrt
//
global Orgnl_N_To_Cnvrt
//clear the register of any residual data
ClearByteDisplay()
//re-initialize the working variable to the desired value to be
converted
Number_to_Convert = Orgnl_N_To_Cnvrt - 1
//convert and display the bit pattern
DecimalToBinaryCnvrsnRvn1()
```

Listing 6-8. DAQFactory Sequence Code for Clearing the Display

```
/ClearByteDisplay
//Nov.14/09
//This sequence just re-zeros the 8 bit byte display
device.ardyRb.Write('z' + Chr(10))
```

Listing 6-9. Arduino Sketch Code for Diode Array Illumination

```
// DAQFactory - Arduino LED Illuminated Digital Bits in Byte
// Register DAQFtry screen bttns D0 to D7 light LEDs in digtal
// array. Total value of illuminated bits calculated and
// register cleared with buttons. DAQFtr uses scripting to
// evaluate digital bits and serial port transmisons to
// illuminate LEDs after selectn by case statement.
//
// digital pins in use 3,4,5,6,7,8,9, and 10
int pv_one = 3;
int pv_two = 4;
int pv_four = 5;
int pv_eight = 6;
int pv_steen = 7;
int pv_threetwo = 8;
int pv_sixfour = 9;
int pv_onetwoeight = 10;
int diod_num;
String inString = "";
//
void setup() {
  Serial.begin(9600);
//
}
//
void loop() {
  while (Serial.available() > 0 ){         // read serial input
  int inChar = Serial.read();
```

```
  if (inChar == '3') {
  pinMode(pv_one, OUTPUT);              // units value 2 exp 0
  digitalWrite(pv_one, HIGH);
 }

  if (inChar == '4') {
    pinMode(pv_two, OUTPUT);            // 2 exp 1 = 2
    digitalWrite(pv_two, HIGH);
 }

  if (inChar == '5') {
    pinMode(pv_four, OUTPUT);           // 2 exp 2 = 4
    digitalWrite(pv_four, HIGH);
 }

  if (inChar == '6') {
    pinMode(pv_eight, OUTPUT);          // 2 exp 3 = 8
    digitalWrite(pv_eight, HIGH);
 }

  if (inChar == '7') {
    pinMode(pv_steen, OUTPUT);          // 2 exp 4 = 16
    digitalWrite(pv_steen, HIGH);
 }

  if (inChar == '8') {
    pinMode(pv_threetwo, OUTPUT);       // 2 exp 5 = 32
    digitalWrite(pv_threetwo, HIGH);
 }

  if (inChar == '9') {
    pinMode(pv_sixfour, OUTPUT);        // 2 exp 6 = 64
    digitalWrite(pv_sixfour, HIGH);
 }

  if (inChar == 'a') {
    pinMode(pv_onetwoeight, OUTPUT);    // 2 exp 7 = 128
    digitalWrite(pv_onetwoeight, HIGH);
 }
```

```
  if (inChar == 'z') {
    // special case to clear array
  pinMode(pv_one, OUTPUT);
  digitalWrite(pv_one, LOW);
  //
  pinMode(pv_two, OUTPUT);
  digitalWrite(pv_two, LOW);
  //
    pinMode(pv_four, OUTPUT);
  digitalWrite(pv_four, LOW);
  //
  pinMode(pv_eight, OUTPUT);
  digitalWrite(pv_eight, LOW);
  //
  pinMode(pv_steen, OUTPUT);
  digitalWrite(pv_steen, LOW);
  //
  pinMode(pv_threetwo, OUTPUT);
  digitalWrite(pv_threetwo, LOW);
  //
  pinMode(pv_sixfour, OUTPUT);
  digitalWrite(pv_sixfour, LOW);
  //
  pinMode(pv_onetwoeight, OUTPUT);
  digitalWrite(pv_onetwoeight, LOW);
   }
 }
}
```

Listing 6-10. DAQFactory "On Receive" Code for the
ArduinoStream Channel

```
if (strIn == Chr(13))
   private string datain = ReadUntil(13)
   Channel.AddValue(strDevice, 0, "Input", 0,
   StrToDouble(DataIn))
   Endif
```

Listing 6-11. Arduino Sketch Code to Read A0 ADC Channel and
Write Data to Serial Port on 50 ms Intervals

```
/*
AnalogReadSerial
Reads an analog input on pin A0, prints the result to the
serial monitor.
Attach the center pin of a potentiometer to pin A0, and the
outside pins to +5V and ground.
*/

// the setup routine runs once when you press reset:
void setup() {
   // initialize serial communication at 9600 bits per second:
   Serial.begin(9600);
}

// the loop routine runs over and over again forever:
void loop() {
   // read the input on analog pin 0:
   int sensorValue = analogRead(A0);
   // print out the value you read:
   Serial.println(sensorValue);
   delay(50);         // delay in between reads for stability
}
```

Code Listings for Raspberry Pi

Listing 6-12. RPi Python Code for Decimal to 12-Bit Binary LED Visual Display

```
# Decimal to 12 Bit Binary LED Visual Display
#
import RPi.GPIO as GPIO
GPIO.setmode(GPIO.BCM)
GPIO.setwarnings(False)
# Ensure all LEDS are OFF and set to output mode
for i in range(2, 15):
    GPIO.setup(i, GPIO.OUT)
    GPIO.output(i, GPIO.LOW)
#
# input dec number to process
#
input_str = input("Decimal to convert to a 12 bit binary
display ",)
dec = int(input_str)
print()
# print out screen display headings
print("Quotient and remainder listing for conversion and
display illumination.")
print()
# first binary digit of 2**0 or 1s
Q1 = dec // 2
rem1 = dec % 2
if rem1 == 1:
    GPIO.output(2, GPIO.HIGH)
print("For LED 1 Q = ", Q1, "and rem = ", rem1)
#
```

```python
# second binary digit of 2**1 or 2s
Q2 = Q1 // 2
rem2 = Q1 % 2
if rem2 == 1:
    GPIO.output(3, GPIO.HIGH)
print("For LED 2 Q = ",  Q2, "and rem = ", rem2)
#
# third binary digit of 2**2 or 4s
Q3 = Q2 // 2
rem3 = Q2 % 2
if rem3 == 1:
    GPIO.output(4, GPIO.HIGH)
print("For LED 3 Q = ",Q3, "and rem = ", rem3)
#
# fourth binary digit of 2**3 or 8s
Q4 = Q3 // 2
rem4 = Q3 % 2
if rem4 == 1:
    GPIO.output(5, GPIO.HIGH)
print("For LED 4 Q = ",Q4, "and rem = ", rem4)
#
# fifth binary digit of 2**4 or 16s#
Q5 = Q4 // 2
rem5 = Q4 % 2
if rem5 == 1:
    GPIO.output(6, GPIO.HIGH)
print("For LED 5 Q = ",Q5, "and rem = ", rem5)
#
# sixth binary digit of 2**5 or 32s
Q6 = Q5 // 2
rem6 = Q5 % 2
```

```
if rem6 == 1:
    GPIO.output(7, GPIO.HIGH)
print("For LED 6 Q = ",Q6, "and rem = ", rem6)
#
# seventh binary digit of 2**6 or 64s
Q7 = Q6 // 2
rem7 = Q6 % 2
if rem7 == 1:
    GPIO.output(8, GPIO.HIGH)
print("For LED 7 Q = ",Q7, "and rem = ", rem7)
#
# eighth binary digit of 2**7 or 128s
Q8 = Q7 // 2
rem8 = Q7 % 2
if rem8 == 1:
    GPIO.output(9, GPIO.HIGH)
print("For LED 8 Q = ",Q8, "and rem = ", rem8)
#
# ninth binary digit of 2**8 or 256s
Q9 = Q8 // 2
rem9 = Q8 % 2
if rem9 == 1:
    GPIO.output(10, GPIO.HIGH)
print("For LED 9 Q = ",Q9, "and rem = ", rem9)
#
# tenth binary digit of 2**9 or 512s
Q10 = Q9 // 2
rem10 = Q9 % 2
if rem10 == 1:
    GPIO.output(11, GPIO.HIGH)
print("For LED 10 Q = ",Q10, "and rem = ", rem10)
#
```

```
# eleventh binary digit of 2**10 or 1024s
Q11 = Q10 // 2
rem11 = Q10 % 2
if rem11 == 1:
    GPIO.output(12, GPIO.HIGH)
print("For LED 11 Q = ",Q11, "and rem = ", rem11)
#
# twelfth binary digit of 2**11 or 2048s
Q12 = Q11 // 2
rem12 = Q11 % 2
if rem12 == 1:
    GPIO.output(13, GPIO.HIGH)
print("For LED 12 Q = ",Q12, "and rem = ", rem12)
```

Listing 6-13. SPI-Based Program to Read an MCP3008 10-Bit ADC

```
# An SPI based program to read an MCP3008 10 Bit ADC
# the referenced voltage range is divided into an integer from
# 0 to 1023 sampled voltage is ADC/1023 * 3.3 volts. A blend of
# GPIO and SPI code is used to run a 10 bit LED display of the
# ADC value.
#
# import the RPi.GPIO low level pin control library
import RPi.GPIO as GPIO
import spidev
import time
# setup the pin identification scheme
GPIO.setmode(GPIO.BCM)
# turn off the array use warnings
GPIO.setwarnings(False)
# ensure all the LED driver outputs are set to output and are zero
```

```python
for i in range(2, 7):
    GPIO.setup(i, GPIO.OUT)
    GPIO.output(i, GPIO.LOW)
for i in range(13, 18):
    GPIO.setup(i, GPIO.OUT)
    GPIO.output(i, GPIO.LOW)
# create required variables
# the delay time
delay = 0.5    # the value of time variable delay is defined
# the channel to use
pot_chnnl = 0
# create a spidev object of the device connected to the
# channel in use
spi = spidev.SpiDev()
spi.open(0, 0)
# create the readadc function that checks for the correct
channel assignment
# if the channel assignment is correct the adc value is read
# the function returns -1 a channel error or the adc value
def readadc(pot_chnnl):
    # check channel
    if pot_chnnl  > 7 or pot_chnnl < 0:
        return -1
    r = spi.xfer2([1,  8 + pot_chnnl << 4, 0])
    data = ((r[1] & 3) << 8) + r[2]
    return data
#
# the while loop, print out and time delay
while True:
    wpr_vlu = int(readadc(pot_chnnl))
    print("--------------------------------")
    print("Pot wiper value = ", wpr_vlu)
```

```python
# The LED Display Code
# Although initially set to low each binary bit
# determination must be reset to low as the code cycles in
# the while loop.
#
# first or least significant bit of 2**0 or 1s
Q1 = wpr_vlu // 2
rem1 = wpr_vlu % 2
GPIO.output(2, GPIO.LOW)
if rem1 == 1:
    print("Q1 = ", Q1, "rem1 = ", rem1)
    GPIO.output(2, GPIO.HIGH)
# second significant bit of 2**1 or 2s
Q2 = Q1 // 2
rem1 = Q1 % 2
GPIO.output(3, GPIO.LOW)
if rem1 == 1:
    print("Q2 = ", Q2, "rem1 = ", rem1)
    GPIO.output(2, GPIO.HIGH)
# third significant bit of 2**2 or 4s
Q3 = Q2 // 2
rem1 = Q2 % 2
GPIO.output(3, GPIO.LOW)
if rem1 == 1:
    print("Q3 = ", Q3, "rem1 = ", rem1)
    GPIO.output(3, GPIO.HIGH)
# fourth significant bit of 2**3 or 8s
Q4 = Q3 // 2
rem1 = Q3 % 2
GPIO.output(4, GPIO.LOW)
```

```python
if rem1 == 1:
    print("Q4 = ", Q4, "rem1 = ", rem1)
    GPIO.output(4, GPIO.HIGH)
# fifth significant bit of 2**4 or 16s
Q5 = Q4 // 2
rem1 = Q4 % 2
GPIO.output(5, GPIO.LOW)
if rem1 == 1:
    print("Q5 = ", Q5, "rem1 = ", rem1)
    GPIO.output(5, GPIO.HIGH)
# sixth significant bit of 2**5 or 32s
Q6 = Q5 // 2
rem1 = Q5 % 2
GPIO.output(6, GPIO.LOW)
if rem1 == 1:
    print("Q6 = ", Q6, "rem1 = ", rem1)
    GPIO.output(6, GPIO.HIGH)
# seventh significant bit of 2**6 or 64s
Q7 = Q6 // 2
rem1 = Q6 % 2
GPIO.output(13, GPIO.LOW)
if rem1 == 1:
    print("Q7 = ", Q7, "rem1 = ", rem1)
    GPIO.output(13, GPIO.HIGH)
# eighth significant bit of 2**7 or 128s
Q8 = Q7 // 2
rem1 = Q7 % 2
GPIO.output(14, GPIO.LOW)
if rem1 == 1:
    print("Q8 = ", Q8, "rem1 = ", rem1)
    GPIO.output(14, GPIO.HIGH)
```

```
# ninth significant bit of 2**8 or 256s
Q9 = Q8 // 2
rem1 = Q8 % 2
GPIO.output(15, GPIO.LOW)
if rem1 == 1:
    print("Q9 = ", Q9, "rem1 = ", rem1)
    GPIO.output(15, GPIO.HIGH)
# tenth or most significant bit of 2**9 or 512s
Q10 = Q9 // 2
rem1 = Q9 % 2
GPIO.output(16, GPIO.LOW)
if rem1 == 1:
    print("Q10 = ", Q10, "rem1 = ", rem1)
    GPIO.output(16, GPIO.HIGH)
# timing delay
time.sleep(delay)
```

Listing 6-14. RPi Code for Testing LEDs on GPIO Pin Array

```
# Test the LED Array on the GPIO pins
#
import RPi.GPIO as GPIO
import time
# set the pin identity mode
GPIO.setmode(GPIO.BCM)
GPIO.setwarnings(False)
# Reset the array pins to on for 3 sec then turn off
for i in range(2, 21):
    GPIO.setup(i, GPIO.OUT)
    GPIO.output(i, GPIO.HIGH)
    print("Testing pin ",i)
    time.sleep(3)
    GPIO.output(i, GPIO.LOW)
```

Listing 6-15. Utility Program to Reset the GPIO Pin Values to Zero

```
# Utility program to reset the GPIO pin values to 0
import RPi.GPIO as GPIO
# set the pin identity mode
GPIO.setmode(GPIO.BCM)
GPIO.setwarnings(False)
# Reset the array pins to off/false/0
chan_list = (2, 3, 4, 5, 6, 7, 8, 9, 10, 11, 12, 13, 14, 15,
16, 17, 18, 19, 20)
GPIO.setup(chan_list, GPIO.OUT)
GPIO.output(chan_list, GPIO.LOW)delay)
```

Summary

- ADC and DAC limitations along with the differences between integer and floating point (decimal-containing numbers) have been presented.

- Serial and parallel signal conversions and the various serial transmission protocols were introduced in both the commercial and less expensive component-assembled systems.

- An important application of digital-to-analog conversions is presented in Chapter 7 dealing with variable intensity and power controls.

CHAPTER 7

Variable Intensity and Power Control

The ability to arbitrarily alter or adjust the settings of either an experimental setup or a process control from the display screen is an integral part of SCADA systems. The DAQFactory software provides variable control icons such as rotating knobs or moveable sliders. The knob or slider page components can be coupled to an analog output channel whose value will be proportional to the rotating position of the control knob or the linear position of the slider index marker.

With proper design, the page component controls can be used to regulate substantial voltages and currents that in turn can activate electro-mechanical devices.

Manipulation of an image on a GUI control screen must at some point be translated into an electrical signal to provide the desired electro-mechanical actions in the experiment or process at hand. As previously introduced, digital systems function in a binary realm in which the required system action is generated in the form of a signal that is either on or off. However, there are many systems that require the ability to continually adjust the amount of action required and are thus in the analog realm. Motor speeds controlling fans, pumps or mixers, heating elements, intensity of illumination, and rotational positioning are some of the operations that may require adjustment by the experimenter or process operator.

© Richard J. Smythe 2021
R. J. Smythe, *Arduino in Science*, https://doi.org/10.1007/978-1-4842-6778-3_7

This exercise demonstrates two methods for exerting variable control over process or experimental setups through voltage control and a technique known as pulse width modulation (PWM).

An increase in the DC voltage of the power being fed to a device such as a motor, heater, or light source generally increases the speed, heat developed (a temperature increase), or luminance in proportion to the additional current passing through the load. It has been stated that PWM is a method for delivering partial power to a load by digital means. In essence, a PWM control application places the full voltage of the power supply across the load in the form of an adjustable-width, higher-frequency (often of several hundred Hz), rectangular pulse stream. Control of the power applied and used by the load is then determined by modifying the width of the full on and off times of the pulse waveform. The ratio between the on time and the width of the rectangular pulse is known as the duty cycle (see Figure 10-5 in Chapter 10). Variation of the duty cycle of the rectangular, full on or off waveform applied to the load is the essence of PWM power control.

PWM is a technique that can be implemented with software or, as presented in the later exercises on current control, with integrated circuitry. For many applications that require precise control, with smooth power transition, hardware-based PWM is much preferred.

For this exercise, PWM is introduced at its simplest level with an entirely software implementation. Restriction of the PWM process to a code-based program limits the techniques that can be used to visually demonstrate the process as is detailed in the following portions of this exercise.

The frequency at which the rectangular waveform is created for PWM must be substantially higher than the response time of the load. Rules of thumb suggest the frequency be twice the reciprocal of the device RC time constant or ten times higher than the control system frequency. In very simplified terms, it can be said that the PWM frequency should be high enough so as not to resonate with the RC time constant of the load. (See resistance-capacitance time constant in the reference.[1])

PWM is an extensively used technique in power control, digital-to-analog conversion, amplifier design, and communications but requires complex circuitry and can create radio frequency interference, voltage spikes, and EMI noise. (See triac control in the reference[1] and Chapter 10.)

Experimental

Variable Voltage Control

Hardware

A 2N3904 NPN transistor, a 10 kΩ resistor to limit the transistor base current, and an LED with the appropriate current limiting resistor are assembled on a breadboard in the configuration shown in Figure 7-1.

---

[1] *Practical Electronics for Inventors* 3rd Edn., Schertz and Monk, McGraw Hill, ISBN 978-0-07-177133-7

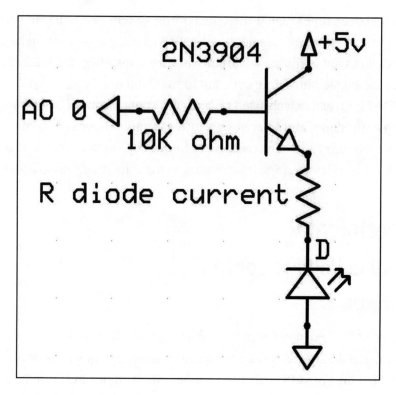

Figure 7-1. *LabJack Analog Output 0 Control of NPN Transistor*

Software

The rotating knob control is selected from the right button pop-up menu as shown in Figure 7-2.

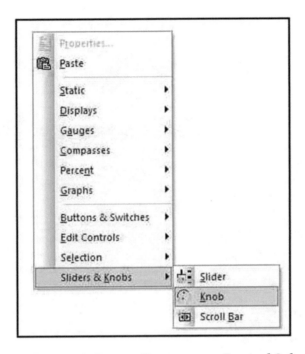

Figure 7-2. *DAQFactory Screen Component Control Selection Menu*

After positioning and sizing the control icon on a page of the display screen, the properties option is selected to gain access to the knob configuration screens.

The visual appearance of the default-valued un-configured screen icon depicted in the following can be altered with the appropriate entries in the boxes displayed in the Main tab. As with all screen icons, the corresponding Help file can be displayed below the screen object being manipulated. Some of the visual effect options presented in the Main tab of the properties window are only evident on larger display images of the icon.

The knob control indicator image defaults to the displayed dot, but with the radio buttons seen to the right in the indicator sub-panel, this can be changed to select a triangle or a conventional line index to mark the degree of control rotation. The default blue indicator image can be changed by selecting the desired color from the palette available by left-clicking the Color box seen in Figure 7-3.

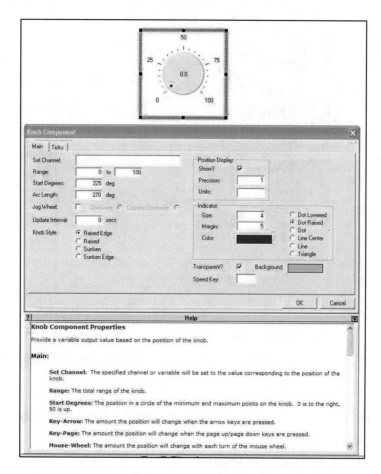

Figure 7-3. *DAQFactory Screen Component Configuration Window*

Figure 7-4 depicts the window opened by selecting the "Ticks" tab seen in Figure 7-3. Within the Ticks window, the investigator can select the nominal aspects of the circular scale and establish the resolution of the display and its appearance in the final window.

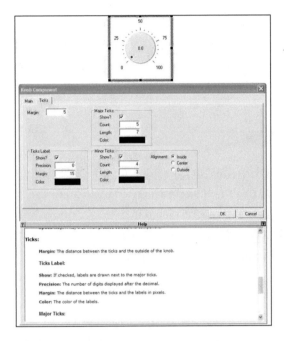

Figure 7-4. *Knob Tick Configuration Window*

The final configuration of the author's screen component is displayed in Figure 7-5.

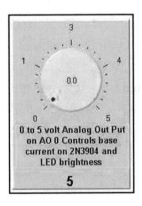

Figure 7-5. *Base Current and LED Intensity Rotating Control Knob with Instruction Panel*

Scripting is not required. The slider or the knob automatically provides a variable output based upon the position of the knob or slider. The channel specified in the Set Channel box of the Main tab of the properties window is set to and outputs the required proportional signal.

Observations

As detailed in the DAQFactory manual, the knob or slider can be set to numerous configurations for controlled activation of the selected channel. Because the control in this exercise has been set up to control the power to an LED, there is a certain amount of "dead band" created by the minimum voltage required to activate the LED at hand.

Discussion

Finer degrees of control for the voltage applied to the transistor base and ultimately to the power delivered by the semiconductor can be realized by configuring the starting position at 225° of rotation and assigning the starting voltage to the breakdown voltage of the LED being used. The forward voltage drop in an LED can vary from 1.2 volts for the infrareds up to 4 or 5 volts for the blues and white devices. The author's setup used a green LED, so depending upon the intended usage of the screen icon, the dial could be configured to start at 3 volts or at zero. The 0–5-volt range could be used and calibrated if the turn on voltage itself is to be estimated, or the dial could be set to indicate from 3.0–5.0 volts to reproduce diode intensity/power applied settings.

Experimental

Pulse Width Modulation of Voltage

Introduction

Typically, the implementation of a software program to demonstrate the fundamentals of PWM uses an LED with a high-frequency variable duty cycle waveform as presented in Chapter 10. In this exercise, the fundamental concept and method of PWM is demonstrated with an electronic-electrical system that has a very simple software signal generator and a relatively slowly responding load consisting of an incandescent light bulb.

In keeping with the simple introduction to creating sequences with the DAQFactory software, an elementary program sequence that coarsely varies current through a 12-volt, battery-powered DC automotive lamp is presented in Listing 7-1 at the end of the chapter.

The code has been reduced to the bare minimum number of statements required to generate the typical rectangular waveform. The duty cycle values must be entered or changed manually by the experimenter as numerical values in the two delay statements in the DAQFactory sequence. The default settings in the code listings are 0.005 and 0.095 that combine to give a total rectangular pulse width of 0.1 seconds.

Figure 7-6 depicts the circuit used to provide a slow-response load for the PWM demonstration.

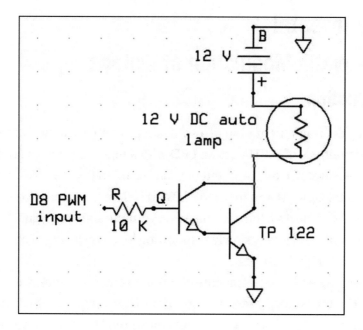

Figure 7-6. *Incandescent Bulb Load for PWM Demonstration*

Observations

Figures 7-7, 7-8, 7-9, and 7-10 depict the varying intensities of brightness of the incandescent bulb and the corresponding low and high duty cycle PWM waveforms.

Figure 7-7. *Incandescent Bulb Load for PWM at low DC power*

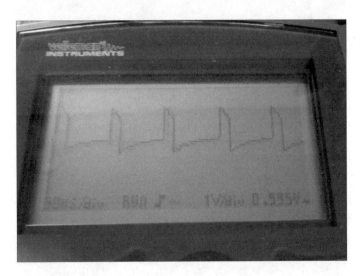

Figure 7-8. *Low PWM DC Waveform for Incandescent Bulb Load*

Figure 7-9. *Incandescent Bulb Load for PWM at High DC Power*

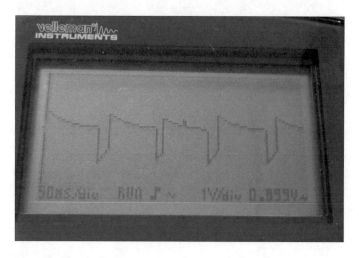

Figure 7-10. *High PWM DC Waveform for Incandescent Bulb Load*

If the pulse code is used with an LED, the flash rate can be seen to be different for the 5 ms and 95 ms time periods, but the eye has difficulty in seeing a difference in the illumination between the two, noticeably flashing, power settings. An incandescent lamp, however, displays a much greater visible response to the different power levels as is evident in Figures 7-7 and 7-9.

Discussion

In the introduction to PWM in this exercise, a point has been made about the need for the frequency of the rectangular wave carrying the power to be substantially higher than the time constant of the system to which the power pulses are applied. In very simplified terms, it can be said that the PWM frequency must be higher than the response time of the load. The incandescent lamp and battery response times are slow enough to visually illustrate the power control ability of a very simple, rudimentary DAQFactory sequence in creating a graphically visual PWM demonstration. The PWM signals for this demonstration are generated by the DAQFactory sequence of just six lines of code. The oscilloscope recordings of Figures 7-8 and 7-10 correspond to a little less than 2 Hz. Although the frequency is not that high, it is sufficient with the time required for the filament to heat up and reach thermal and illumination stability that a two-cycle PWM illumination control technique produces the desired results. Using a software program such as the first entry in the code listings to vary the times at which the signal is on and off is often referred to as "bit banging" PWM.

PWM techniques are a very important part of many digital electronics and electro-mechanical systems and in many cases are implemented from hardware devices as will be encountered in several of the exercises to follow using the Arduino microcontroller.

Virtually all microcontroller boards as have been used in previous exercises as inexpensive substitutions for DAQ systems are equipped with digital pin outputs capable of outputting hardware-implemented PWM signals (see Chapter 10).

Raspberry Pi Variable Intensity Control

Introduction

Physical computing with the RPi is only possible through the general-purpose input and output pin array seen as the double row of 13 or 20 male pins along the upper portion of the RPi circuit board in Figure 1-16 in Chapter 1. The digital nature of the programmable pins on the array allows the implementation of software PWM operations from either experimenter-written code or from libraries containing various forms of PWM operations.

Intensity variation screen control icons or components are available from the tkinter graphical image library available from online sources as discussed in the documentation provided online by the Raspberry Pi and Python Foundations.[2]

To accommodate the ever-increasing interest in and development of physical computing and the "Internet of things," the RPi Foundation has approved three open source Python libraries to facilitate the use of the GPIO array in connecting to the outside world. The initial library release was of a more fundamental or lower-level code with the import designation of RPi.GPIO, while the later more sophisticated codes can be accessed by importing the gpiozero and pigpio libraries. RPi.GPIO contains the code required to work with mechanical devices using either the polling method or interrupts to detect mechanical motions such as button or switch contact closings, "debouncing" these events, and

---

[2]docs/python.org/3/library/tk.html

using the contact actions to initiate electrical activity on the GPIO pin array. It is reported in the RPi documentation that the gpiozero library is built upon the RPi.GPIO library and contains many elements of very easy-to-use objects derived from the use of very well-explained, object-oriented programming code. A detailed listing of library use and the objects available can be found online.[3] Researchers and educators will find the list of objects created in the gpiozero library is extensive, and the documentation detailing their implementation and wiring is so very detailed that a printout of the archive may aid greatly in further work.

The third and most recently released physical computing library, imported as pigpio, is very different from the previous two facilities as it is written in C for implementation on several operating systems. For use on the RPi's Linux operating system, an interfacing program must be running in order for the Python interpreter to access the pigpio library. The program also called a daemon is started from the Linux terminal with a sudo pigpiod command.

The pigpio facility has extensive documentation that encompasses detailed code syntax, the numerous testing and visualization utilities available, and a large assortment of simple and very sophisticated codes for interfacing to all manner of sensors and hardware. The library also provides code for several of the more popular communications protocols.

C code is well known for its very fast execution, and the pigpio library uses both software and hardware to provide single-digit microsecond time resolution for its PWM and rectangular waveform generation and voltage transition detection operations.

PWM applications are available through all the libraries, and several RPi code listings from the three libraries are presented at the end of this chapter to demonstrate the facets of software PWM power control using the three different facilities.

---

[3] http://gpiozero.readthedocs.org/ and https://sourceforge.net/p/ raspberry-gpio-python/wiki/Examples

Experimental

Software PWM signal generation and applications using the RPi physical computing libraries are presented in a series of six programs. Observations of the desired PWM effects can be achieved by using the Run Module in the IDLE screen menu to access and process the stored program code. Program execution can be halted by using the Ctrl+C key combination.

In addition to the demonstration programs, a very short utility program is also provided to aid in the development and testing of the pigpio physical computing code.

PWM Signals with the RPi.GPIO Library

Listing 7-2 can be used to demonstrate the basics of PWM waveform generation with the circuit of Figure 7-11.

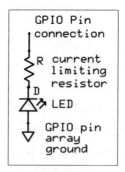

Figure 7-11. *LED–GPIO Pin Connection Schematic*

It has been noted in previous exercises that the RPi.GPIO array is limited in the current that it is able to safely supply to any peripherals connected to the pins. Figure 7-11 depicts the generic connections that are required to display the effects created by the programs under study and development. It is left to the experimenter to safely configure the electronic components so the power draw from the GPIO pin or pins in use and the array ground are safely within the operating limits of both the computer and the LED.

The program code PWM_tst1 raises and then lowers the #6 pin of the GPIO array between 3.3 and 0 volts. The width of the on-off pulse or its duty cycle (DC) is defined and entered into the program code by the investigator as the variable prcnt_on. The actual PWM waveform is generated by two loops, a continuous outer loop controlled by a "while" statement that sets the #6 pin to a high value and an inner "if loop" that counts out the number of units in the prcnt_on variable before resetting the pin to 0 volts.

Setting the prcnt_on variable to 5, 50, and 95 can be used to demonstrate the variation in intensity of the LED illumination.

A demonstration of the effects of the frequency of the PWM signal on the observed illumination intensity of the LED at hand is given in Listing 7-3 written with the RPi.GPIO library. When developing the RPi. GPIO PWM frequency effect demonstration program, a suitable visual effect was obtained when five different array pin–LED channels were used to demonstrate the effects of PWM frequency on the observed LED illuminations. The demonstration program set the duty cycle to a constant value of 95%, and only the frequency of the PWM power signal was changed.

Prior to loading and running the PWM frequency effect code, five LEDs and current limiting resistors must be wired to the GPIO array as depicted in Figure 7-11. GPIO pins 3, 4, 5, 6, and 7 that are found at physical positions (see Chapter 1, Figure 1-16) 5, 7, 29, 31, and 26 of the 40-pin array can be used.

PWM Signals with the gpiozero Library

Listing 7-4 from the gpiozero documentation is a very simple single-LED PWM illumination variation program demonstrating the advanced interfacing available with the gpiozero library. The pulsed LED PWM program that varies the power applied to an LED to alter the intensity or brightness of its output consists of five lines of code, of which two are import statements. A circuit to demonstrate software PWM is configured as depicted in Figure 7-11. The author used a 5 mm LED and a 220 Ω current limiting resistor and connected the circuit to GPIO pin 21 (physical pin #40) and ground (physical pin #34). To see the control possible with the technique, the program code is loaded into the Python IDLE editor screen and the Run menu used to launch or process the code.

The gpiozero library contains numerous objects for interfacing the RPi output array and the MCP3008, eight-channel, 10-bit ADC, as depicted in the circuit diagram of Chapter 6, Figure 6-17, which can be used in a PWM demonstration using a RGB LED.

Listings 7-5 and 7-6 use three potentiometers biased between the positive RPi power output and ground to provide three signals to the first three channels of the MCP ADC that in turn function as three PWM signals to vary the intensity of the individual red, green, and blue outputs of the LED. The programs differ by the code used to implement the PWM function. In theory, any desired color of light can be produced by the three-potentiometer color control circuit configuration as depicted in Figure 7-12.

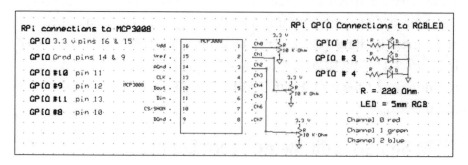

Figure 7-12. *PWM Three-Potentiometer RGB LED Color Control Circuit*

Although the first three channels of the MCP3008 are used with 220 Ω resistors to limit the currents through the diode, the typical output intensity of a green LED can be five times that of the red and blue devices. To "balance" or equalize the sensitivity of the green channel, a higher value resistance may be desired by the experimenter.

PWM Signals with the pigpio Library

To load, activate, and access the pigpio library on operating system images or operating system code installations that do not have the library already included in the code, a number of commands have to be entered at the terminal. (Raspbian Jessie 2016-05-10 or newer comes with the pigpio C library pre-installed.)

The author's RPi has been in use for several years, and the newer library had to be loaded at the terminal as detailed in the following:

1) Enter at the terminal prompt – wget abyz.co.uk/rpi/pigpio/pigpio.zip

2) unzip pigpio.zip

3) cd PIGPIO

4) make

5) make install

The first two lines download the zipped file and unzip the Python code to create the file PIGPIO in the home / pi directory fairly quickly. The "make" and "make install" can take a minute or so to process depending upon the speed of the Pi on which the library is being installed. Three programs are created in the /home / pi / PIGPIO file: "pigpio.py" is a documentation program explaining the Python pigpio module, which is slightly over a hundred printed pages that define and explain all the module functions and variables and provide short typical coded applications. In addition to the documentation are "setup.py," an RPi access module for the pigpio daemon, and "x_pigpio.py," a 15–20-page coding of an extensive full test program of all the library functions available from the pigpio library.

Listing 7-7 is a simple program demonstrating pigpio basic operations that access the pigpio library through the running interface (pigpiod) to turn an LED on and off and then vary the brightness with a four-step PWM illumination intensity increase and decrease. Listing 7-8 is a pigpio test utility that prints out the status of the GPIO pins in the array.

Observations

PWM_tst1

The LED illumination intensity variation is readily seen between the low, medium, and high experiments when the three simulated duty cycle values are entered into the program and the code is run. During the three illumination periods, the code appears to be cycling fast enough to produce a flicker rate that is not immediately perceptible.

Figure 7-13 is the output from the RPi.GPIO PWM frequency effect demonstration program.

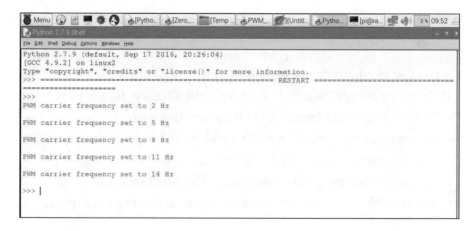

Figure 7-13. *PWM Frequency Variation Effect with RPi.GPIO Library Code*

An LED is capable of switching on and off in the mega-Hz range; and as expected, the 2, 5, and 8 Hz PWM signals flash on and off and flicker noticeably, while the 11 and 14 Hz signals are reasonably stable with minimal perceivable flicker or "jitter." (See "Discussion" for jitter description and origin.)

PWM Control of RGB LED Output

The various diode colors can be seen to predominate the device output as the shafts on the variable resistors are individually turned from their off to full on positions. Although the circuit of Figure 7-12 has three equal resistance values that allow the green to dominate the LED output, a distinct sporadic and irregular variation of the intensity of the diode output is visually discernible.

The pigpio library program produces a bright steady illumination when the LED is powered on and during the four-step increase and decrease of the diode illumination intensity. (See "Discussion.")

Included in the code listings is the utility program that tests the status of the first 32 pins of the RPi GPIO array and prints out their status in a tabular form as depicted in Figure 7-14.

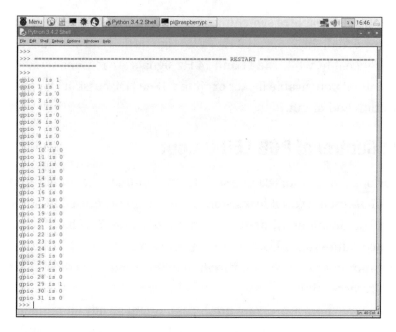

Figure 7-14. *Tested Status of the GPIO Pins*

The test program not only prints out the status of each of the 32 pins of the array but also confirms the operation of the Linux daemon interfacing of the Python interpreter with the C code library.

The preceding tabulation was run after the "reset array to zero" utility of Chapter 6 was used to clear the RPi array (Listing 6-15 in Chapter 6). Pins 1, 2, and 29 are the power supply pins of the array.

Discussion

A portion of the RPi.GPIO library is devoted to the implementation of interfacing lower-level devices such as mechanical switches to the RPi's GPIO pin array. The library has functions for determining if the current state of any pin is high or low (+ system logic voltage level of 5 or 3.3 V or at system ground potential of 0 V.) detecting changes in the pin state and for determining when or how the transitions are to be monitored or detected.

The RPi uses a Linux-based multitasking operating system that may temporarily take control away from lower-level priority input/output operations. On a normal time scale as encountered in the operation of a mouse or keyboard, the I/O operation may not be significantly affected by the delay; but for higher-precision operations on shorter time scales such as with graphics displays, it may become quite evident. In this exercise, the visual effects of the irregular timing can be seen as the flickering in the LED intensity or, as it is sometimes called, "jitter."

When using the change frequency function of the RPi.GPIO library, it is much easier to use a different pin array–LED channel for each new frequency than it is to try and use the same channel and change its frequency five times.

A distinct increase in capability and flexibility is evident in the applications possible with the three GPIO physical computing libraries. The pigpio is more complex to use but is far more powerful than the simpler libraries. As noted previously, the C-based library is able to use the Linux operating system and system hardware to achieve single-digit microsecond time resolutions on many of the library operations. The simple demonstration program used in this exercise is completely flicker- or jitter-free.

In addition to the simple LED illumination function program, a very short but useful utility program is included at the end of the code listings that produces a printout of the state of each of the GPIO pins from 0 to 31. The printout to the console lists all of the pins and their current high/low values as 1 or 0. In addition to displaying the high/low voltage level of the individual pins, the utility confirms the functioning of the Python pigpio interfacing daemon program.

A majority of the pigpio library functions and capabilities will be encountered, demonstrated, and discussed as required in later more advanced exercises in RPi physical computing dealing with advanced PWM applications; sensor initiation or monitoring; Serial, I2C, and SPI communications; and motor or servo controls.

Code Listings

Listing 7-1. DAQFactory Sequence Program for PWM

```
while(1)
    sftwr_pwm = 5
    delay(0.095)
    sftwr_pwm = 0
    delay(0.005)
endwhile
```

Listing 7-2. RPi Python PWM_tst1

```
Python Code for Raspberry Pi PWM_tst1
# A software PWM demonstration on GPIO - 6
import RPi.GPIO as GPIO
GPIO.setmode(GPIO.BCM)
GPIO.setwarnings(False)
GPIO.setup(6, GPIO.OUT)
#
# set the duty cycle
prcnt_on = 10
#
# the outer loop to provide the continuous application of the
    modulated power signal
while True:
    # start the duty cycle loop and set the output pin to ON
    GPIO.output(6, 1)
    for i in range(1, 100):
        if i == prcnt_on:
            GPIO.output(6, 0)
```

Listing 7-3. RPI.GPIO PWM Frequency Effect Demonstration

```
# RPi PWM Frequency Demonstration with the RPi.GPIO Library
# 5 LEDs are used to illustrate the effects of the frequency of
the carrier wave on PWM techniques. Different carrier
# frequencies are used at a constant duty cycle to illustrate
# the effects of frequency om PWM
import RPi.GPIO as GPIO
import time
# Array set up
GPIO.setmode(GPIO.BCM) # Use BCM pin reference
GPIO.setwarnings(False) # turn off the array use warnings
GPIO.setup(3, GPIO.OUT) # set pin #3 for output
#
pwm = GPIO.PWM(3, 2) # a PWM instance on pin 3 to operate at
                        2 Hz is setup
print("PWM carrier frequency set to 2 Hz")
print(" ")# print a blank line in the output
dc = 95 # the duty cycle is set close to full on
pwm.start(dc)# start the application of PWM power
time.sleep(5)# Keep the LED illuminated for 5 seconds
pwm.stop()# stop the power application
#
# carrier frequency increased to 5 Hz
print("PWM carrier frequency set to 5 Hz")
print(" ")
GPIO.setup(4, GPIO.OUT) # set pin #4 for output
pwm = GPIO.PWM(4, 5) # a PWM instance on pin 4 to operate at
                        5 Hz is setup
dc = 95 # the duty cycle is set close to full on
pwm.start(dc)
time.sleep(5)
```

```python
#
# carrier frequency increased to 8 Hz
print("PWM carrier frequency set to 8 Hz")
print(" ")
GPIO.setup(5, GPIO.OUT) # set pin #5 for output
pwm = GPIO.PWM(5, 8) # a PWM instance on pin 5 to operate at
                      8 Hz is setup
dc = 95 # the duty cycle is set close to full on
pwm.start(dc)
time.sleep(5)
pwm.stop()
#
# carrier frequency increased to 11 Hz
print("PWM carrier frequency set to 11 Hz")
print(" ")
GPIO.setup(6, GPIO.OUT) # set pin #6 for output
pwm = GPIO.PWM(6, 11) # a PWM instance on pin 6 to operate at
                       11 Hz is setup
dc = 95 # the duty cycle is set close to full on
pwm.start(dc)
time.sleep(5)
pwm.stop()
#
# carrier frequency increased to 14 Hz
print("PWM carrier frequency set to 14 Hz")
print(" ")
GPIO.setup(7, GPIO.OUT) # set pin #7 for output
pwm = GPIO.PWM(7, 14) # a PWM instance on pin 7 to operate at
                       14 Hz is setup
dc = 95 # the duty cycle is set close to full on
pwm.start(dc)
```

```
time.sleep(5)
pwm.stop()
```

Listing 7-4. Single-LED PWM with the gpiozero Library

```
from gpiozero import PWMLED
from signal import pause

led = PWMLED(21)

led.pulse()

pause()
```

Listing 7-5. Control of a RGB LED with gpiozero PWM Library and Three Potentiometers

```
# PWM Control of RGB Led Diode Pgm 1
from gpiozero import RGBLED, MCP3008
#
led = RGBLED(red=2, green=3, blue=4)
#
red_pot = MCP3008(channel=0)
green_pot = MCP3008(channel=1)
blue_pot = MCP3008(channel=2)
#
while True:
    led.red = red_pot.value
    led.green = green_pot.value
    led.blue = blue_pot.value
```

Listing 7-6. PWM Control of RGB LED with Three ADC Channels and Pause()

```
# PWM Control of RGB Led Diode Pgm 2
# PWM Control of RGB Led Diode
from gpiozero import RGBLED, MCP3008
from signal import pause
#
led = RGBLED(2, 3, 4)
#
red_pot = MCP3008(channel=0)
green_pot = MCP3008(channel=1)
blue_pot = MCP3008(channel=2)
#
led.source = zip(red_pot.values, green_pot.values, blue_pot.
values)
#
pause()
```

Listing 7-7. *pigpio Basic Operations Program*

```
# A simple demonstration of some basic pigpio capabilities.
# The PIGPIO library must be d/l, installed and available on
  the RPi in use.
# The requirements for use of the library code must be met and
  the interface
# often called a daemon must be running to provide an interface
  between the pigpio library written in C and the
# Python interpreter. (see PIGPIO documentation)
#
import pigpio
import time
#
```

```
pi = pigpio.pi()# create a instance of the pigpio class
#
# Simple LED illumination
pi.set_mode(4, pigpio.OUTPUT) #set gpio 4 for output
pi.write(4,1) # set gpio pin 4 high
time.sleep(0.5)# delay for 1/2 sec
pi.write(4,0) # turn LED off
#
time.sleep(2) # delay for 2 sec between displays
#
# simple PWM controlled variable brightness scaled from 0 - off
to 255 - full on
pi.set_PWM_dutycycle(4,  0)  #PWM off
time.sleep(0.5)# delay for 1/2 sec
pi.set_PWM_dutycycle(4, 64) # PWM power at 1/4 on
time.sleep(0.5)
pi.set_PWM_dutycycle(4,128) # PWM power at 1/2 on
time.sleep(0.5)
pi.set_PWM_dutycycle(4,192) # PWM power 3/4 on
time.sleep(0.5)
pi.set_PWM_dutycycle(4, 255) # PWM power full on
time.sleep(0.5)
pi.set_PWM_dutycycle(4,192) # PWM power 3/4 on
time.sleep(0.5)
pi.set_PWM_dutycycle(4,128) # PWM power 1/2 on
time.sleep(0.5)
pi.set_PWM_dutycycle(4, 64) #  PWM power 1/4 on
time.sleep(0.5)
pi.set_PWM_dutycycle(4, 0) # PWM power off
#
pi.stop()
```

Listing 7-8. pigpio Test Utility

```
# pigpio pin status and test utility
# ensure that the pigpio daemon is running and run the following
code from the run menu in the Python 3 IDLE facility.
#
import pigpio
pi = pigpio.pi() # create an instance of the library
for g in range(0, 32):  # recall range must be the required
                         number of iterations + 1
    print("gpio {} is {}".format(g, pigio.read(g))) # print out
    a tabulated status report
pigpio.stop()
```

Summary

- Variable intensity controls in the commercial software are used to implement PWM methods in software to demonstrate how the technique functions.

- Several methods are presented for implementation of PWM techniques with the inexpensive RPi computing platform.

- In Chapter 8, the detection of events that occur outside of the host computer in the SCADA system and how the time between multiple events is measured are presented.

CHAPTER 8

Counting Events and Timing

This exercise considers the methods available for dealing with time measurements in physical computing. Software or hardware can be used to directly measure time or time intervals. Time intervals can then be used to make frequency measurements by counting the number of events that occur in fixed units of time or determine speeds and accelerations when distances traveled in time intervals are evaluated.

Determinations of time of day and the time between events are important parameters for gathering scientific data and in process control. Turning a light on or collecting data from 9:05 till 9:35 could be classified as an "absolute" or "time of day" format, while measuring the time required for a ball to fall a fixed distance through a viscous liquid may be termed a differential time measurement.

The user manual for DAQFactory advises against attempting to work in time frames of less than a half or quarter of a second with software scripting. Fractions of a second are at about the limit of a high-level software's ability to process threads of code for data processing while maintaining a system status display screen user interface. Measurement of millisecond, microsecond, or lower time frames usually requires the use of assembly language programming for software timing or a physical timing device for hardware timing. There are several hardware timing devices available such as the LabJack HMI, Arduino microcontroller boards, or

© Richard J. Smythe 2021
R. J. Smythe, *Arduino in Science*, https://doi.org/10.1007/978-1-4842-6778-3_8

555 timer integrated circuits, all of which are able to work in time frames measured in milli- and microseconds. This first portion of the chapter examines the basics of digital time concepts and demonstrates software limitations. The remaining portions of the chapter and exercises deal with short time scales available through integrated circuitry hardware and the introductory concepts of frequency.

Electronically, time is measured with oscillator clocks generating fixed-voltage (5.0 or 3.3 volts) square wave signals that may have frequencies in the mega- and giga-Hertz ranges. (MHz are 10^6 cycles per second, and GHz are 10^9 cycles per second.) The PC on which this manuscript is being written has a 1.48 GHz clock speed, while an Arduino microcontroller has a 16 MHz clock speed, and the various models of the Raspberry Pi have clock speeds from 800 MHz to 1.5 GHz.

Electronic oscillators, regulated to a high degree of precision and accuracy by quartz crystals, can be configured to generate a pulse train of square waves that can be counted individually to measure time. With very stable oscillator frequencies of MHz and GHz and individual pulse counting capability, time frames of micro- and nanoseconds can be measured very accurately.

Desktop, portable, and network-connected computing devices are able to keep track of the time of day through either the network connection or a battery backup system when the computing device is switched off. Some devices such as the Raspberry Pi and the Arduino microcontrollers require the addition of an accessory called a "real-time clock" (RTC) that has a battery backup to keep an accurate track of the time of day when the device is powered down.

Software Time and Timing

DAQFactory SCADA software is a self-contained program written to run on Windows-based operating systems. Batteries are used to maintain the operating system time counts when the computer is shut down between operating sessions. Time in DAQFactory is measured in seconds since 1970 with microsecond resolution. When a DAQFactory session is started, the program takes the date and time from the operating system, initializes an internal counter, and maintains a time count in seconds from January 1, 1970. The DAQFactory clock runs independently of the operating system timer and produces a decimal second time resolution. Time functions available in DAQFactory are detailed in the "Expressions" section of the user manual. The software time functions available are used in the first part of this exercise to create two, one-second-resolution, screen-activated timers that start and stop electronic operations on the external breadboard and measure the elapsed or cumulative times between manually observed events much like a handheld stopwatch. The basic software time evaluation screen is depicted in Figure 8-1.

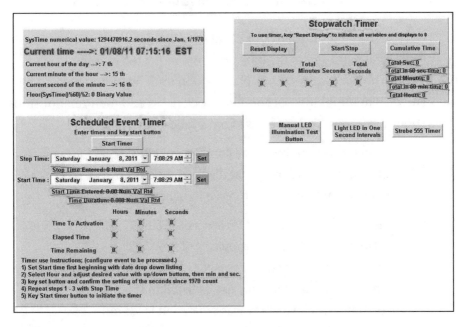

Figure 8-1. *GUI for Three Timing Operations*

Basic Time Variables

Figure 8-2 depicts several of the basic current DAQFactory time values.

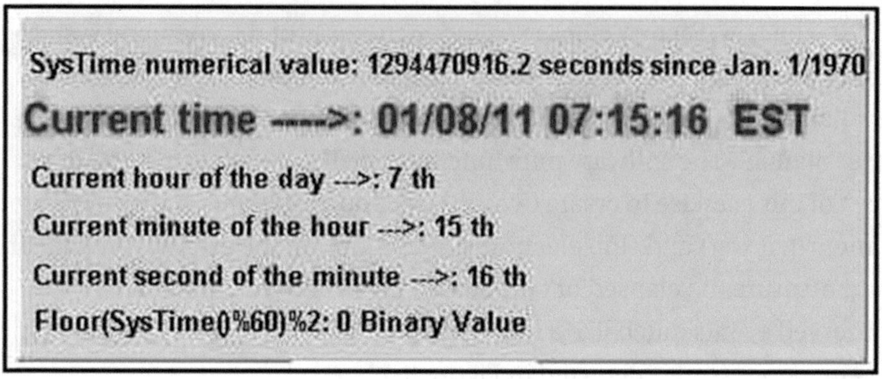

Figure 8-2. *GUI for Current Timing Operations and Values*

The basic variables screen consists of six variable value components (VVCs) and was captured at the date and time indicated in red. Configuring the entries on the panel will aid in understanding the mathematical manipulation of counter "clock ticks" and their relationships to our hours, minutes, and seconds of our cyclic time concepts:

1) The first line variable value component (VVC) expression is SysTime() that displays the number of seconds that have elapsed since January 1, 1970.

2) Line 2 uses the statement "FormatDateTime("%c", SysTime())" in the expression box of the VVC to generate the time of day displayed. A large number of formats are available for use as listed in the user manual. The display was created in large red characters for visual emphasis.

3) Lines 3–5 use modulo notation to convert the total tick counts of SysTime() into various timekeeping values, while line 6 produces a one-second modulated switching between logic one and zero.

Scheduled Event Timer

The scripting of Listing 8-1 (provided at the end of the chapter with all others) titled Scheduled Time Timer controls the GUI panel shown in Figure 8-3.

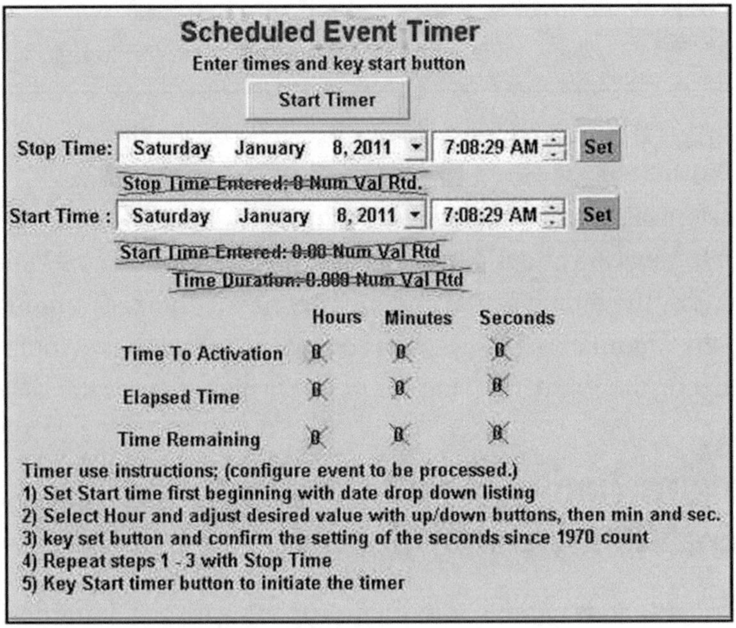

Figure 8-3. *A DAQFactory Scheduled Event Timer GUI*

The Stopwatch Timer

The nominal group of controls depicted in Figure 8-4 implements stopwatch-style timing and is controlled by the code of Listing 8-2.

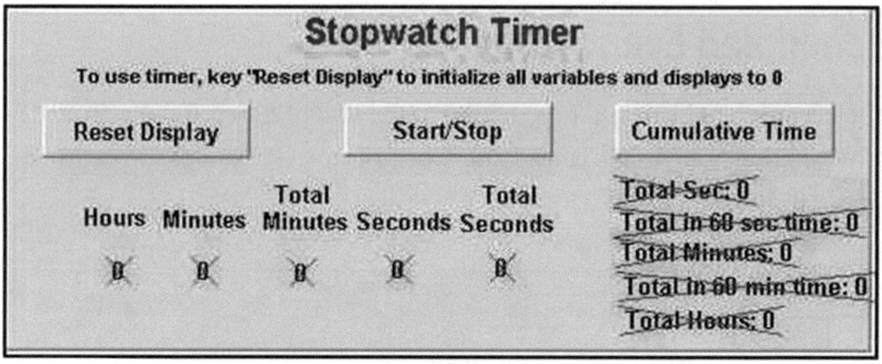

Figure 8-4. *A Stopwatch Timer GUI*

The stopwatch timer is activated by three DAQFactory sequences found in Listings 8-3 and 8-4. The Start/Stop button (Listing 8-2) initiates or terminates the timing action and thus defines an interval. A mouse click on the Cumulative Time button adds the current interval into the accumulating time sum. Clicking the Reset Display re-zeros the GUI.

Hardware Timing, Event Counting, and Frequency Determination

Any physical actions in our world such as opening a door, entering a room, and turning on a light can be translated by sensors into electrical transitions that can be monitored and recorded by electronic systems. Activation of a typical light switch causes the electrical power applied to a light source to jump from the on to the off extreme. The electrical waveform that results from the act of turning the light on, leaving it on for a time t, and switching it off can be considered as a "pulse of duration t." Electrical pulses can be created by the conversions of mechanical, optical, and electromagnetic events into sharp changes in electronic signal levels.

Pulse counting is accomplished by the use of bipolar transistor or CMOS integrated circuitry in which interconnected transistor switches are able to record, in binary format, the number of transitions between 0 and 5 (or 3.3) volts that occur in the electronic signal applied to the chip input pin. Counting the number of electronic transitions in a given period of time is a measure of the input signal frequency, while counting the total number of pulses that have occurred since a starting point in the past is a measure of elapsed or total time passage.

The fundamental unit used to store binary information is known as the "flip-flop" or "latch." A flip-flop is a configuration of switches stable in one of two states in which the inputs to the latch or flip-flop cause the output to change between the two binary logic states of one and zero. A basic circuit for a flip-flop, multivibrator, or latch is depicted in Figure 8-5.

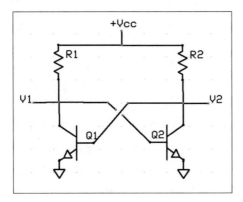

Figure 8-5. *A Base Junction Transistor Flip-Flop*

Simple flip-flops were made initially from current-controlled devices such as vacuum tubes, then later from bipolar transistors, and finally from very-low-current-draw voltage-controlled devices such as field effect transistors (FETs) and metal oxide semiconductor field effect transistors

(MOSFETs). These are often termed multivibrators and are known as a bistable circuit. The circuit stays in either of its two stable states until a control signal is applied to switch it to the other stable state.

To understand how the basic circuit operates, we can see in Figure 8-5 that if V1 is grounded, then there will be no base current through the base of Q2. In bipolar transistors, the current through the collector and emitter (emitter arrow indicates positive current flow) is controlled by the base current. The transistor Q2 with no base current will have no collector-emitter current. The current through R2 from Vcc all flows into the base of Q1 that then causes a much larger current to flow through Q1. With the symmetrical circuit, if V2 is grounded, then the base current in Q1 is shut off, and the current through R1 flows into the base of Q2, causing a much larger current to flow through Q2 as the circuit switches to the second stable state.

The simple flip-flop is the basic building block of a very large number of mainly very-low-current-draw complementary metal oxide semiconductor voltage-controlled integrated circuits that provide functions such as memory storage, logic, and mathematical functions. (See Chapter 1, Figure 1-15.)

Details of latches, flip-flops, digital logic counting, oscillator clocks, and the applications of various families of integrated circuit logic chip sets can be found in several reference works.[1]

A terminal on the LabJack HMI labeled CNT provides access to an integrated circuit that is capable of counting the number of times a voltage level is changed from +5 to 0 and back to +5 volts. Such event counting is conducted in binary by the integrated circuitry of the device

---

[1] 1) Digital Electronics for Scientists and Engineers, Malmstadt and Enke, W. A. Benjamin Inc. NY, NY, ISBN 0-80536899-X

2) *CMOS Cookbook* 2nd Edn. , Lancaster, Howard W. Sams & Co., ISBN 0 672-22459-3

3) *The Art of Electronics* 2nd Edn, Horowitz and Hill, Cambridge University Press, ISBN-13 978-0-521-37095-0

with results being displayed on the system screen in base ten format. The events to be counted must be converted into the voltage-level changes noted previously. The LabJack counter has a 32-bit capacity that allows a total count of 2^{32} or 4,294,967,296 events. Because the event counter is an integrated circuit, it can count at frequencies up to 1 MHz.

In the following exercise, a manual event counter that can be incremented by any number of sensors such as a change in daylight levels, objects passing a point, or clicking a system screen icon will be created. Configurations of experimental setups or process control systems involving time spans of durations measured in seconds and longer are not a problem with the LabJack and DAQFactory software combination. Documentation in the user manual indicates that many instructions have an execution time of 20 ms that creates a lower limit with respect to the shortest time responses that can be reasonably expected from the visually based SCADA system. High-speed signal changes are best recorded with techniques called streaming or burst-mode operations. High-speed signal changes at speeds or frequencies well beyond what the eye can resolve are acquired with very fast hardware speeds for post-collection processing. High-speed operations are detailed in the user manuals and are dealt with in subsequent chapters and exercises.

The LabJack counter is considered a hardware device and thus is not limited by software execution times. An integrated circuit device known as a 555 timer can be used in conjunction with the counter to work in time spans shorter than those imposed by software execution overhead. The 555 timer is also a "hardware"-based integrated circuit and thus, like the LabJack counter, able to work in time scales varying from microseconds to hours. The details of both the bipolar transistor and CMOS 555 timer ICs are found in numerous references including those referenced earlier. The differences between the various forms of the timer lie in their power handling capability with the bipolar forms being high-current types and the CMOS forms being low voltage based.

Experimental

Hardware

1) Simple manual counting of events

2) Simple continuous event counting or frequency determination

A blue LED and a 470 Ω current limiting resistor can be used to demonstrate manual counting of screen-initiated events.

Circuit Schematic

The diode and current limiting resistor are configured as depicted in Chapter 1, Figure 1-3, for the red diode with the junction of the serial pair being wired to D9 on the CB25 terminal board.

Software

For demonstration of the two modes of counter usage, the panel with two buttons, two variable value components, and a descriptive text component of Figure 8-6 was created.

For counting manually activated events, a screen button icon is created, appropriately labeled, and linked to an output channel. The author's button was labeled "Initiate Event" configured to activate the script of Listing 8-5 "A_Counter_Event," which applies a 5–0–5-volt transition through a channel created as "DigOut_9_EvntCntr," wired to output pin 9, on the CB25 board terminal. Clicking the screen button thus drives the D9 output from 5 to 0 and back to 5 volts that in turn switches the blue LED off and then back on. The counter terminal CNT is wired to monitor the voltage level at the junction of the blue LED and its 470 Ω current limiting resistor. Manually clicking the "Initiate Event" button thus increments the counter through the Listing 8-5 DAQFactory sequence.

Section 10 of the DAQFactory LabJack manual[2] details the single LabJack counter operation. Having only a single counter, all data is passed through counter channel 0. By default the counter value is reset to 0 each time the channel is read, so for the first part of this exercise, the default must be turned off, to continuously increment its value until manually resetting it to 0. For this exercise, we create a channel named "EventsCounted" with Counter I/O type; and in the "Channel Table View," under the Quick Note / Special / OPC heading, a button along the right-hand side of the cell with three dots (...) should be visible. Click the button to bring up the Channel Parameters window with a drop-down list from which Reset is selected. The only parameter is "Reset?", and selections of Yes or No, OK, and Apply will immediately configure the counter channel not to reset to zero when the channel value is read for display.

A second button labeled "Reset Counter" is configured to start the short "ResetCounter" script of Listing 8-6, which sets the most recent value of the "EventsCounted" channel EventsCounted[0] to zero. A variable value component display of EventsCounted[0] has been placed below the buttons to indicate the number of events counted. The panel created to demonstrate simple counter usage is depicted in Figure 8-6.

---

[2] azeotech.com/dl/labjackguide.pdf

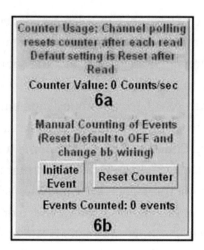

Figure 8-6. *A LabJack U12 Counter Usage Demonstration*

Listing 8-5 in the exercise code listings is activated by clicking the Initiate Event button.

Clicking the screen button "Initiate Event" causes the blue light to light up and the event counter to increment. Clicking "Reset Counter" (Listing 8-6) sets the "Events Counted" variable value display back to 0.

Scripting

Listing 8-5 and Listing 8-6 are DAQFactory sequences whose scripting creates the square waveform signal used for frequency measurement with a time - goto script and the code used to manually clear the counter and turn off any LED that may be left in the on configuration.

As noted previously, the "Reset Counter" button activates the short sequence of Listing 8-6 that consists of a single line of active code to set the value of the counter channel to 0.

By switching the LabJack counter channel back to the default setting of "Reset after reading a counted value" and configuring a new counter channel with a one-second counting interval, the new counter channel is configured to read a per-second frequency.

Circuit

A white LED and 470 Ω current limiting resistor are configured as depicted in Chapter 1, Figure 1-3, for the red diode with the junction of the serial pair at hand being wired to D8 on the CB25 terminal board.

Software

A pulse train must be created to form a repetitive signal with a measurable frequency. The script of Listing 8-7 is a PWM or variable pulse width generator that can be used in conjunction with a screen button and instruction text as seen in Figure 8-7, to start and stop the square wave pulse train.

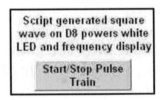

Figure 8-7. *A DAQFactory Pulse Train Generator Panel*

The Start/Stop button is configured to activate the DAQFactory sequence PWM_Script that is Listing 8-7 in the code listings of this chapter.

Scripting and Action

Although usage of the "time - goto" statement is not considered good programming practice, it does simplify creation of the square wave signal. Once the two panels for the counting exercise have been created, change the values in the "Delay (0.5)" statements to 0.25 and 0.1. While the square wave is being generated and the frequency is being displayed, move the mouse cursor rapidly back and forth and watch the LED and the frequency value being displayed.

Observations

The inclusion of the blue and white LEDs in the two counter exercises is used as a visual aid in following the operation of the system. (See "Discussion.")

Discussion

Time Determination

Digital electronic circuits are activated by crystal-controlled oscillator "clocks." Crystal oscillators generate a very stable, fixed-frequency, square wave pulse train providing nanosecond time resolution (10^{-9} s). The square wave consists of a sequential series of transitions from 0 to +5 volts or from logic zero to logic one in binary format. Time can be divided into relative time as determined by the spacing of the clock square wave fronts and absolute time from a fixed event. Absolute time for the DAQFactory program is determined by the number of seconds from January 1, 1970. The time variables of Figure 8-2 and their syntax are discussed in detail in the user manual.

Manual and Automated Event Counting

The button-initiated manual events are created in time frames that are usually not in conflict with DAQFactory software timing. However, it can be shown that attempts to create a waveform with a script generating a signal that changes with sufficient rapidity can conflict with the operating system software timing.

As part of this exercise, a script has been used to generate the voltage waveform required to increment the LabJack counter. A blue LED has been included in the exercise as a visual indicator of system validation. However, the counter hardware records an event as a two-transition operation in which a high signal drops to a low value, which then is followed by a low signal being raised to a high voltage value. The two-transition "event" is effected by a script that leaves the pin voltage level at 5 V that in turn powers the blue LED in the circuit. To turn the LED off, we include a line of code in the script activated by the Reset Counter button to set pin 9 back to 0 V without it being recorded as half of an "event."

By altering the delay values in the PWM_Script, the width of the time the signal is held at either 0 or the nominal 5 V can be varied. The LabJack counter only registers the +5- to 0- to +5-volt transitions as a single event for the purpose of counter increment, so the width of the residence time at 0 volts is the parameter that is counted as a single event or a cycle in frequency determinations.

Any graphical display must be composed of a two-dimensional array of elements that can be individually illuminated to form an image. The updating of a GUI consumes a large amount of computational resources as the individual elements of the array are constantly being scanned to implement any required changes. If a program such as the pulse generator used to drive the pulse generator panel of Figure 8-7 is invoked with delay times involving fractions of a second, software conflicts can arise.

When the pulse generation program was used to power the white LED as the delay times became very short into the range of fractions of a second, both the LED pulse rate and the cursor movement became erratic. The observed hardware and software conflicts demonstrate the limitations of using software scripting in time spans of less than a second.

Hardware Time and Timing

Our discussion of the hardware control of time is centered on the 555 integrated circuit timer chip that has been manufactured, improved, and used for over 40 years. The chip functions by causing its output to change from high to low voltage levels at controlled time intervals. The timing intervals may be easily varied over numerous orders of magnitude to create long delays (the monostable mode of operation) or generate high-speed pulse trains (the astable mode of operation). Simple external components consisting of resistors and capacitors can be used to generate the desired time intervals. The 555 chip is available in bipolar transistor and CMOS formats that differ in power consumption, power output, and high-frequency operation.

The 555 chip is named for the series string of three 5 kΩ resistors that are connected to the supply voltage and ground to establish the 1/3 and 2/3 supply voltage reference levels used by the circuit logic. The circuit contains two comparator op-amps that feed their output signals to a digital set-reset flip-flop. The analog comparators use the 1/3 and 2/3 voltage reference points to change their output state that causes the flip-flop to change state based upon the comparator inputs. The digital flip-flop output controls the output driver circuitry.

Figures 8-8 and 8-9 illustrate some of the operations and configurations for the timer circuit.

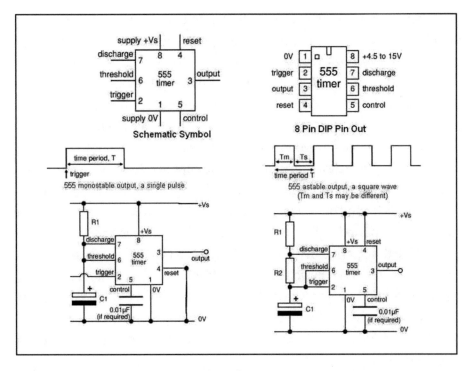

Figure 8-8. *555 IC Timer Modes of Operation*

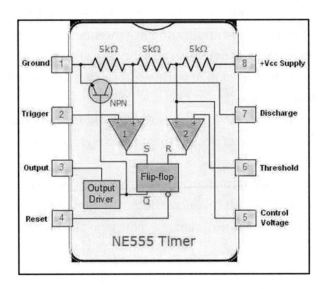

Figure 8-9. *A 555 Timer IC Block Diagram*

When power is applied to a 555 IC configured as depicted in the astable mode schematic in the bottom-right of Figure 8-8, the capacitor begins to charge as the current flows through R1 and R2. As the voltage rises on pins 2 and 6 and then reaches 2/3 of the supply, as determined by the internal voltage divider, the output goes low. As the output goes low, the NPN transistor is turned on, and the discharge pin of the 555 is effectively connected to ground that discharges C1 through R2. As the voltage on the capacitor drops to 1/3 of the supply value, the transistor is turned off, the capacitor begins charging through the series pair, and the cycle repeats itself. The voltage on C thus cycles between 1/3 and 2/3 of the supply with a period of T = 0.693(R1 + 2R2)C or a frequency of f = 1.4/(R1 + 2R2)C. The time period of the output signal can be divided into two parts consisting of the time the voltage is high (see Figure 8-8, bottom right) and the time the signal is low. The high time is often called the "mark time" and the low the "space time" with the duty cycle being defined as the ratio of the high or mark time to the sum or time period of the signal, expressed as a percentage value.

The ability of the 555 timer to generate a pulse train whose electronic characteristics are determined by external resistance and capacitance values has a very important application in experimental science. The following exercise visually demonstrates the concept of square wave or clock signals and the variation of pulse widths with physical changes in external sensors.

Numerous websites, references, and textbooks contain detailed discussions of the characteristics of the timer chip together with tables of circuit design parameter values.

In the following exercise, the concept of square wave output signals and duty cycle and the basis of pulse width variation using the timer chip are demonstrated. Using the design procedures available from the data sheets made available online by the major IC suppliers, a circuit with an output frequency of 6–7 Hertz can be assembled to power different colored LEDs for a visual display of the circuit operation.

Experimental

1) A 555 timer chip configured in the astable mode (see Figure 8-8, bottom right).

2) A 100 kΩ variable resistor is used as R2, and a 10 kΩ resistor is used as R1.

3) A 1 uF capacitor is used as the timing capacitor or C1. An electrolytic capacitor can be used as the higher current leakage rate of the component is not critical to the performance of the circuit.

4) Two different colored LEDs with 470 Ω current limiting resistors are connected between the output pin of the chip and the power supply rails in order to produce alternately flashing indications of the high and low output states.

5) The schematic diagram of Figure 8-10 has been drawn with +5 V power, but the circuit can be powered with any supply between 3 and 18 volts (adjust CLR values for voltages > +5).

Schematic

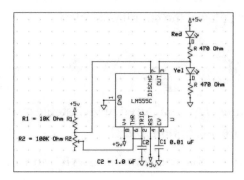

Figure 8-10. *Schematic for Controlled High and Low 555 Timer IC Output Variation*

Observations

Using the circuit shown in Figure 8-10, the red-yellow pair alternately flashed ten times in 13 seconds when the 100 kΩ potentiometer was near its maximum limit, and the circuit flashed continuously when near the zero value.

Discussion

In the "astable" configuration, the timer chip is able to vary the time at which output is on or off. The measured ratio between the time on and off or the "duty cycle" is shown to be dependent upon the resistance of R2 that in this case is the mechanical position of the shaft on the variable resistor. Rotary mechanical motion of the potentiometer shaft can thus be transformed into a varying electronic square wave signal. Any transducer capable of transforming a physical phenomenon into a varying resistance can also be used to produce a square wave signal with a ratio of on/off time that is proportional to the resistance created by the physical phenomenon being monitored. Thermistors are heat sensitive resistors. Negative temperature coefficient (NTC) thermistors exhibit a lower proportional resistance to an increase in their ambient temperature. Inserting an NTC thermistor into the timing circuitry of a 555 timer IC will cause the frequency of the output square wave to vary in proportion to the thermal environment of the thermistor bead thus forming a digital thermometer. By using the output signal to turn on and off a power transistor, a heavier current can be controlled. With a fixed frequency, the variable "duty cycle" format signal functions as a "pulse width modulation" technique. The PWM current control can be used to vary the speed of a motor or control the current applied to a heater.

In the astable mode, the frequency of the square wave generated by the 555 depends upon the values of R1, R2, and C. The frequency is given by the following formula:

$$f = 1/\ln(2) * C * (R1 + R2) \; (\ln(2) = 0.6931)$$

Figure 8-11 shows the 555 astable cycle.

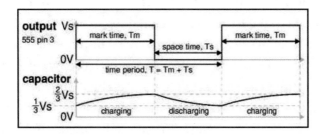

Figure 8-11. *The 555 Astable Cycle*

The frequency of the output can be controlled by the three values of the RC network. The duty cycle or the ratio of the high time to low time is illustrated in Figure 8-12 as a percentage value.

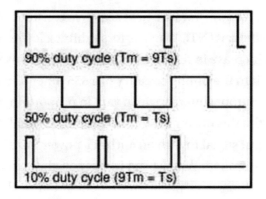

Figure 8-12. *Duty Cycle Variation of the 555 Timer Output*

The high time of the output is given by

$$\text{high time} = \ln(2) * (R1 + R2) * C$$

and the low time is given by

$$\text{low time} = \ln(2)\, R2 * C \qquad\qquad (\ln(2) = 0.6931)\ (R\ \text{is in}\ \Omega\ \text{and}\ C\ \text{in uF})$$

The output signal is high as the capacitor is charged by current flowing through R1 and R2. When it discharges, it does so only through R2, and thus there is a limit to the variation that can be introduced into the duty cycle by the value of R2. If the resistor pair is replaced by a potentiometer whose wiper terminal is connected to pin 7 of the timer, then the total resistance of R1 + R2 is constant, and the duty cycle can be varied by changing the position of the wiper. To avoid unwanted problems should R2 be set to 0, connect a small value resistor in series with the capacitor and the variable resistor to avoid the possibility of unpredictable results at low potentiometer resistance values. If fixed resistors are to be used to establish the desired duty cycle at less than 50%, then a diode pointing toward the capacitor will allow the capacitor to charge through the R1 resistor only, during the high time portion of the cycle.

Microcontroller Clocks, Timekeeping, and Event Counting

Virtually all microcontrollers that are communicating with host computers and peripheral devices such as sensors or process controls are equipped with an onboard crystal-controlled oscillator that functions as a system clock. Usually the hardware-based clock signal can be accessed with the microcontroller software and used for timing and event counting.

Arduino microcontrollers use a crystal-controlled 16 MHz oscillator as the system clock. When power is applied to the operating system, it begins to count the number of milliseconds ($1/1,000$ or 10^{-3} s) as the value of the function millis() and the number of microseconds ($1/1,000,000$ or 10^{-6} s) as value of the function micros(). (Due to binary counting and hardware constraints when invoking micros(), microsecond time resolution is limited to the nearest 4 μs or 4×10^{-6} s.)

The two functions are stored as unsigned long integers, which have maximum values of 4,294,967,295 before rolling over to 0. The maximum value limitation provides for a time span of approximately 50 days for a millis() count and a 70-minute time span for micros(). Millis counts are accurate to the nearest single digit, but micros values are expressed to the nearest four digits (2^2). The timing error in millis() is 0.18 s/hour, 4.32 s/day, and 129.6 s/month.

DAQFactory provides an alternate method for demonstrating the concepts of timing and event counting with microcontrollers such as the Arduino. There are many published programs that create countdown, stopwatch, and other timing applications for microcontrollers using mechanical switches and a corresponding large number of library and other methods for dealing with mechanical "switch contact bouncing.[3]"

---

[3] 1) https://github.com/j-bellavance/EdgeDebounceLite/blob/master/README.md
2) https://www.allaboutcircuits.com/technical-articles/switch-bounce-how-to-deal-with-it/

A DAQFactory screen button and the serial port eliminate the need for both mechanical switches and having to deal with mechanical switch contact bouncing.

Experimental

To demonstrate the basic timing functions available with the inexpensive, serial port–connected microcontroller, two programs are required, the first to display the timer control panel in the SCADA software on the host computer screen and the second to implement the selected timing functions on the microcontroller. See Listings 8-8 for the Arduino code and 8-9 for the DAQFactory Quick Sequence.

Figure 8-13 illustrates a simple basic configuration for the simple stopwatch timer set up in the DAQFactory SCADA software.

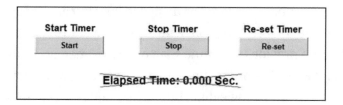

Figure 8-13. *A Simple DAQFactory Stopwatch Control Panel*

Each of the three buttons has been configured to activate a Quick Sequence code that writes a "b," "s," or "r" to the serial port to begin a timing session, stop the timing session and transmit the millis() count back to the SCADA software, or reset the timer to zero and begin another timing session.

The inactive (red X) variable value display seen in Figure 8-13 receives the total millis() count from the Arduino when the timing session is halted with the "s" command. Figure 8-14 illustrates the DAQFactory serial monitor activity during a simple start and stop timing session run for validation during the development of the combined timing system.

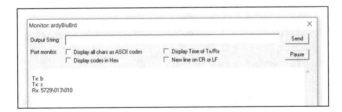

Figure 8-14. *DAQFactory Serial Port Monitor Record of a Simple Arduino Timing Session*

Recall that the DAQFactory serial port code expects both a carriage return (CR, ASCII code 13) and a line feed (LF, ASCII code 10) after the data sent to the serial port. The data passing through the DAQFactory serial port can be read into a channel or a global variable. In the primary code development process, a channel named millisVlu was configured in the DAQFactory software, and the variable value screen component was then set to divide the millis() value received from the Arduino by 1000 to get the number of whole seconds and a milliseconds fraction that the timer had recorded. Later revisions of the code used a global variable "elapsed" and Quick Sequence to implement the simple timing function (see Figure 8-15 in "Observations" and Listings 8-8 and 8-9).

The DAQFactory serial port uses the "On Receive" code in Listing 6-10 in Chapter 6 to read the numerical value from the serial port into a channel or for use as a value for a global variable.

Observations

In Figure 8-15 the Arduino serial port has been programmed to aid in validating command interpretation by the microcontroller, and a typical timing result display is depicted in Figure 8-16.

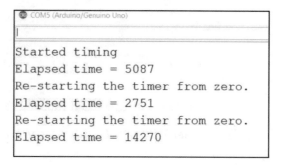

Figure 8-15. *Arduino Serial Port Output for Stopwatch Program Development*

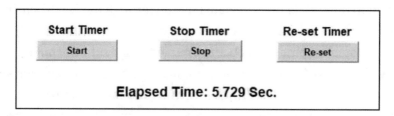

Figure 8-16. *A Typical Simple Millisecond Resolution Timing Session*

The simple stopwatch timer has been developed by first getting the Arduino to function as a stand-alone timer by using the Arduino's own serial port to manually send the "b," "s," and "r" commands to generate the output seen in Figure 8-15. With a functioning Arduino program, the code was refined down to that presented in Listing 8-8 in which the only output is the Arduino line of code "Serial.println(elapsed)" that sends the contents of the elapsed time variable to the serial port with the requisite CR and LF.

Examination of Listings 8-8 and 8-9 will reveal that the reset functions in the two programs are different. It is simpler to isolate the reset code into two actions on either side of the serial port. The Arduino code resets the state flags for the begin timing loop and the stop timing and print to the serial port action, while the DAQFactory Quick Sequence code actually sets the elapsed time variable and timed seconds display back to zero.

Once an initial timing measurement has been made, the reset button should be used to reset the single action–only flags in the Arduino code.

Discussion

Figure 8-15 illustrates a simple technique for developing the Arduino code that is to respond to the single-letter commands that will be written to the serial port by the SCADA software in the final iteration of this exercise. The Arduino code was completely developed by using the serial monitor "send" feature of the IDE and writing into the developing code the responses in Figure 8-15 to validate the operation of the code before finally combining the SCADA and microcontroller operations. The reduction of the functioning stopwatch code to that to be used in combination with the DAQFactory panel can be done by rewriting or just commenting out the unwanted lines.

More elaborate timer functions can also be configured by converting the elapsed millisecond time values that can extend out to close to 50 days into minutes, hours, and days subject to the time errors noted previously.

Where possible, a screen-activated button can be used to avoid problems caused by mechanical switch contact bounce.

Counting Events and Timing with Python and Raspberry Pi

Time measurement for the Python language interpreter is derived from the host computer on which the program is running. The basic concept for the Raspberry Pi is oriented around Internet access. An Internet connection can be used to transfer operating systems, application software, and updates. An Internet connection provides accurate timekeeping through Internet time servers. If the RPi is to be used in a time-dependent experiment or measurement application where Internet access is not possible, then the installation of a real-time clock (RTC) will be required to supply an accurate timekeeping base.[4]

In Figure 8-17, the timekeeping basis is shown in a very simple console request for the number of "ticks" that have occurred since the January 1, 1970, timekeeping starting point.

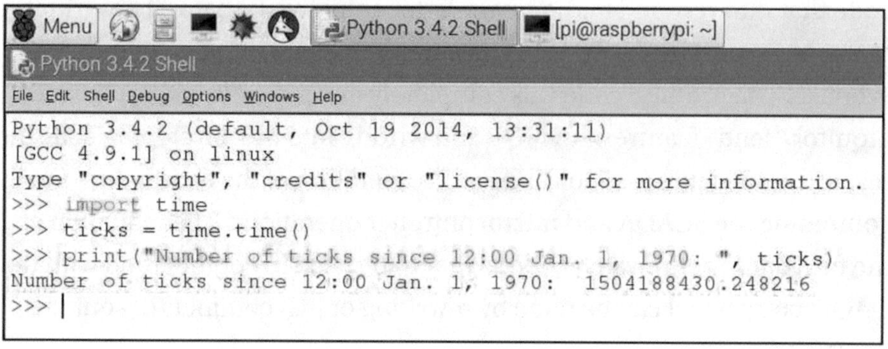

Figure 8-17. *A Console Request for the Tick Count*

In the Unix/Linux operating systems, the number of ticks can be converted into seconds, minutes, hours, and days to provide any timekeeping operations required. Figure 8-18 is a console conversion of ticks into a current time display.

---

[4] 1) *Raspberry Pi Cookbook* 2nd Edn., Monk, O'Reilly Media Inc., ISBN 978-1-491-93910-9

2) *Practical Raspberry Pi*, Horan, Apress, ISBN 978-1-4302-4971-9

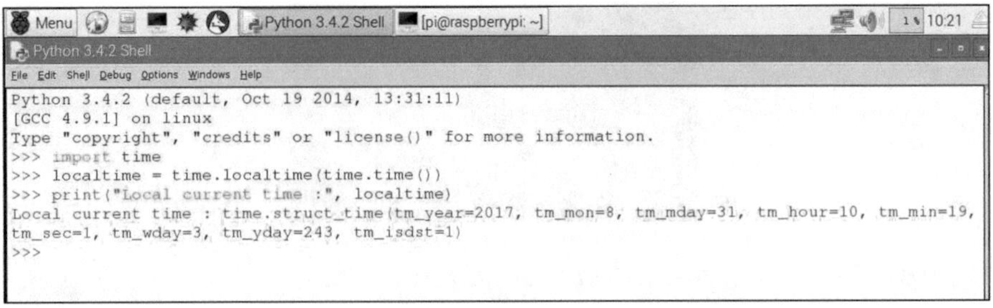

Figure 8-18. *A Console Request for the Current Time from the Tick Count*

A more familiar format for the time can be obtained at the interactive console with the asctime() function as depicted in Figure 8-19.

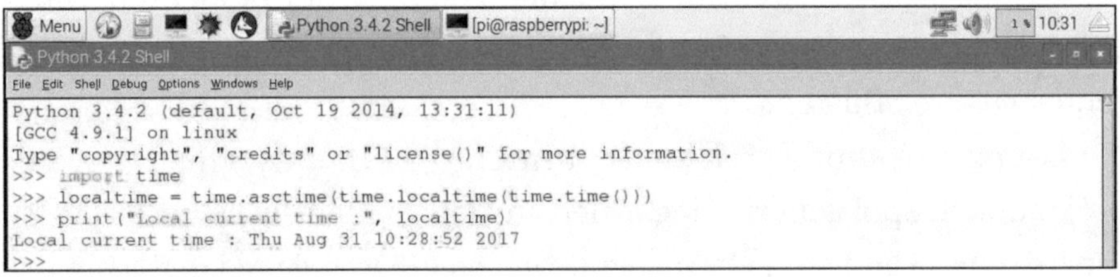

Figure 8-19. *A Familiar Current Time Format*

There are a number of simple push button timer GUI and timer modules that have been published for coding timer applications in Python, and a three-button GUI using the tkinter Python module is depicted in Figure 8-20. The code is listed in Listing 8-10. The code has been modified from the original published in 2002.[5]

---

[5] HTTP://CODE.ACTIVESTATE.COM/RECIPIES/124894/

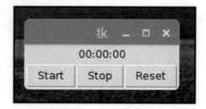

Figure 8-20. *A Three-Button Stopwatch Timer*

Scheduling Events

In addition to the time display functions listed previously, Python has several libraries such as sched and schedule that use the time module as a base for scheduling events. In essence, the sched and schedule modules provide the experimenter with a programmable starting point from which delays can be specified before individual events or programming code sequences are initiated.

Listing 8-11 entitled Scheduled_PgmCntrl_LED.py uses the programmed application of logic high and low to the GPIO pins 20 and 21 (board pins 38 and 40) to turn on and off two LEDs attached to the pins through current limiting resistors as "events."

Examination of the code shows a typical creation of a scheduler object instance with the line scheduler = sched.scheduler(time.time, time.sleep). The two events to be run in the future are defined in the following two lines:

scheduler.enter(2, 1, actvt_GrnLed, ("Green led activated first",))

scheduler.enter(5, 1, actvt_RedLed, ("Red led is activated second",))

The documentation for the sched module stipulates four arguments for the enter() function consisting of the numerical value of the time delay in seconds from the processing of the initiating function start(), a numerical value specifying the priority of the event, the name of the event function to be called, and data to be passed into the function being called, if required. Listing 8-11 is an example of overlapping events in which the time during which the LEDs are illuminated is longer than the desired start times of the events. The shed module executes all the called functions and none are lost, but the timing of the events is displaced further out in time by the amount of the process overlap.

Figure 8-21 is a typical output from the scheduler program. The red and green LEDs to be illuminated are wired as depicted in circuit A of Figure 8-22.

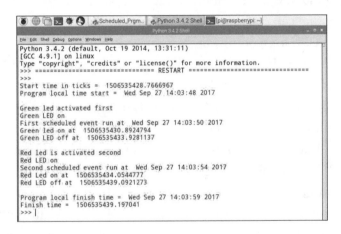

Figure 8-21. *Scheduler Program Output from Overlapped Events*

Scheduling events can be a complex problem, and the Python reference documentation should be examined for further details when using these modules.[6]

_____

[6] 1) docspython.org/3/library/sched.html
2) https://pypi.python.org/pypi/schedule - schedule 0.4.3

Detecting and Counting Events

Detection and counting of external events on the RPi require both the ability to determine the presence or absence of a voltage on the individual pins of the GPIO array and the ability to detect a transition in the pin voltage. Electrical voltage transitions on the GPIO pins can be monitored by two techniques, known as "polling" and using "interrupts." Looking for a voltage change at any arbitrary point in time is called "polling" the pin. The disadvantage of polling lies in the fact that the event to be monitored could occur before or after the time frame in which the pin status observation is made. Polling is often implemented with software loop coding that can consume significant amounts of processor time while blocking the CPU from doing other task processing.

The second method for determining electrical voltage transitions uses interrupts or "edge detection" in which the change from high to low (a falling edge) or low to high (a rising edge) is recorded.

In very simplified terms, it can be said that most modern operating systems are time-sharing operations managing multiple programs that appear to the user to be running simultaneously. Each program being run by the operating system is termed a process in Unix (a task in Windows) and is only run for a short period of time. Periodically the currently running program uses up its allocated "time slice" as determined by the generation of interrupt signals sent to the central processing unit from either a hardware or software timer. The interrupts cause the CPU to suspend or "interrupt" the normal tasks at hand to attend to, or service, high-priority events. An interrupt causes the CPU to save its current computation, switch to processing an interrupt service routine (ISR) (or event handler), and resume normal operation after completion of the ISR. Input-output operations can be coded into ISRs, and the CPU thus is able to divide its processing resources between monitoring I/O operations and normal computational functions. The processing of the first program slice of CPU time, the generation of the interrupt signal, the processing of the ISR, and the switch to the next program to be processed are all happening in such short times that, to the user, several programs appear to be running at the same time.

Threads are smaller portions of a program's code that can be interleaved to produce the desired effect of having the two code portions appear to run simultaneously. (Only multicore processing hardware can actually run multiple threads simultaneously.) Threading can be used to avoid the shortcomings of polling in GPIO operations. An interrupt and ISR can be used to examine the status of a GPIO pin and, if it is inactive, continue on seamlessly with normal program processing. Polling involves continuous checking for events, while interrupts do so periodically. Polling consumes all the resources, while interrupts consume only some. Polling uses a single thread focused on event detection, but Python and the RPi.GPIO library allow the creation of two or more threads in which event detection code can run independently. Detection of an event in the secondary threads activates code that calls back to the primary thread to initiate an interrupt service routine. There are numerous, very simple, easy-to-implement, multiple push button, threaded callback demonstration programs that have been published to support the library documentation describing GPIO array input and output use. Documentation for a simple threading library is available online.[7]

In previous exercises, the three libraries that can be used to work with the RPi.GPIO pins have been introduced, and these different modules will be used as required to generate simple timer programs or to monitor pin status and record times between pin state changes throughout the remainder of the manuscript.

The RPi.GPIO and gpiozero libraries are very easy to use and are supported by extensive documentation of code that has been developed for a large number of common devices that can be interfaced to the RPi through the GPIO pins.

---

[7] http://sourceforge.net/p/raspberry-gpio-python/wiki/BasicUsage

The first two libraries are however not capable of accurate, short-period, timekeeping. In previous exercises, the "jitter" that can be seen in simple LED power control applications is caused by the Unix-based Linux operating system halting GPIO operations to deal with internal processes that have a higher priority than the RPi input-output code.

A third library imported as pigpio has been developed for use on the RPi that is capable of providing microsecond timekeeping accuracies. Timekeeping accuracy in the pigpio module has been achieved by using C code to write the library and using a Python-Linux/Unix interface program running on the RPi to access the GPIO pins. Unix utility or service programs running in the system background are often known as "daemons."

As noted, physical computing with the GPIO pins on the RPi can be considered as the interfacing of the computer with the outside world. The RPi is able to detect the status of each pin in the array by measuring its voltage at virtually any point in time. System and software overheads limit the response time of the RPi to changes in the voltage on any GPIO pin when the Python interpreter uses either the RPi.GPIO or gpiozero library. As noted, in order to improve the short time response of the RPi to its GPIO pin array, a library written in the very fast-executing C language has been interfaced to the Python interpreter with the Linux/Unix daemon or utility program called "pigpiod." Microsecond time scales are reliably accessible in GPIO pin operations with the C library module.

The pigpio library can be used by investigators at all levels of programming capability, and the extensive documentation should be consulted as required.

Timing and low-frequency event counting can be realized with Python programs written using the appropriate GPIO pin management library for the task at hand. Simple, low-level, easy-to-code-and-implement interfacing can be achieved with the RPi.GPIO library, while more complex sensors are best interfaced using the gpiozero library. Moderate- to

advanced-level programming skills are required to use the pigpio library
with its fast accurate time management capabilities and the interfacing
utility daemon running in the background of the RPi operating system.

Experimental

Implementation of the software GUI-based stopwatch timers requires no
interaction with the GPIO array.

Scheduling events may be used in both ordinary Python code
application programming or a physical computing process utilizing the
GPIO array as is described in the following portions of this exercise.

Since all input and output actions from sensors, actuators, motors, and
switches must be in the form of transitions from 0 to 3.3 or 5 volts, the two
circuits depicted in Figure 8-22 can be used to either source or sink the
electrical activation signals in the form of circuit A or B, respectively.

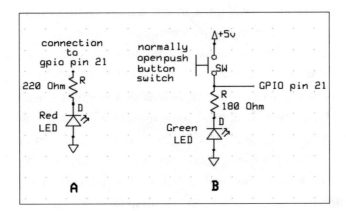

Figure 8-22. *Circuits for Sinking or Sourcing Electrical Signals for*
GPIO Programming Demonstrations

The use of an LED in circuit B of Figure 8-22, although not required
for the activation of the RPi GPIO code, does provide the investigator with
an additional diagnostic capability in the event of a section of code not

responding to a button click. A button click should cause the LED to light and the code waiting for the button click to be activated as expected. A failure of the LED to illuminate when the button is clicked can thus identify the root cause of the code not responding (see "Observations" and "Discussion").

Listing 8-12 uses a push button mechanical switch configured as depicted in circuit B of Figure 8-22 to provide "rising edge events" to trigger the actions of the time measurement program.

The program uses two rising edge detection functions that block all computing operations while the RPi waits for the edge to appear. If activation of the push button switch is the only operation on which the program is to focus, as is the case in the timer example, then a blocking function is both simple to implement and adequate for the problem at hand. Figure 8-24 is a typical output from the rising edge timer program, while Figure 8-25 caught a switch contact "bounce" during programming code development.

As previously noted, high-speed digital timers and counters monitoring mechanical switches such as push buttons, toggles, or magnetically activated reeds must accommodate contact bounce that occurs before a switch provides a continuous closed contact. The RPI. GPIO libraries all have provisions for estimating the switch contact bounce that may be encountered in the experiment at hand and will accept the experimenter's millisecond time scale in which to ignore the second event.

When higher-speed events are to be monitored, such as those encountered in optical beam blocking configurations, a capacitor can often be used to dampen spurious noise or electromagnetic interference.

Polling and interrupt event detections, although easy to implement for educational purposes with push button devices, are of limited value for detecting and counting higher-speed events. Motor rotational speeds, high-speed object counting, and accurate timing over fixed distances, as are to be encountered in subsequent physical computing exercises and measurements, can all be implemented with break beam optical techniques. In Chapter 10 an IR break beam detector is used to count motor rotations to determine motor rotational speed.

Figure 8-23 depicts an invisible infrared (IR at 940 nm wavelength) break beam circuit that can be configured on a prototyping breadboard and connected to the RPi 40-pin GPIO array. (BCM GPIO values and BN or board number values are both provided in the circuit description.)

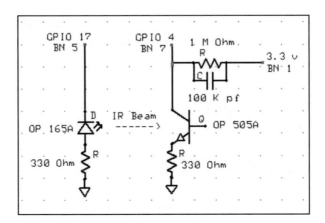

Figure 8-23. *An IR Break Beam Circuit*

A break beam system does not have metal contacts and does not "bounce" but can experience an electrical spike or noise that can generate spurious signal responses. Implementation of a bounce time for second signal rejection or the use of a capacitor to absorb spurious signals is thus a matter of either judgement or experimentation for the investigator when assembling and writing code for the experiment at hand.

The following break beam programs are designed for continuous operation and use a while loop to monitor the beam integrity. The loop software has built-in code for a clean exit scheme that uses the Ctrl+C keystroke combination to terminate the main program beam scanning loop and execute a proper circuit shutdown procedure that, in general, turns off the IR beam, removes code no longer in use, and resets port configurations.

Listings 8-13, 8-14, and 8-15 of the three RPi programs monitoring the IR beam have additional code in the main while loop that activates two diodes, a red and a green, connected to pins 38 and 40 on the board array (BCM GPIO 20 and 21) in accordance with Figure 8-22 A. An IR beam is invisible, and the added code turns the red diode on when the beam is broken and illuminates the green when the beam is intact. The two diodes serve as a remote indicator of the invisible IR beam status.

Listings 8-13 and 8-14 are two ways in which an IR diode and a photo-transistor detector can be used to demonstrate higher-speed event monitoring and present a practical application of the technology.

Observations

Output from the rising edge timer program is heavily commented to describe the events that occur during the elapsed time measurement as seen in Figure 8-24.

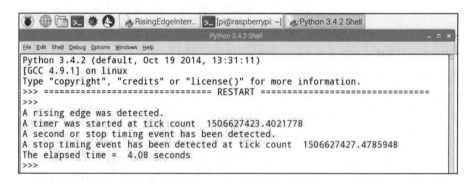

Figure 8-24. *A Typical Rising Edge Push Button Timer Output*

Occasionally the button click does not produce the expected results with the code awaiting the electrical transition. As seen in Figure 8-25, when attempting to activate the timer programs that use two sequential clicks of the button to measure an elapsed time, the code acknowledges and acts upon the "start a timing session" initial event and then, virtually immediately, properly ends the timing session, recording a fractional second elapsed time. (See "Discussion.")

```
A rising edge was detected.
A timer was started at tick count   1504709817.4018524
A second or stop timing event has been detected.
A stop timing event has been detected at tick count   1504709817.450809
>>> |
```

Figure 8-25. *An Unexpectedly Short Elapsed Time Determination*

In Figure 8-25, a 0.049 or a 49 ms (millisecond) elapsed time has been measured that is characteristic of mechanical switch "bounce".

On occasion an initial click of a button does not activate the code awaiting the transition. The phenomenon is random in nature and has on occasion fortuitously been traced to the switch contacts either not closing or not closing with sufficient surface area contact to provide the energy needed to light the diode or activate the transition recognition code. (See "Discussion.")

Figure 8-26 is the output of a simple program that uses a simple while loop polling method to monitor the status of the IR beam. As can be seen from the output that was generated by the author rapidly hand-vibrating a pen in the beam, when the beam is unbroken, the photo-transistor or diode acts as a short circuit to ground, and the GPIO pin attached to the IR-sensitive element is pulled down to virtually 0 V. Beam blockage removes the short circuit to ground, and the GPIO pin rises to 3.3 V driving the input pin high.

The while loop constantly cycles as fast as the system's software-hardware combination will allow and outputs the high/low value of the pin.

```
Python 3.4.2 (default, Oct 19 2014, 13:31:11)
[GCC 4.9.1] on linux
Type "copyright", "credits" or "license()" for more information.
>>> ============================== RESTART ==================================
>>>
Beam off, photodiode off input hi
Beam on, photodiode on, input low
Beam on, photodiode on, input low
Beam on, photodiode on, input low
Beam on, photodiode on, input low
Beam on, photodiode on, input low
Beam off, photodiode off input hi
Beam off, photodiode off input hi
Beam off, photodiode off input hi
Beam on, photodiode on, input low
Beam off, photodiode off input hi
Beam off, photodiode off input hi
Beam on, photodiode on, input low
Beam off, photodiode off input hi
Beam off, photodiode off input hi
Beam on, photodiode on, input low
Beam off, photodiode off input hi
Beam on, photodiode on, input low
Beam off, photodiode off input hi
Beam on, photodiode on, input low
Beam off, photodiode off input hi
Beam on, photodiode on, input low
Diode OFF
>>>
```

Figure 8-26. *A Polling Program Output*

The continuous loop that is only polling the input pin is properly terminated by using the "Ctrl+C" keystroke sequence. The sequence is recognized by encasing the while loop in a try-except keyboard interrupt combination that allows the loop to terminate and passes control to the remainder of the program. After loop termination, the program code turns off diodes that may be on, resets the GPIO configuration that may have been modified, and signals the program termination. Rapidly vibrating motions of the pen in the beam do not change the rate at which data is printed out in the interactive terminal. The polling can be seen to be missing beam breaking events.

Figure 8-27 displays the output from the rising edge detection interrupt code of Listing 8-13.

```
File Edit Shell Debug Options Windows Help
Input  =   0  Photodiode ON
Input  =   0  Photodiode ON
Input  =   0  Photodiode ON
Input  =   0  Photodiode ON
Input  =   0  Photodiode ON
Input  =   0  Photodiode ON
Input  =   0  Photodiode ON
Input  =   0  Photodiode ON
Input  =   0  Photodiode ON
Input  =   0  Photodiode ON
Input  =   0  Photodiode ON
Input pin status changed to  1
Input pin status changed to  0
Input pin status changed to  1
Input = 1 Photodiode OFFInput pin status changed to
 0
Input pin status changed to  1
Input pin status changed to  0
Input pin status changed to  1
Input pin status changed to  0
Input pin status changed to  1
Input pin status changed to Input =    00
 Photodiode ONInput pin status changed to
 1
Input pin status changed to  0
Input pin status changed to  1
Input pin status changed to  0
Input pin status changed to  1
Input pin status changed to  0
Input =Input pin status changed to    11
Photodiode OFFInput pin status changed to
 0
Led Off, event detect interrupt removed and GPIO cleanup run
>>> |
```

Figure 8-27. *An Interrupt Event Detection Program Output*

Rapid vibration of a pen shaft in the IR beam causes a corresponding rapid increase in the data output rate. The garbled output, as seen in the preceding data output, appears to be due to the interactive screen output not being able to respond to the rapid interrupt detection of beam blockage events.

An interrupt on event detection process has been created in the program by using the add_event_detect function of the RPi.GPIO library. The added function takes several arguments that specify the GPIO pin number; the event condition on which to act, a rising/falling edge or both; and the name of the function to branch to or "call back to" when the interrupt signal is received.

279

Until the selected electronic transition is encountered on the GPIO pin being monitored, the main loop of the program prints out the expected "Input = 0 Photodiode ON" and program control does not branch to the function created specifically for use when the transition is encountered. With no activity on the GPIO pin, the interrupt runs virtually invisible in the background. Electronic activity however triggers a branching to occur, and program control is transferred to a "jump to, execute, and return from" function that conducts the actions required by the investigator. In Figure 8-27, the input pin status is printed out until a rising edge is encountered that causes the program to branch to the specially created function that examines the pin status, prints it out, and returns to the original program looping routine. The add_event_detect function of the RPI.GPIO library is executed so quickly that the slower code controlling the output display is unable to keep up with rapid pen movements in the IR beam, and the corrupted output seen in Figure 8-27 results. The high speed of the interrupt technique is made possible by the use of threading.

Listing 8-15 uses an interrupt technique to drive an event counter. The counter runs in a separate thread from the main program and is accessed only when a specified electronic transition occurs on the pin being monitored. The counter value is stored in a Python global variable so as to be visible to the output portion of the main program loop, outside of the thread in which the counter increment function works. The main loop prints out the counter value on a regular timed basis as determined by the program code execution, but the counter value is increased by the interrupt-activated event detection that branches to the thread in which the counter is incremented. As can be seen in Figure 8-28, by vibrating a pen in the IR beam, the counter records the number of beam interruptions and adds them to the total count during the normal, virtually constant rate, data output intervals of the main program.

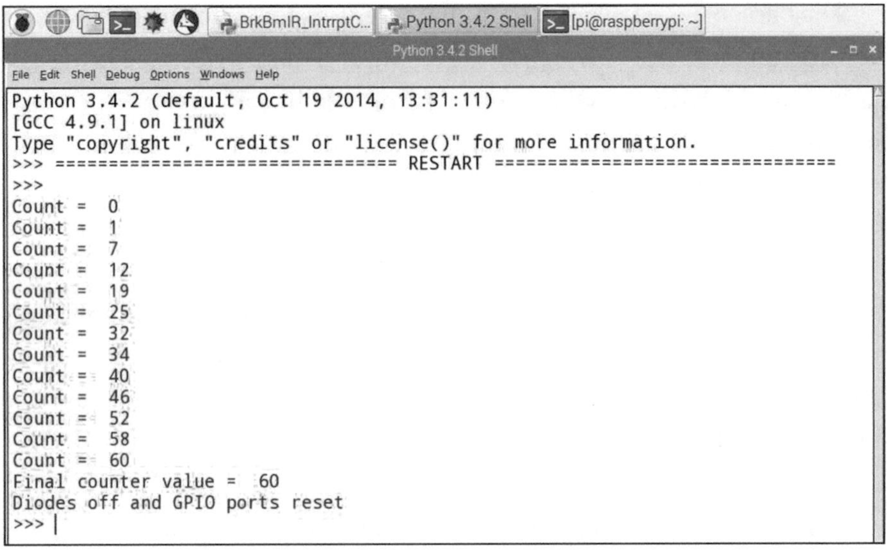
BrkBmIR_IntrrptC...
Python 3.4.2 Shell
[pi@raspberrypi: ~]
Python 3.4.2 Shell
File Edit Shell Debug Options Windows Help
Python 3.4.2 (default, Oct 19 2014, 13:31:11)
[GCC 4.9.1] on linux
Type "copyright", "credits" or "license()" for more information.
>>> ================================ RESTART ================================
>>>
Count = 0
Count = 1
Count = 7
Count = 12
Count = 19
Count = 25
Count = 32
Count = 34
Count = 40
Count = 46
Count = 52
Count = 58
Count = 60
Final counter value = 60
Diodes off and GPIO ports reset
>>> |

Figure 8-28. *An Interrupt-Driven Event Counter Output*

Discussion

A direct interfacing of sensors to the RPi through the GPIO pins and one of the three interfacing libraries is one of the less expensive and simplest of the options available for collecting data or monitoring sensors. Each of the three libraries has unique features and a differing degree of complexity. GPIO is best for simple digital systems, gpiozero is for integrated circuits, sensors, or sensing devices and robotics motor control, while pigpio is more complex, very fast, and chronologically accurate while able to interface a wide variety of electro-mechanical systems.

All three I/O libraries are able to accommodate mechanical switch "bounce" that is probably best estimated empirically in the system at hand. The magnitude of the time window in which second or third signals are to be ignored is determined by the time width of the smallest signal that the investigator wishes to measure.

The choice between a program that monitors for events with a polling loop and an interrupt-driven routine is simply a matter of considering the rate at which data is sent to the GPIO pin. Polling at once or twice per second is perfectly adequate for monitoring a door opening sensor, while an interrupt-driven monitor should be used for high-speed rotational measurements.

Python time-based measurements are all based upon tick counts of the system on which the program is running. The time base of the system is derived from Internet time as supplied by Internet time servers. As previously noted for time measurements that are to be made "off-line" such as in field measurements, a real-time clock (RTC) must be installed on the RPi.

Complete descriptions of the use of the scheduler modules can be found at the URLs in footnote 6 and should be consulted when using these Python functions. The use of the modules with minutes, hours, days, and hours of the day for all the days of the week requires care in application to function as desired and should be carefully set up for real-world applications.

The rapid response rate of an optical break beam circuit can be used to measure the frequency of a signal by using the appropriately scaled signal of interest, to power the IR diode source. The counter software can then be coded to measure, with an interrupt-driven counter, the number of events that accumulate over a timed and defined number of iterations of the program's main output loop.

Code Listings

Listing 8-1. DAQFactory Sequence Scheduled Time Timer

```
// Scheduled Time Timer
// Oct. 2 to 15, 2010
// A screen Start/Stop button is used to initiate the
// Schdld_Time_Tmr sequence. The sequence accepts a start and
// stop time at which to run a "scheduled event" from two,
// labelled, date and time edit boxes.
// The sequence verifies that both times are in the future and
// that the start time is before the finish time. Beneath the edit
// entry boxes a panel display shows the time left before event
// activation together with the elapsed and remaining times of
// the scheduled event.
//
//
global EvStartTime  // the starting time of the scheduled event
global EvEndTime    // the ending time of the event
global EvElapsedTime // time the event has been running
global EvRemainingTime // the time remaining in the timed event
global CurrentTime // the current time
global TimeToGo    // the variable for the count down timer
global HrsToGo
global MinToGo
global SecToGo
global EvHrsToGo
global EvMinToGo
global EvSecToGo
global EvElpsdHrs
global EvElpsdMin
global EvElpsdSec
```

```
//
// verify validity of entered time values
//if (EvStartTime < EvEndTime)
//if (CurrentTime < EvStartTime)
//
// Count down to start of timed event
//
CurrentTime = SysTime()
while (EvStartTime - CurrentTime > 0)
CurrentTime = SysTime()
TimeToGo = EvStartTime - CurrentTime
//Calculate the count down times for display
HrsToGo = floor(TimeToGo/3600)
MinToGo = floor(TimeToGo - (floor(HrsToGo) * 3600))/60
SecToGo = TimeToGo - (floor(HrsToGo * 3600) + (floor(MinToGo) * 60))
delay(0.01)
// zero count down timer display
HrsToGo = 0
MinToGo = 0
SecToGo = 0
endwhile
//
// Start Scheduled Event Timer
//
While (EvEndTime - CurrentTime > 0 )
CurrentTime = SysTime()
// Start actual event
RedLed = 5
//
TimeToGo = EvEndTime - CurrentTime
```

```
//Calculate the count down times to the end of the scheduled
event for display
EvElapsedTime = CurrentTime - EvStartTime
EvElpsdSec = (EvElapsedTime)%60
EvElpsdMin = (EvElapsedTime/60)%60
EvElpsdSec = (EvElapsedTime/3600)
EvHrsToGo = floor(TimeToGo/3600)
EvMinToGo = floor(TimeToGo - (floor(EvHrsToGo) * 3600))/60
EvSecToGo = TimeToGo - (floor(EvHrsToGo * 3600) +
(floor(EvMinToGo) * 60))
delay (0.01)
endwhile
// Stop Timed Event
RedLed = 0
```

Listing 8-2. DAQFactory Stopwatch Timer

```
The Stopwatch Timer DAQFactory Sequence Code
// Stop Watch Timer Oct.6 - Nov. 17 2010  (Min is a reserved
// word!) The timer sequence is started and stopped by a screen
// button that simultaneously sets a timing flag for a while
// loop and starts the sequence StopWatchTimer. The SysTime()
// function is used in a wait(0.05) delayed while loop, that
// calculates the total number of clock ticks between the current
// value of SysTime() and the initial interval starting value.
// The total elapsed time in seconds is calculated then divided
// into hours, minutes and seconds for display. The main screen
// display provides the operator with two modes of timing
// operation that record either a single interval time or the
// cumulative total of multiple intervals. The cumulative total
// option must determine the number of seconds that have elapsed
// in the current interval and keep track of the sum of the
// accumulated interval times.
```

```
//
//
//
global InitialTime // the start of the current interval
global ElapsedTime // the elapsed time of the current interval
global Hrs = 0
global Minutes = 0
global SxtyMinTm
global Sec = 0
global SxtySecTm
global TimingFlg // the main while timer loop condition flag

//
//
InitialTime = SysTime() // Set the initial time value
//
while(TimingFlg) // start the main program loop
   ElapsedTime = SysTime() - InitialTime
   wait (0.05)
   Hrs = Floor(ElapsedTime/3600) // just divide total time in
                                 seconds by 3600 to get hours
   Minutes = Floor(ElapsedTime/60) // total minutes is calculated
   SxtyMinTm = (Floor(ElapsedTime/60))%60
   Sec = (ElapsedTime - ((ElapsedTime - (ElapsedTime % 3600)) % 60))
   SxtySecTm = (ElapsedTime - ((ElapsedTime - (ElapsedTime %
   3600)) % 60)) % 60
   Endwhile
```

Listing 8-3. DAQFactory Sequence Reset Stopwatch

```
// Reset Stopwatch Display Oct. 6, 2010
// The sequence resets the timer variables
//
InitialTime = 0
CurrentTime = 0
ElapsedTime = 0
Hrs = 0
Minutes = 0
Sec = 0
SxtySecTm = 0
TSixtySecTm = 0
SxtyMinTm = 0
TSxtyMinTm = 0
TtlHrs = 0
TtlMin = 0
TtlSec = 0
```

Listing 8-4. DAQFactory Sequence Cumulative Time of Intervals

```
// CumulativeTimeOfIntervals Nov. 27, 2010 is a summation of
// the previous collected intervals Each interval timed is
// measured in clock ticks that are converted into sec, min
// and hrs for display. When the current interval is to be
// summed into the accumulation the Cumulative Time button is
// used to add the current interval's total seconds to the
// accumulating sum of total seconds. The previous hrs, min.
// and seconds used for the previous display are discarded and
// a new total time is calculated for an up-dated display.
//
```

```
global TtlHrs
global TtlMin
global TtlSec
global Hrs
global Minutes
global Sec
global TSixtySecTm
global TSxtyMinTm
global ElapsedTime
global IntrvlMin
//
TtlSec = TtlSec + Sec
TtlHrs = Floor(TtlSec/3600) // just divide total time in
seconds by 3600 to get hours
TtlMin = Floor(TtlSec/60) // total minutes is calculated
   TSxtyMinTm = (Floor(TtlSec/60))%60
   Sec = (TtlSec - ((TtlSec - (TtlSec % 3600)) % 60))
   TSixtySecTm = (TtlSec - ((TtlSec - (TtlSec % 3600)) % 60)) % 60
```

Listing 8-5. DAQFactory Sequence Counting Events

```
// A_Counter_Event - Jan. 1/11 - The LabJack counter is activated
// by a 5 to 0 volt falling edge followed by a 0 to 5 volt
// rising edge. The following script applies the 5 - 0 - 5 volt
// profile to the DigOut_9_EventCntr channel that activates
// pin D9 onthe CB-25 board. This script is activated by
// clicking on the screen button labelled "Initiate Event".
//
// Set the pin voltage to 5 volts
DigOut_9_EventCntr = 5
// Create the falling edge by setting the pin voltage to 0
DigOut_9_EventCntr = 0
```

```
// Create the rising edge by setting the pin voltage back to 5
   DigOut_9_EventCntr = 5
// For ease of configuration the voltage is left on for 1/2 a
   second so as the lit LED can be
// used to validate a functioning system.
//Delay(0.5)
//DigOut_9_EventCntr = 0
```

Listing 8-6. DAQFactory Sequence Reset Counter

```
// ResetCounter - Fall/09 Revn Jan 1/11 The script manually
// resets the displayed number of events counted, by the LabJack
// counter after the defaut "Reset after polling" has been
// turned off. The counter is activated after it detects a
// falling edge waveform followed by a rising edge waveform.
// The "event" counted thus consists of a 5 to 0 - 0 to 5 volt
// transition which leaves the Pin 9 at 5 volts. For the manually
// activated counter exercise the blue LED thus remains ON as
// long as the manually activated counting session is in
// progress, re-setting the counter then turns the LED off.
//
EventsCounted[0] = 0
DigOut_9_EventCntr = 0
// By using the default setting of "Reset" after polling (reading)
// the number of 5-0-5 volt transitions in a given period of
// time, the frequency can be determined.
RawCounts[0] = 0
DigOut_8_PWM = 0
```

Listing 8-7. DAQFactory Sequence PWM Script

```
// PWM_Script (Pulse Width Manipulation) Script for pulse
// width variation - Oct. 21/09 Rvn. Jan. 2/11, Aug. 3/17
// A "time - goto" loop is used with delay statements to set
// D8 to 1 then 0 thus raising and lowering the channel
// DigOut_8_PWM output between 0 and 5 volts in a continuous
// manner. The continuously varying voltage creates a square
// wave train. The 0.002 and 0.098 can be considered as the
// time on time off duty cycle. With the lower duty cycle the
// pulsing of a powered light source is quite evident.
// Various duty cycles must be entered manually into the simple
// program which is started and stopped with the sequence
// pop-up menu displayed by right clocking on the sequence name.
time 0
DigOut_8_PWM = 1
Delay (0.002)
DigOut_8_PWM = 0
Delay (0.098)
goto 0
```

Listing 8-8. Arduino Stopwatch Timer Code

```
/* A stopwatch program using a DAQFactory panel and the serial
port to avoid the debouncing problems associated with
mechanical switches. The program uses the letters b, s, and r
to branch in an Arduion case statement using b for begin,
s for stop and r for re-set. Always ensure that data sent
from the Arduino to the DAQFactory software code is
Serial.println(data);
*/
```

```
char incmngByte;                           // a variableto hold
                                           //   the incoming byte
                                           //   from the serial port
unsigned long start, finished, elapsed;    // timing variables
bool tsipFlg = LOW;                        // timing session in
                                           //   progress flag
bool wtspFlg = LOW;                        // write to serial port
                                           //   once only flag
bool rstFlg = LOW;                         // re-set b and s flags
//
void setup() {
  Serial.begin(9600);                      // start the serial port
}
//
void loop() {
  if(Serial.available() > 0) {             // check port for
                                           //   incoming character

  incmngByte = Serial.read();              // set character into
                                           //   variable

  }
switch(incmngByte) {                       // the case statement
                                           //   for decisions

  case'b':                                 // begin a timing
                                           //   session
  if (tsipFlg == LOW) {                    // check the status flag
  start = millis();                        // set the start time
  //Serial.print(start);                   // diagnostic
  tsipFlg = HIGH;                          // set the status
                                           //   flag to timing in
                                           //   progress

  }
```

```
  rstFlg = LOW;
  break;
  case's':                              // stop the timer
  if (wtspFlg == LOW) {                 // check the status flag
  finished = millis();                  // set the finish time
  //Serial.println(finished);           // diagnostic
  elapsed = finished - start;           // calculate the
                                        //    elapsed time

  Serial.println(elapsed);              // write the elapsed
                                        //    time to the serial
                                        //    port

  wtspFlg = HIGH;                       // set the status flag
                                        //    to write only once

  }
  rstFlg = LOW;
  break;
  case'r':                              // re-set b and s
                                        //    functions

  if (rstFlg == LOW) {                  // check the status flag
  tsipFlg = LOW;
  wtspFlg = LOW;
  rstFlg = HIGH;
  }
  break;
 }
}
```

Listing 8-9. DAQFactory Quick Sequences for b, s, and r

```
// send begin signal b
device.ardyBluBrd.Write('b')

// send stop signal s
global Elapsed
device.ardyBluBrd.Write('s')
private string datain
datain = device.ardyBluBrd.ReadUntil(13)
Elapsed = strToDouble(datain)

// send re-set signal r
device.ardyBluBrd.Write('r')
Elapsed = 0
```

Raspberry Pi Program Code

Listing 8-10. A RPi Three-Button Stopwatch Timer GUI

```
from tkinter import *
import time

class StopWatch(Frame):
    """ Implements a stop watch frame widget. """
    def __init__(self, parent=None, **kw):
        Frame.__init__(self, parent, kw)
        self._start = 0.0
        self._elapsedtime = 0.0
        self._running = 0
        self.timestr = StringVar()
        self.makeWidgets()
```

```python
def makeWidgets(self):
    """ Make the time label. """
    l = Label(self, textvariable=self.timestr)
    self._setTime(self._elapsedtime)
    l.pack(fill=X, expand=NO, pady=2, padx=2)

def _update(self):
    """ Update the label with elapsed time. """
    self._elapsedtime = time.time() - self._start
    self._setTime(self._elapsedtime)
    self._timer = self.after(50, self._update)

def _setTime(self, elap):
    """ Set the time string to Minutes:Seconds:Hundreths """
    minutes = int(elap/60)
    seconds = int(elap - minutes*60.0)
    hseconds = int((elap - minutes*60.0 - seconds)*100)
    self.timestr.set('%02d:%02d:%02d' % (minutes, seconds,
    hseconds))

def Start(self):
    """ Start the stopwatch, ignore if running. """
    if not self._running:
        self._start = time.time() - self._elapsedtime
        self._update()
        self._running = 1

def Stop(self):
    """ Stop the stopwatch, ignore if stopped. """
    if self._running:
        self.after_cancel(self._timer)
        self._elapsedtime = time.time() - self._start
        self._setTime(self._elapsedtime)
        self._running = 0
```

```python
    def Reset(self):
        """ Reset the stopwatch. """
        self._start = time.time()
        self._elapsedtime = 0.0
        self._setTime(self._elapsedtime)

def main():
    root = Tk()
    sw = StopWatch(root)
    sw.pack(side=TOP)

    Button(root, text='Start', command=sw.Start).pack(side=LEFT)
    Button(root, text='Stop', command=sw.Stop).pack(side=LEFT)
    Button(root, text='Reset', command=sw.Reset).pack(side=LEFT)

    root.mainloop()

if __name__ == '__main__':
    main()
```

Listing 8-11. A Python Scheduled Event Program

```python
# Scheduled Program Control of LEDs, green and red LEDs wth
  CLRs are connected
# to GPIO pins 20 and 21 or pins 38 and 40 of the RPi array.
  Pgm calls two
# sequential events with defined delays between events to light
  the leds and
# print out tick time and current times.
#
import RPi.GPIO as GPIO
import sched
import time
#
```

```python
scheduler = sched.scheduler(time.time, time.sleep)
# create an instance of scheduler
#
GPIO.setmode(GPIO.BCM)
GPIO.setwarnings(False)
GPIO.setup(20, GPIO.OUT)
GPIO.setup(21, GPIO.OUT)
#
# Activate green led for a measured length of time, timestamp
  event, pass in text
# and document actions
def actvt_GrnLed(name):
    print(name) # text or data passed in --> Green led
    activated firt
    print("Green LED on")
    frstsched_tm = time.asctime(time.localtime(time.time()))
    # local time code processed
    print("First scheduled event run at ", frstsched_tm)
    print("Green led on at ", time.time()) # the tick count at
    grn led on
    GPIO.output(20,GPIO.HIGH)
    time.sleep(3)
    print("Green LED off at ", time.time()) # tick count at grn
    led off
    GPIO.output(20,GPIO.LOW)
    print() # format spacing for output
#
# Activate red led for a measured length of time, timestamp
event, pass in text # and document actions
def actvt_RedLed(name):
    print(name)
    print("Red LED on")
```

```
    scndsched_tm = time.asctime(time.localtime(time.time()))
    print("Second scheduled event run at ", scndsched_tm)
    print("Red Led on at ", time.time())
    GPIO.output(21,GPIO.HIGH)
    time.sleep(5)
    print("Red LED off at ", time.time())
    GPIO.output(21,GPIO.LOW)
    print() # format output spacing
    fnsh_tm = time.asctime(time.localtime(time.time()))
    print("Program local finish time = ", fnsh_tm)
    print("Finish time = ", time.time())
#
print("Start time in ticks = ", time.time())
pgm_strt_tm = time.asctime(time.localtime(time.time()))
print("Program local time start = ", pgm_strt_tm)
print()
#
scheduler.enter(2, 1, actvt_GrnLed, ("Green led activated
first",))
scheduler.enter(5, 1, actvt_RedLed, ("Red led is activated
second",))
#
scheduler.run() # start the program
```

Listing 8-12. A Raspberry Pi RPi.GPIO Push Button Timer

```
# A push button activated rising edge transition starts a timer
  and a second
# stops the elapsed time measurement. GPIO 21 is pin 40 on the
  pi board and
# is connected to the junction of the series connected PBS and
  LED CLR circuit
```

```
# A bounce time of 100 ms is used to avoid false triggering.
#
import time
import RPi.GPIO as GPIO
GPIO.setmode(GPIO.BCM)
GPIO.setwarnings(False)
# set up the pin-channel, board is 40 bcm is 21
GPIO.setup(21, GPIO.IN)
#
GPIO.wait_for_edge(21, GPIO.RISING, bouncetime=100)
# a blocking action while waiting
#
# wait for the event, print an alert and start a timer
#
if GPIO.input(21):
    print("A rising edge was detected.")
    # start a timer to count ticks
    ticks_initl = time.time()
    print("A timer was started at tick count ", ticks_initl)
    GPIO.setup(21, GPIO.IN, pull_up_down=GPIO.PUD_DOWN)
# reset the GPIO pin low
#
# wait for the second event to occur and measure the elapsed time
GPIO.wait_for_edge(21, GPIO.RISING, bouncetime=100)
# again a blocking action while waiting
#
if GPIO.input(21):
    print("A second or stop timing event has been detected.")
    ticks_fnl = time.time()
    print("A stop timing event has been detected at tick count ",
    ticks_fnl)
```

```
#
# calculate and display the elapsed time.
print("The elapsed time = ", round(ticks_fnl - ticks_initl, 2),
"seconds")
```

Listing 8-13. A Polling IR Break Beam Monitor Program

```
# Code for PRi Detecting Input Events by Polling
# Program to get input from pin 7 (board) Gnd is pin 6
import RPi.GPIO as GPIO
import time
#
GPIO.setmode(GPIO.BOARD)    # get library
GPIO.setwarnings(False)
GPIO.setup(11, GPIO.OUT)    # set pin 11 as output to power IR LED
GPIO.setup(38, GPIO.OUT)    # green led beam intact indicator
GPIO.setup(40, GPIO.OUT)    # red led beam broken indicator
GPIO.setup(7, GPIO.IN)      # set pin 7 as IR Photodiode input
#
#  Main program loop
GPIO.output(11, True)       # turn LED on
try:
    while (1):              # continuous loop
        if GPIO.input(7):
            print("Beam off, photodiode off input pulled hi ")
            # detects 3.3v power from pin 1
            GPIO.output(38, 0)   # grn led off as beam has been
                                 broken
            GPIO.output(40, 1)   # red led on to indicate beam
                                 is broken
            time.sleep(0.5)
```

```
        else:
            print("Beam on, photodiode on, input pulled low ")
            # detects 0v (diode-on acts like short)
            GPIO.output(40, 0)    # red led off as beam restored
            GPIO.output(38, 1)    # grn led on as beam intact
            time.sleep(0.5);      # wait time before next loop
except KeyboardInterrupt:
    pass
#
#
GPIO.output(11, False)                      # turn OFF the IR LED
GPIO.cleanup()                              # reset ports
print("Diodes off and ports reset ")       # indicate end of pgm
```

Listing 8-14. An IR Break Beam Monitor with Interrupt Activity

```
# PRi Detecting Input Events with Interrupts
# Program to get input from pin 7 (board) Gnd is pin 6
import RPi.GPIO as GPIO
import time
#
GPIO.setmode(GPIO.BOARD)    # get library
GPIO.setup(11, GPIO.OUT)    # set pin 11 as output to power IR LED
GPIO.setup(38, GPIO.OUT)    # green led beam intact indicator
GPIO.setup(40, GPIO.OUT)    # red led beam broken indicator
GPIO.setup(7, GPIO.IN)      # set pin 7 as IR Photodiode input
#
#   Function that "add event detect" runs at input change
def inputChng(channel):
    print("Input pin status changed to ", GPIO.input(7))
#
# On input change, run input change function
GPIO.add_event_detect(7, GPIO.RISING, callback=inputChng)
```

```
#
GPIO.output(11, True)           # turn IR LED on
time.sleep(1)
try:
    while True:
        if GPIO.input(7) > 0.5:
            print("Input =", GPIO.input(7), "Photodiode
            OFF")  # detects 3.3v power from pin 1
            GPIO.output(38, 0)  # grn led off as beam has been
                                  broken
            GPIO.output(40, 1)  # red led on to indicate beam
                                  is broken
            time.sleep(0.5)     # wait time before next
                                  iteration
        else:
            print("Input = ",GPIO.input(7), "Photodiode ON")
              # detects 0v (diode-on acts like short)
            GPIO.output(40, 0)  # red led off as beam restored
            GPIO.output(38, 1)  # grn led on as beam intact
            time.sleep(0.5)     # wait time before next
                                  iteration
except KeyboardInterrupt:
    pass
#
#
GPIO.output(11, False)          # turn OFF the LED
GPIO.remove_event_detect(7)     # Turn off event detect interrupt
GPIO.cleanup()                  # reset ports
print("Led Off, event detect interrupt removed and GPIO cleanup run")
```

Listing 8-15. An IR Break Beam Interrupt-Driven Counter

```
# Break Beam Interrupt Driven Counter: counts & prints number
of interruptions in beam
# Input from pin 7 (board) (GPIO 4) system ground at pin 6
# IR photodiode pull-up with 1M ohm pullup btwn 7 & 1 (3.3v)
# IR LED pin 11 supplies IR illumination gnd pin 6
#
import RPi.GPIO as GPIO    # get GPIO library
import time
#
GPIO.setmode(GPIO.BOARD)        # use RPi board pin numbers
GPIO.setup(11, GPIO.OUT)        # set pin 11 (GPIO 17) as output
                                  to power IR LED
GPIO.setup(7, GPIO.IN)          # set pin 7 (GPIO 4) as input
#
counter = 0 # declare and initialize counter variable
#
# Function "add_event_detect" runs at input change
def counterPlus(channel):
    global counter                  # declared global to share
                                      with system & threads

    if GPIO.input(channel) > 0.5:  # pin 7 = 3.3v. photodiode off
        counter += 1                # recognize blocked beam
    else:
        counter += 0                # 0v, no-op
#
# On input change, run input change function
GPIO.add_event_detect(7, GPIO.RISING, callback=counterPlus)
#
GPIO.output(11, True)           # turn on the IR LED
time.sleep(1)                   # give LED time to turn fully on
```

```
try:
    while True:
        print("Count = ", counter)    # output current counter
                                         value
        time.sleep(1)                   # time delay before
                                          looping
except KeyboardInterrupt:
    pass
#
print("Final counter value = ", counter)  # output final
counter value
GPIO.output(11, False)                      # turn IR source off
GPIO.cleanup()                              # reset ports
print("Diodes off and GPIO ports reset")
```

Summary

- Integrated circuits based upon "latches" with crystal-regulated oscillators acting as timing clocks are able to count and determine the time between events with microsecond resolution.

- Time of day measurements are based upon "tick" counts since January 1, 1970, and allow for day time determination, timing coordination, and scheduling for events in the future through the SCADA GUI.

- Stopwatch timing can be configured with both the commercial and component-assembled SCADA systems.

- Several solutions are provided for monitoring for events and compensating for the false or erroneous triggering of event detectors during experimental sessions.

- In Chapter 9, the advantages of graphical data recording are presented that in some experiments can detect false triggering of event detection.

CHAPTER 9

Graphical Data Recording

An old Far Eastern proverb advises that "a picture is worth a thousand words." The truth of the proverb is fully realized in chemical analysis and medical imaging where not only the numerical values but the shape of the recorded data conveys information. Numerous techniques in medical, physical, and many other experimental sciences depend upon the graphical presentation of data. Clinical and chemical analysis has traditionally used chemically sensitive transducers to generate a millivolt signal in response to changing chemical process values. The small signal was amplified electronically and used with a servomotor to mechanically drive a pen across a paper chart to provide a visual record of the chemical process being monitored. Although both x-y and x vs. time plotting systems are extensively employed in the manufacturing process industries, chemical analysis, and other sciences, the electro-mechanical plotting instruments, much like the typewriter, have been replaced by the PC.

x-y plotting is used extensively in analytical spectroscopies and electrochemical analysis, while x vs. time charting is used for following titrations, in biochemical kinetics, and in both chromatographic and spectroscopic analysis.

DAQFactory is being used for this application because of its powerful graphical recording and display capabilities. A graphical display tutorial is included with the DAQFactory user manual along with a detailed chapter on

© Richard J. Smythe 2021
R. J. Smythe, *Arduino in Science*, https://doi.org/10.1007/978-1-4842-6778-3_9

the DAQFactory graphical display capabilities. Both the tutorial and the user manual should be reviewed before starting this exercise for those researchers using either the free Express or full version of the SCADA software.

In this exercise, several very important concepts and circuit configurations are demonstrated. The 555 timer configured as an astable multivibrator will be used to create square, sawtooth, and nonsymmetrical triangular signal waveforms as a prelude to visually examining the very important concept of pulse width modulation (PWM). Exponential and linear voltage waveforms from capacitor charging and discharging will be demonstrated, and the creation of symmetrical voltage waveform outputs from special ICs will be used for creating graphical data recordings.

In the first timer configuration examined, two resistors and a capacitor will be used to form a "timing network" on the oscillator chip. The RC component values will be chosen so the timer chip generates waveforms compatible with our recording software. One of the resistance components chosen will be of a variable nature to model a resistance-based chemical or physical transducer. Variation of the transducer resistance with some physical phenomenon, such as the intensity of the light falling on the sensor surface or temperature, will then cause the frequency and wavelength of the timer output signal to vary, and the output variation will be displayed on the PC screen in a graphical format. Signal variation can then be transformed into pulse width variation to form the basis of the extensively used pulse width modulation (PWM) concept.

In the second timer configuration examined, the use of a constant current source to charge the timing capacitor will be demonstrated, and the creation of "sawtooth" and triangular output waveforms will be graphically recorded. The triangular waveform or voltage ramp has an important use in some sensor monitoring and in chemical analysis. A third circuit is assembled to demonstrate a simplified method for creating a dual-slope analog ramp that is used frequently in electrochemical, corrosion, and biophysiology investigations.

A simple x-y recording system constitutes the last portion of the chapter.

Experimental: Linear Graphical Data Recording

Part 1: Hardware and Component Selection – Square Wave Output

Previous work in Chapter 8 has shown the limitations imposed by software overhead, and hence the rate of change of signal shape that can be displayed as it occurs or in "real time" is limited by the computer performance. The bipolar transistor 555 timer in astable mode can produce an output signal that can be made to vary from 70 kHz to about four cycles per minute. CMOS versions of the timer can generate frequencies in the megacycle range. Most 555 timer manufacturers include a standard nomograph of the relationship between the capacitance and the R1-R2 values of the resistors in the IC's timing network. Figure 9-1 is an extended graphic that accommodates the newer versions of the CMOS-based ICs that are able to oscillate at the higher frequencies. The approximate timing network values and resulting free running output frequencies are depicted in Figure 9-1 for the astable configuration of the timer.

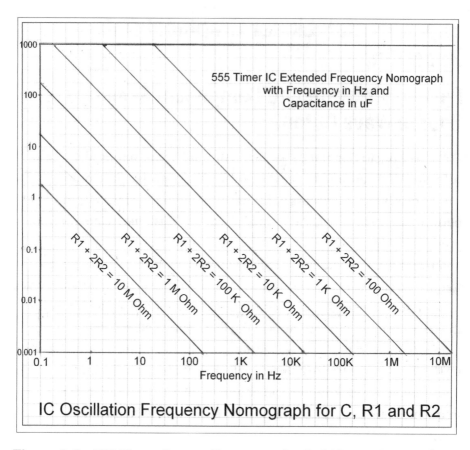

Figure 9-1. *555 Timer Output Frequency for R-C Timing Network Values*

In order to keep the output signal from the timer chip in the low frequency range that should be suitable for the DAQFactory graphics, the resistance values should be in the megohm range (million or 10^6 ohms) and the capacitance value in the 0.1–10 uF (micro or 1/1,000,000 F) range. The graphical data of Figure 9-1 is an approximation, and the actual resistance values chosen for use are somewhat dependent upon the capacitance value selected or available.

An electrolytic capacitor with a value of 1–10 uF should be suitable for this graphics display exercise, but for more accurate work, a higher-quality low-leakage type of capacitor may be required as detailed in the following discussion.

Electronic Components Required

1) 555 timer integrated circuit

2) Variable and fixed resistors to sum into the low megohm range preferably with the fixed and variable values being in the same order of magnitude of resistance

3) A suitable "timing" capacitor in the 1–10 uF range, a 0.01 uF bypass capacitor, and a 9 V battery supply

Circuit Schematic

Figure 9-2 depicts the circuit configuration for the astable 555 timer.

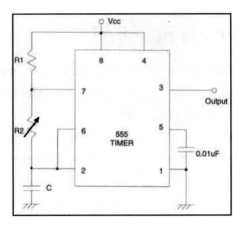

Figure 9-2. *555 Timer Astable Configuration*

The preceding circuit shows a single variable resistance between pins 7 and 2. The circuit will work when the variable resistor is in its mid-travel position but will produce erratic results when at the low end of its resistance value. To avoid any problems with circuit malfunctions, place a fixed value resistor in series with the variable unit to limit the lower end value of the second timing network resistance. The author used a 10 kΩ value for a 1.2 MΩ R1 + R2 network sum value.

Software

After having assembled the astable oscillator, connect the output to a differential input channel on the LabJack and configure a channel for receiving the square wave output. The graphical page component can then be created. For long-duration graphical displays, make sure the channel storage capability is large enough to support the length of the desired time display. The number of values in memory is defined by the value in the channel's "History" box. (The default entry is 3600 that can be filled quite quickly when working in experimental time frames of tens of minutes or fractions of hours.)

Page Components Required

A two-dimensional graphical screen component is created by selecting, on a new page, the 2D Graph entry from the right-click pop-up page component menu, as shown in Figure 9-3.

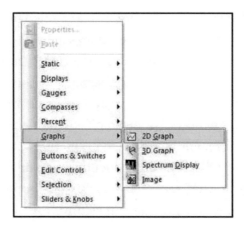

Figure 9-3. *DAQFactory Selection of a 2D Graphical Recorder Screen Display*

The default graphical screen component configuration for an x-y graph is displayed in Figure 9-4.

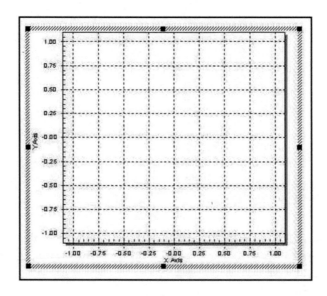

Figure 9-4. *The Default X-Y Graphical Screen Display*

The graphical component is positioned and fitted to the page by pressing the Ctrl key and dragging the squares in the centers of the hatched edge lines to the desired locations on the page. Once the component has been sized, the properties menu for the screen component can be opened by right-clicking the screen component and selecting the "Properties" entry. The properties window for the graph is a multi-tabbed display with multiple entry forms for adding traces to the graph, defining the axis values used for the graphical display, adding identification titles, and selecting colors for the display. The Traces tab of the six-tab properties window, for defining the name entry, is illustrated in Figure 9-5.

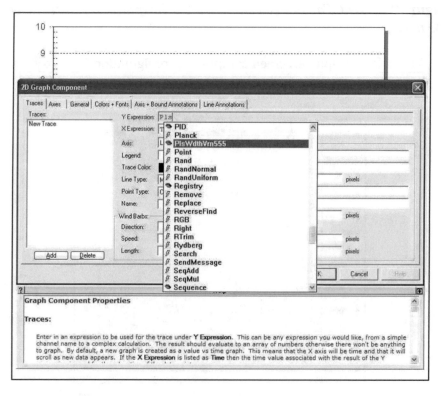

Figure 9-5. *Recorder Trace Name Selection*

A Help screen at the bottom of the properties window explains all of the data entry boxes and tabs that are found in the graphical screen component.

For the square wave being generated by the 9-volt battery-powered 555 timer oscillator, the voltage range was offset to display values from –1 to 9 volts to more clearly depict the time the waveform is at 0 V.

Part 1: Observations

With a 392 kΩ R1, a 900 kΩ R2, and a 10 kΩ series resistance limiting unit, charging a 22 uF, 25 V electrolytic capacitor from a 9 V battery, a graphical display of four high time cycles in 60 seconds was obtained with a midrange setting on R2.

Between the two extremes as depicted in Figures 9-6 and 9-7, the number of signal waveforms being generated on a unit time basis changes.

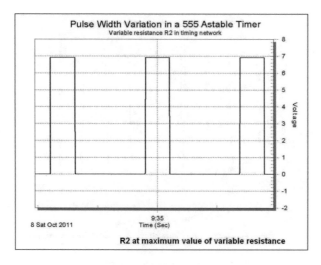

Figure 9-6. *Timer Output at Maximum Resistance*

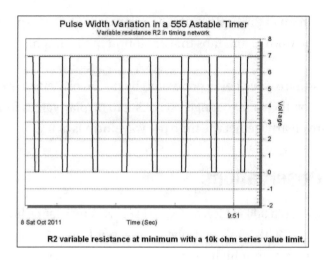

Figure 9-7. *Timer Output at Minimum Resistance*

If the circuit is operated without a series resistor to limit the minimum value of R2, then waveforms such as those of Figure 9-8 may be created.

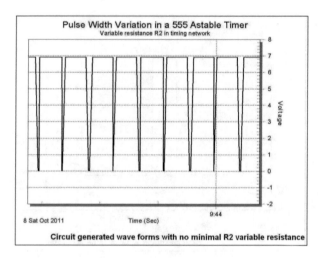

Figure 9-8. *Waveform Without Minimal Resistance*

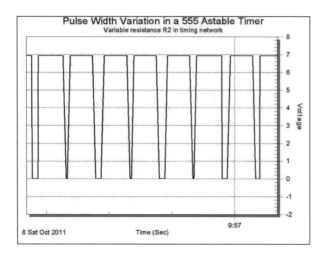

Figure 9-9. *Erratic Output Signal or "Aliasing"*

Experimental

Part 2: Hardware and Component Selection – Triangular and "Sawtooth" Outputs

In addition to the creation of a square wave signal with a varying duty cycle, the astable 555 timer can be used to generate a "sawtooth" and asymmetrical triangular wave. Basic electronics teaches that when a capacitor is charged or discharged through a fixed value resistor, an increasing or decreasing exponential voltage value is seen across the terminals of the capacitor. When a capacitor is charged with a constant current source, a linear voltage increase is seen across the capacitor terminals. The linear voltage change forms a triangular waveform that can be used to generate a voltage ramp having several applications in chemical analysis and other experimental work.

By assembling the circuit depicted in Figure 9-10, two additional waveforms can be generated.

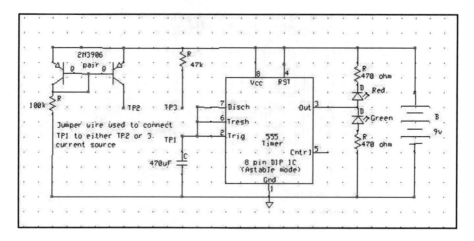

Figure 9-10. *A Constant Current Charging Source*

Part 2: Observations

When the capacitor is charged through a series resistor, the familiar
exponential voltage change is observed and recorded as seen in Figure 9-11,
between test points 1 and 3.

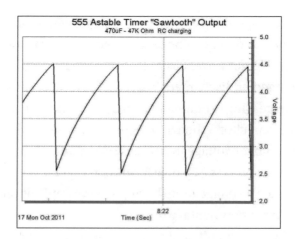

Figure 9-11. *Typical 555 Timer "Sawtooth" Output Voltage
Waveform*

When the voltage between TP1 and TP2 is measured, a triangular waveform is recorded as illustrated in Figure 9-12.

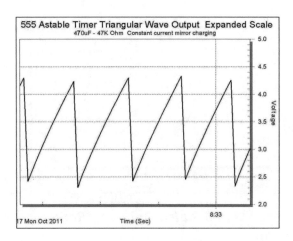

Figure 9-12. *A 555 Timer Triangular Wave Expanded Scale*

The charging of the capacitor with a constant current generates the linear voltage ramp across the capacitor plates as seen on the left-hand side of the waveform. The steep right-hand portion of the signal is caused by the rapid discharge of the capacitor when the discharge pin of the timer is connected to ground through the emitter of an internal NPN switching transistor in the 555 timer IC. Although the discharge trace appears to be a straight line, it is in reality the initial portion of the inverse exponential curve of the positive charging curvature seen in Figure 9-11. Figures 9-12 and 9-13 illustrate the effects of adding a fixed series resistance between the capacitor and the discharge pin of the timer IC.

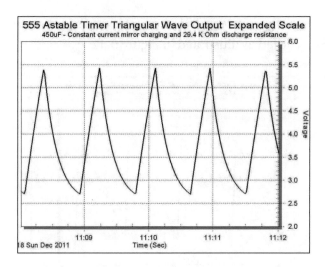

Figure 9-13. *The Effect of Added Discharge Resistance on the Timer Output Waveform*

Simple logic would suggest that to obtain a linear triangular waveform, charging and discharging a capacitor through constant current sources and sinks would achieve the desired result, but a simpler solution can be found by using "function generators" that can produce signals of various shapes and frequencies.

Part 3: Hardware and Component Selection – Dual-Slope Triangular Waveform

To obtain a symmetrical triangular waveform, it is easier to use a "function generator." Like the 741 and 555 ICs, a very successful function generator is the Exar XR-2209 that has been available in an eight-pin dual in-line package (DIP) since 1975. The integrated circuit is built around a circuit known as a voltage-controlled oscillator (VCO). The XR-2209 VCO can simultaneously generate both a square and triangular voltage waveform signal from a single eight-pin DIP. The chip can be powered from a single- or dual-voltage supply as required by the application at hand.

(See "Discussion.") The function generator chip requires some care when single-ended or dual-voltage supplies are used for power as detailed in the manufacturer's data sheets. The recommended circuit schematic for using the 2209 function generator with a dual-voltage power supply, in the author's case +/–9-volt batteries, is depicted in Figure 9-14.

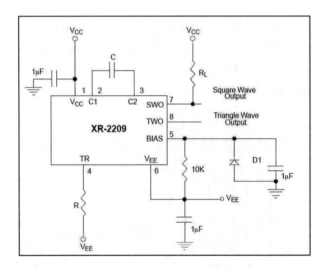

Figure 9-14. *Schematic for Function Generator Configuration*

To create the positive and negative voltage ramps, the circuit is powered by a pair of 9 V batteries configured as a bipolar +/–9 V supply with a common ground as depicted in Figure 9-15.

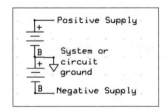

Figure 9-15. *A Dual-Battery Bipolar Power Supply*

If the circuit, when properly assembled on a breadboard, fails to operate as expected, consult the manufacturer's data sheets and the "Discussion" section.

Part 3: Observations

The XR-2209 can produce symmetrical triangular waveforms as depicted in Figure 9-16 and with an appropriate "pull-up" resistor the square waveform of Figure 9-17. (See discussion on design limitations for "pull-up" resistor selection.)

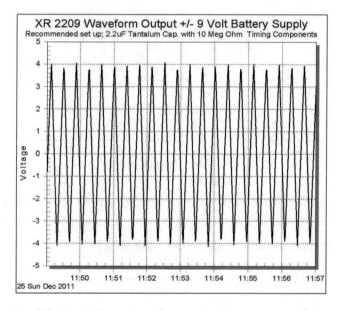

Figure 9-16. *XR-2209 Function Generator Symmetrical Triangular Wave Output*

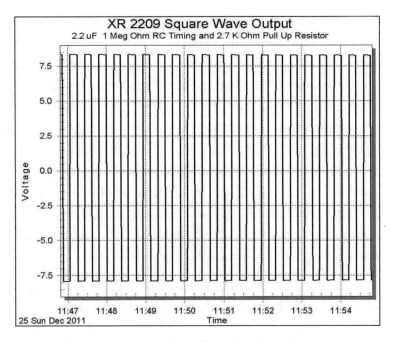

Figure 9-17. *Square Wave Output with Pull-Up Resistor*

X-Y Data Recording

As can be seen in Figure 9-4, the default format for the two-dimensional plotting, graphical display screen component is x vs. y. The constant current charging circuit of Figure 9-10 can be used to produce an x-y plotting of the voltage across the capacitor and its square as would be used in measuring the energy developed across the capacitor. $E = CV^2/2$. The constant current circuit can be used for this demonstration exercise because an asymmetrical voltage ramp is created on the capacitor by the constant current charging and the exponential discharging of the component.

To create the desired display, the voltage across the 470 uF electrolytic capacitor of the constant current charging circuit can be recorded in the channel created for the PWM data collection display. The breadboard electronics causes the voltage on the capacitor to linearly cycle between 1/3 and 2/3 of the supply voltage and then exponentially discharge, when the timer chip connects the charged capacitor to ground. A graphical display of the cyclic charging and discharging voltages should thus be different. The channel name is entered into the x axis box, and the square of the voltage is computed in the y axis expression box. The voltages displayed on the two axes must be adjusted for the power supply being used to drive the voltage change, and in the author's case, the values depicted in Figures 9-18, 9-19, and 9-20 were used to record the data in Figure 9-21.

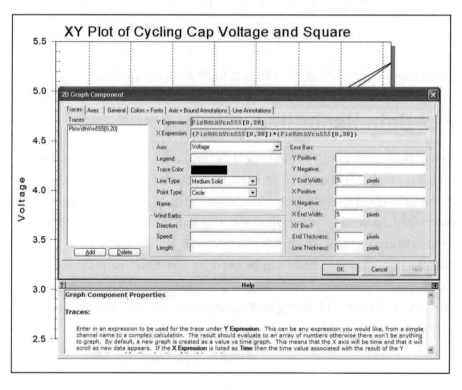

Figure 9-18. *x-y Graph Traces Tab*

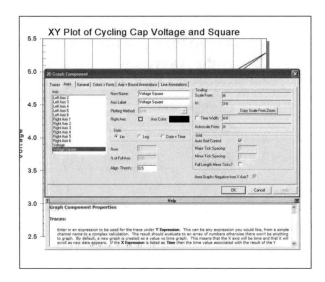

Figure 9-19. *x-y Graph Axes Tab*

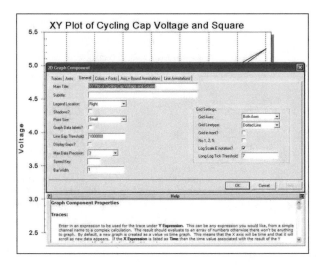

Figure 9-20. *x-y Graph General Tab*

Take note of the data being displayed for this graphical image. It is not PlsWdthVrn555 but PlsWdthVrn555[0,20] in both the x and y axes as seen in Figure 9-18. Because this is a cyclic phenomenon, we need only a limited portion of the channel's data to be displayed, that is, a limited "field of view" or "persistence of vision."

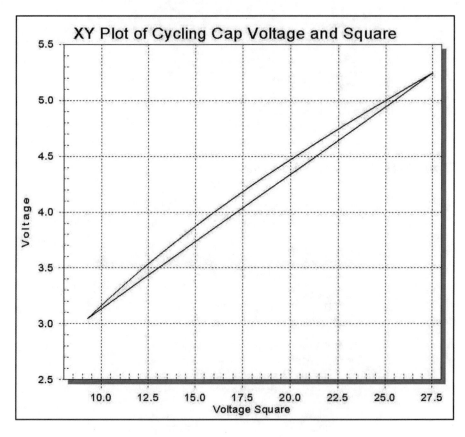

Figure 9-21. *A Plot of Capacitor Voltage and Voltage Square*

Observations: x-y Plotting

The trace shown in Figure 9-21 is a typical recording that may remain stable and reproducible for several minutes before a distortion or altered trace is recorded. Figures 9-22 and 9-23 have captured two instances of errant tracings.

In Figure 9-22, the voltage square discharge trace recorded at the 5 V and 25 V intersection has split into two. Careful examination of Figure 9-23 will reveal that the discharge trace has not only split in two at the high voltage portion of the cycle but also at the 3 and 9 V low end of the cycle.

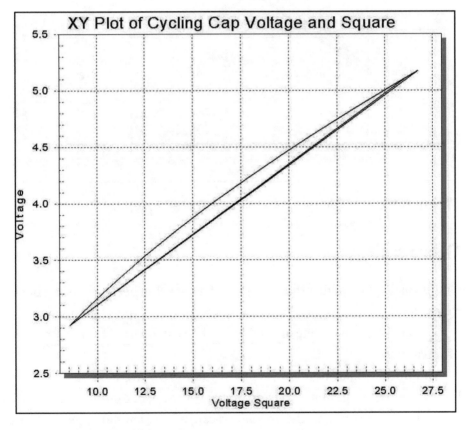

Figure 9-22. *A Higher Voltage Trace Variation*

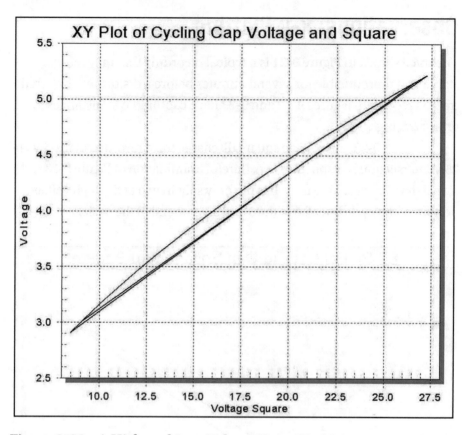

Figure 9-23. *A High and Low Voltage Trace Variation*

Discussion

Graphical displays of recorded data are of great value because of the ability to see trends in the display. Experimental science is dependent upon reproducibility, and graphical displays of data can be used to validate observations.

Graphical display permits the investigator to see events or trends hidden from the "real-time" observations. However, in examining the trends in data recordings, the deviations caused by material imperfections, temperature variation from self-heating, light-induced variations, poor choice of experimental conditions, and a host of other sources of error must be taken into account before judgments regarding data validity can be made. Quite frequently in analytical chemical procedures, and this exercise in particular, the researcher must deal with graphical representations of "analog" data that involve or require very long or short time periods of recording. Long or short time frames may require special components, special electronic circuits or configurations, and protection of the operational circuitry from stray electrical signals and disturbances to be reproducible. Very long and ultrashort time constants may be approaching the limitations of the original design parameters for the traditional IC building blocks, and hence greater care must be taken when using these devices at or close to their operating extremes.

Common sources of variation in data derived from electronic sources can include the following:

1) Variations due to the power delivered by battery or "mains" energized supplies.

2) Component imperfections and variations such as in resistor noise, which is least in wire-wound units, moderate in metal films, and greatest in carbon units, capacitor leakage currents, and memory effects that are greatest in electrolytic, lower in tantalum, and least in plastic film–type components.

3) Temperature effects caused by environmental variation and internal heating caused by current passage through resistive electronic components all cause electronic signals to drift.

4) Long wires can accumulate radio frequency interference (RFI) by acting like antennas for mains power line radiation. Wires should be as short as possible and encased in a Faraday cage if required. Breadboards with their long strips of metallic contacts and the long leads of components pushed into the board should be used for experimental development only and then replaced with printed circuit boards for actual experimental service.

5) Aliasing in digital sampling (or analog-to-digital conversion) for channel storage. Data from the experimental setups created in these exercises is converted into a digital format by the LabJack or microcontrollers and is read by the DAQFactory software at a rate controlled by the channel timing values entered into the channel timing value boxes. Any electrical signals of a repetitive or periodic nature that might be picked up or created by the controlling computer electronics, the LabJack electronics, the experimental setup itself, or the mains wiring of the building in which the experiments may be located present the possibility of "aliasing" with the true signal being generated by the setup being monitored. The signal thus being monitored over extended times may contain "false or artifact" waveforms superimposed over the true or original signal when displayed in long-term graphical formats.

X vs. Time Recordings

The operating sequence for the 555 timer has been outlined in Chapter 8, and from that summation together with the information in Figures 9-6 and 9-7, we can see that the waveform generated in the astable mode changes frequencies as the R2 resistance value in the timing network varies.

When wired in the astable configuration, the capacitor charge time is determined by the total resistance of the RC timing network as indicated in the following:

$$t_1 = 0.693(R1 + R2)C \quad \text{(output high time)}$$

And the discharge time is

$$t_2 = 0.693(R2)C \quad \text{(output low time)}$$

Thus, the total signal period is

$$T = t_1 + t_2 = 0.693(R1 + 2R2)C$$

and the frequency of operation is

$$f = 1/T = 1.44/(R1 + 2R2)C$$

The capacitor charges through both resistors while discharging through only one. When the R2 resistor in the network is a variable resistance, then the time that the output is low is proportional to the value of the varying resistance. The varying analog resistance in the 555 timing network could thus be digitized by measuring the width of the recording during which the output is low.

There are limitations as to the relative width of both the high and low times that can be generated with the circuit shown in Figure 9-2. Special circuitry is required to keep the oscillator frequency relatively constant, while the widths of the high and low times (the duty cycle) of the oscillator are varied.

Expanding or contracting the time scale of the graphical display can vary the resolution of the waveform displayed.

Graphical displays require a large amount of computer processing resources and, as noted in the previous exercises dealing with time and timing, have a limited ability to respond to a rapidly changing signal. Rapidly changing signals are best digitized with hardware for storage in memory and then, after collection, converted into a graphical format for display.

For slower signal changes, DAQFactory's ability to store graphical data in its channels and then be able to display it as a strip chart recording can be very useful in revealing hidden information. If the triangular waveform of Figure 9-12 is recorded for 8 to 10 minutes and then the time scale of the graphical display is reconfigured to display an 8-minute window of the data (i.e., an 8-minute window would be 8 minutes × 60 = 480 for the time base), then a host of variations become evident, as displayed in Figures 9-24 and 9-25.

In Figures 9-24 and 9-25, extending the time scale over which the repetitive voltage cycles are displayed has brought out visually the influences of several ubiquitous experimental sources of error.

Most individuals are familiar with the propagation of water waves in a body of still water. Water waves from two sources caused by stones thrown into a pond appear to our eyes to pass through one another without interference. However, if an object is floating on the surface of the water at the same point where the waves pass through one another, a violent pitching of the object is seen. The violent pitching is caused by the superposition principle that sums the amplitudes of the two water displacement waves passing through one another. The distortions visible at 7:14:30 and 7:19:00 in Figure 9-24 could be caused by a second voltage variation wave with an amplitude of ½ volt and a frequency of one cycle in 4 1/2 minutes blending with or interfering with the main signal.

An additional source of pattern distortion caused by a more complex electronics problem involving timed repetitive digital sampling of cyclic analog waveforms is known as aliasing and is discussed in some electronics textbooks.[1] (Aliases are a RPi-Python programming code utility concept.)

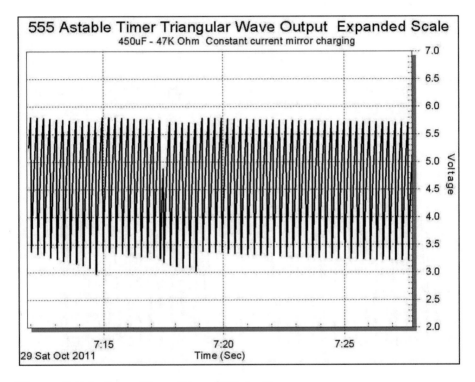

Figure 9-24. *Long-Term Signal Distortions*

The recorded triangular waveforms are reasonably reproducible with respect to their frequency of occurrence as the author's breadboarded circuit can be seen to be producing 19 cycles in 5 minutes. The reproducibility of the voltage levels however can be seen to be both

---

[1] *The Art of Electronics*, Horowitz and Hill, Cambridge University Press, ISBN 0-521-37095-7

drifting and oscillating. The lower values for the voltage vary from 3.0 to 3.4, while the upper values vary from 5.7 to 5.0. Although the upper and lower voltage values are varying, the display has a distinct pattern that suggests the system is both drifting and oscillating due to the factors discussed previously.

Finger heat applied to the left- and right-hand transistors in the constant current source produces the expansion and compression in cycle time illustrated in Figures 9-25 and 9-26.

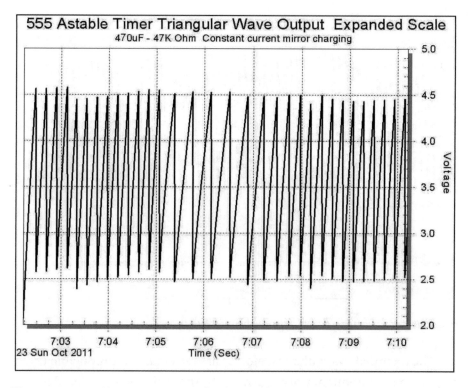

Figure 9-25. *Finger Heat Applied to Left Transistor of Current Mirror*

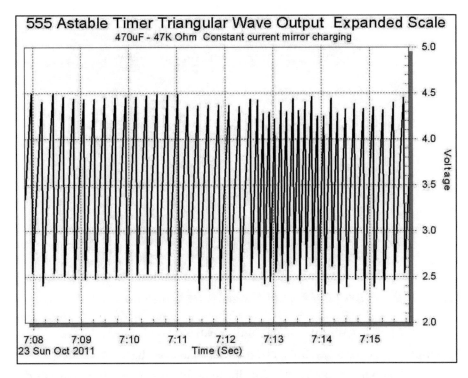

Figure 9-26. *Finger Heat Applied to Right Transistor of Current Mirror*

The erratic amplitude seen in addition to the altered cycle time is also a result of thermal effects.

The materials from which electronic components are fabricated also contribute to the noise seen in electronic circuits. Wire-wound resistors are the least noisy, metal films are intermediate, and carbon-based components exhibit the greatest contribution to resistor circuit noise.

Electrolytic capacitors are inexpensive and available in higher values, but virtually all high-value electrolytic units have sizable leakage currents. Leakage currents can cause problems in systems that require cyclic or repetitive reproducibility. Traditional low-leakage capacitors are generally not available in high capacitance values, but when the limited higher-value units are located, they are usually very expensive and large in physical size as depicted in the photo of Figure 9-27.

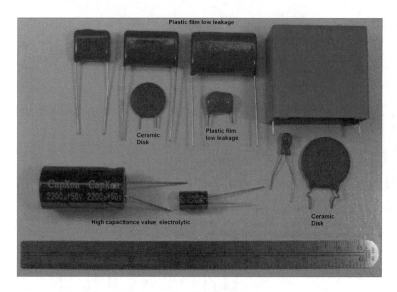

Figure 9-27. *Various Types of Fixed Value Capacitors*

Creation of a symmetrical triangular waveform can be done with op-amps and capacitors, but a circuit known as a voltage-controlled oscillator has been designed to simultaneously produce both square and symmetrical triangular waveforms. The Exar XR-2209 IC is a module that with an external capacitor and resistor can be powered by dual or single, 4- to +/–13-volt supplies to produce the required signal. Figures 9-16 and 9-17 are typical outputs from the IC. The triangular wave in the author's breadboard setup can be seen to systematically vary in the peak voltages achieved. The breadboard setup also proved to be very sensitive to the value of the "pull-up" resistor used to develop the square waveform. The component sensitivity is probably due to operating the circuitry in an area near to the extremes of the circuit design.

X-Y Recordings

x-y recordings are often used when the signal to be recorded is cyclic in nature. Because of the cyclic nature of the signal, it is desirable to clear old traces from the x-y screen as new ones will be overlaid on the older data traces. By specifying the number of data points to plot, using the [n] channel value notation, any fraction or multiple of signal cycles can be displayed.

The effects of non-reproducible signals that are seen in Figures 9-22 and 9-23 arise from the same causes that are evident in the variations of the recorded x vs. time signals of Figures 9-24, 9-25, and 9-26.

Microcontroller Data Plotting

Programmable microcontrollers supported by open source, online communities are constantly having their base capabilities expanded, and a data plotting facility has been added to the Arduino IDE from version 1.6.6 onward.

In previous exercises, the Arduino microcontroller has been used as a smart data acquisition device, a power source for sensors or displays, and a clock; and in this chapter, it will be used to provide a visual graphical display of data.

Since revision 1.6.6 and 7 of the Arduino's IDE, there has been a serial plotter selection available in the Tools menu as depicted in Figure 9-28 for initially a single plot but as of version 7 for multiple–data point plotting.

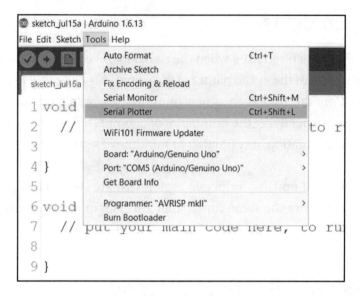

Figure 9-28. *Arduino IDE Tools Menu Serial Plotter Selection*

Invoking the serial plotter output converts the serial port window display into an x-y plotter. Individual data points directed to the serial port for display with a print statement are plotted on the vertical y axis. The x axis auto-scrolls from left to right in the form of a 500-point moving window. The metric for the x axis is the processing of the line of code with the line feed print instruction. Line 15 in Figure 9-29 contains the println code that is counted as processed and whose total value forms the numerical values displayed on the x axis.

For multiple-point plotting, each data value to display with a separate trace is separated from the next with either a print white space instruction or a tab instruction: (print(" "); or print("/t);). Lines 10, 12, and 14 in Figure 9-29 form the separation markers for the four-trace plot seen in Figure 9-30.

Experimental

The code presented in Figure 9-29 plots two straight lines and two sinusoidal traces with different frequencies that are graphically displayed in Figure 9-30.

```
SineCosRdBluWaveGenWthAxes | Arduino 1.6.13
File Edit Sketch Tools Help

SineCosRdBluWaveGenWthAxes §

1 // Plotter demo, sawtooth, sin and cos
2 byte b = 0;   // sawtooth between 1 and 0
3 void setup() {
4    Serial.begin(9600);
5 }
6
7 void loop() {
8    for (int j = 0; j < 360; j++) {
9      Serial.print(2.5);
10     Serial.print(" ");
11     Serial.print(sin(j * (PI / 3)));
12     Serial.print(" ");
13     Serial.print(cos(j * (PI / 60)));
14     Serial.print(" ");
15     Serial.println(-2.5);
16    }
17 }
```

Figure 9-29. *Arduino IDE Typical Plotter Program*

Observations

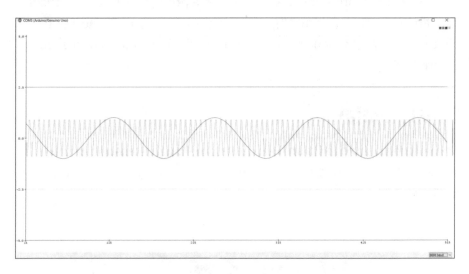

Figure 9-30. *Arduino Serial Plotter Output*

Examination of the microprocessor plotter demonstration code and the displayed frequencies of the sinusoids validates the expected 20:1 frequency ratio between the sine wave and cosine. The constant values plot as the expected straight lines.

Discussion

Inclusion of the plotter in the Arduino's IDE has made a very powerful visualization technique available to the experimental investigator. The plotter is both very easy to use and useful. Plots generated by an experimental process being controlled by the microprocessor can be recorded for archiving with the print screen function available on host computers. Experimental plot archiving has been used in experimental work involving the measurements of temperature, motion, and vibration and in light and optics investigations.

Although the plotter is a very useful function, it is at the time of manuscript preparation limited in several aspects of operation. The colors of the traces are fixed by the operating system of the IDE and can be difficult to see at times. The scales are auto-adjusting and unlike the DAQFactory plotter cannot be independently set to different values.

Occasionally on initial start-up, the plotter will produce spurious images such as depicted on the left in Figure 9-31 or improperly auto-scale the y axis.

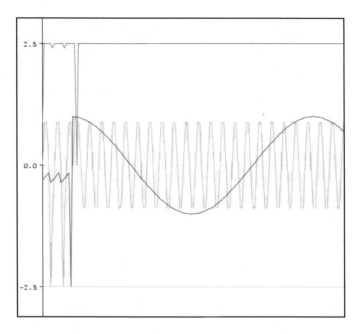

Figure 9-31. *Arduino Serial Plotter Start-Up Noise*

As is seen in the preceding figure, the plotter settles into reproducibility reasonably quickly but on occasion may plot erroneously until the 500-point window refreshes itself and the auto-scale functions also settle into a reproducible plot mode.

Graphical Data Recording with Python and the Raspberry Pi

Introduction

As noted, graphical plotting of experimental data can take two forms. If the data is generated at a high rate, it is best saved by streaming into memory for storage and analyzed graphically at a later time. Experimental data generated at a slower rate can often be displayed as it is created in a "live" or "real-time" display. Python and the RPi use a graphical plotting library called matplotlib for display of both live and stored data.

An example of a Python matplotlib code that plots out the values of the voltage at the wiper arm of a 10 kΩ potentiometer biased between the 3.3-volt RPi power source on the GPIO array and its ground is provided in Listing 9-1 at the end of the chapter. The code has been modified from the strip chart recorder program that can be found as "animation example code: strip_chart_demo.py" in the matplotlib documentation. The documentation contains a full development tutorial for the use of this type of animated graphical display.

Although the RPi does not have an extensive selection of commercial graphical display software applications available, the matplotlib can provide a substantial basis from which the required application can be developed. The relatively short program used to monitor the varying potentiometer voltage in this exercise is equipped with several advanced utilities for in-depth examination of the recorded graphical presentation. A section of the matplotlib documentation entitled "Interactive Navigation" describes the actions of the seven buttons seen in the bottom-left corner of the plotting display as seen in Figures 9-32 and 9-34. The left button restores the focus of the display when any of the display manipulation or storage buttons has been used. Buttons allow sections of the recorded trace to be saved as seen in Figure 9-33 and enlarged as seen in Figures 9-34, 9-35, and 9-36. In addition to the button-activated utilities, the library example also displays the coordinates of the mouse cursor so that exact points can be identified by placing the cursor pointer at a point of interest in the tracing and reading the x and y coordinates of the point in terms of the display time and the measured data value from the numerical values displayed in the lower right-hand corner of the plotter frame.

The matplotlib program is also very easy to alter the scale of either plotting axis, but because of the time scale inconsistencies seen in previous exercises, the plotter time base displayed needs to be calibrated as described in the following experimental section.

Experimental

To demonstrate the plotting facility available with the RPi, an example can be created from the gpiozero library and an MCP3008 ADC IC reading the voltage from the wiper of a biased potentiometer. The wiper voltage is digitized by an MCP3008, 10-bit ADC configured as described in Chapter 6, Figure 6-17. To facilitate programming with the ADC, the gpiozero library has been used to provide the plotting data through accessing the "pot. value" attribute of the object instantiated in the line "pot = MCP3008(0)". The creation of the pot object with the gpiozero library enables the programmer to access the wiper voltage value connected to the first channel on the ADC chip. The value is automatically normalized to a dimensionless floating-point value between 0 and 1 by setting the code variable to be plotted equal to the pot.value attribute.

The configuration of the RPi with the gpiozero library to access the MCP3008 ADC also allows the plotting program to be modified to accept any sensor or transducer that is able to supply a voltage value of 3.3 V or less. Figures 35 and 36 are two traces that have been made from the output of a 555 IC timer that has been wired to the first or 0 channel of the digital converter. The configuration of the 555 IC is illustrated in the right-hand drawings and circuitry of Chapter 8, Figure 8-8. For this experiment, R1 and R2 were 4.7 kΩ, and C1 was a 100 µF electrolytic capacitor in the 555 timer RC network. The output circuitry also included an LED and current limiting resistor to aid in circuitry assembly, verification of electrical operation, and validation of recorder display by observing a continuous LED flashing at a rate of 59 flashes in 60 s. The final two expanded scale figures, Figures 9-37 and 9-38, were made with the "save a trace" button of the options row at the bottom left of the plotter display.

In order to aid in the development of the adaptation of the published matplotlib strip chart recorder code that uses an internal random number generator to create the y values for the plotter example output, the author inserted a number of diagnostic print statements in the code being modified. The print statements stream out the values of certain variables at points in the executing code to the Python console to aid in the development of different methods for adapting the code to follow data from different sources. Commenting out the diagnostic print lines will clear the console display. The streamed-out variable data is seen in the console displays as the left-hand screens in Figures 9-32 to 9-34. When no longer required, the print lines can be commented out.

Several factors must be taken into account when using graphical data displays on the RPi. As has been noted in previous exercises and previously, the time base of the system is not constant, and hence the time scale at the bottom of the plotter display is of limited reliability and must be semi-quantitatively calibrated for semi-quantitative use (see "Discussion").

Once a desired experimental time frame has been established, a stopwatch must be used to measure the actual time the system takes to plot out the data for the nominal desired window time width. Table 9-1 is an example of the data collected by the author when developing a procedure to be used to calibrate a nominal 2-minute-wide plotting window.

Table 9-1. *Adjusting Plotter Time Base*

Dt Setting	Time Width (sec)
0.02	25
0.01	41
0.005	127
0.0055	116
0.00525	129
0.005	125

Observations

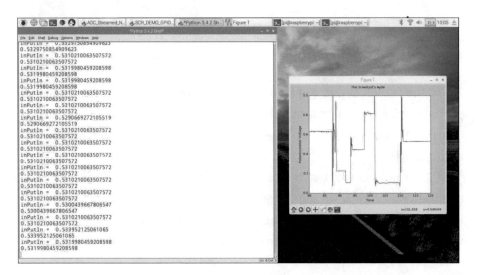

Figure 9-32. *A Data Recording of Potentiometer Wiper Voltage*

Figure 9-32 displays the voltage value trace from 80 to 120 minutes into the experiment in which the author has manually turned the potentiometer shaft at the times recorded on the un-calibrated relative time axis of the display. The trace is relatively quick to respond, but rapid twisting of the shaft can overrun the display's ability to keep up with the changing data value.

343

Figure 9-33 illustrates the actions invoked when the "save a figure" icon at the extreme right of the row of options is clicked. The graphical figure is saved as a png image in the documents file of the RPi.

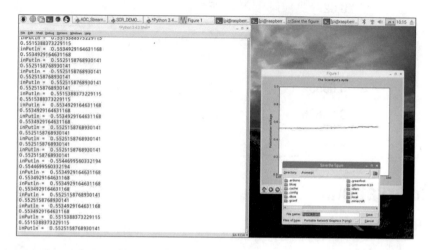

Figure 9-33. *The "Save a Figure" Option Window*

In the screen capture of Figure 9-34, the cursor of the mouse had been placed on the vertical response line just past 17 minutes, and the exact coordinates of the point were then printed in the bottom right-hand corner of the display.

Figure 9-34 illustrates the scale expansion option that expands the area enclosed by a mouse-drawn box to a full-screen display. The expanded image can then be saved as noted previously, or the "return to previous view" icon can be used to restore or resume the normal plotting action.

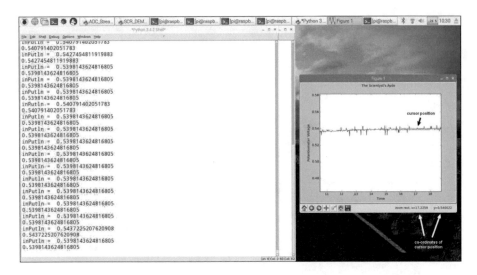

Figure 9-34. *The "Scale Expansion" Option*

In the following two figures, the output from a 555 timer configured as detailed was recorded at expanded scales with the "save a figure" option. Figures 9-35 and 9-36 illustrate the ability of the software to save the plotted data in shorter time scales from external voltage-generating sources.

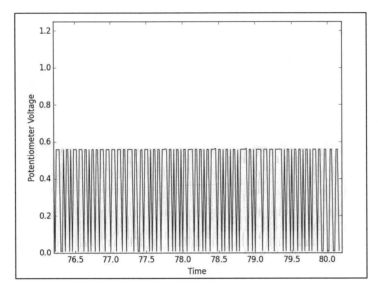

Figure 9-35. *Expanded Time Scale 555 Timer Data Recording*

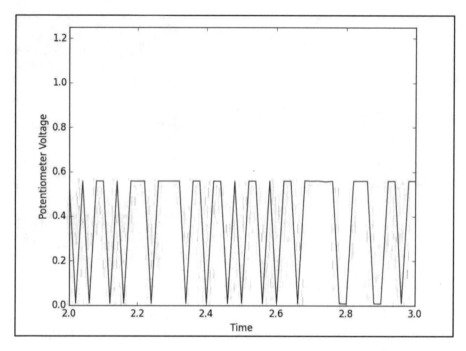

Figure 9-36. *One-Minute Time Scale Expansion of 555 Timer Data Recording*

Discussion

Graphical data recording with the strip chart recorder program from the Python matplot library is a very adaptable and flexible system that can be used to display data directly from sensors attached to the GPIO array or from the Python serial port.

In Figure 37, the output from a 555 timer configured with R1 = 5.83 kΩ, R2 = 4.7 kΩ, and a 420 μF C1 timing capacitor created ten LED flashes in 33 sec. The timer was powered by the 3.3 V supply of the GPIO array and calibrated for a 4-minute display window as detailed in the "Experimental" section.

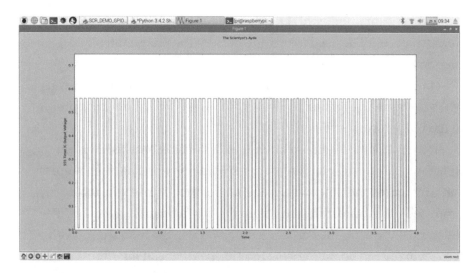

Figure 9-37. *A Calibrated Time Base 555 Timer Voltage Output Recording*

Figure 9-38 illustrates the scale expansion capability available with the display option buttons of the data plotting program.

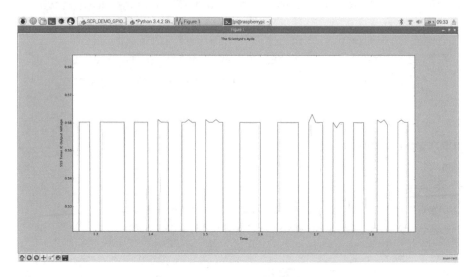

Figure 9-38. *A Time-Calibrated Plotted Trace Expansion*

347

A significant number of sensors have been coded into the gpiozero library that could be used to provide data for the matplotlib plotting program.

One of the advantages of graphical data displays becomes obvious when the variation in the time width of the rectangular pulses is presented in the visual format of Figure 9-38.

Table 9-1 demonstrates a limitation of the time base used for the RPi graphical data displays. A progressive incremental halving of the Dt value increased the time measurement, but the return to the 0.005 value produced a 2-second difference from the original measured value. The differential validates the earlier caution noted in the manuscript with respect to the RPi operating system priorities that can interfere with the timekeeping of the input and output operations of the computer.

Code Listing

Listing 9-1. Python Code for Live or Real-Time Data Plotting with Raspberry Pi

```
# SCR Plotting of Normalized Potentiometer Voltage Value from
    an MCP3008 gpiozero used to configure MCP3008 and attributes
# for plotting
#
import matplotlib
import numpy as np
from matplotlib.lines import Line2D
import matplotlib.pyplot as plt
import matplotlib.animation as animation
import time
from gpiozero import MCP3008
```

```
#
pot = MCP3008(0)
#
#
class Scope:
    def __init__(self, ax, maxt=40, dt=0.02):
        """maxt time width of display"""
        self.ax = ax
        self.dt = dt
        self.maxt = maxt
        self.tdata = [0]
        self.ydata = [0]
        self.line = Line2D(self.tdata, self.ydata)
        self.ax.add_line(self.line)
        self.ax.set_ylim(0.0,1.0)  # y axis scale
        self.ax.set_xlim(0, self.maxt)

    def update(self, y):
        lastt = self.tdata[-1]
        if lastt > self.tdata[0] + self.maxt: # reset the arrays
            self.tdata = [self.tdata[-1]]
            self.ydata = [self.ydata[-1]]
            self.ax.set_xlim(self.tdata[0], self.tdata[0] +
            self.maxt)
            self.ax.figure.canvas.draw()

        t = self.tdata[-1] + self.dt
        self.tdata.append(t)
        self.ydata.append(y)
        self.line.set_data(self.tdata, self.ydata)
        return self.line,
```

```python
#
#
def rd_data():
    inPutln = pot.value
    #print("inPutln = ", inPutln)
    line = inPutln
    #print(line)
    yield (line)

    fig = plt.figure()
fig.suptitle("Pot Wiper Voltage", fontsize = 12)
ax = fig.add_subplot(111)
ax.set_xlabel("Time")
ax.set_ylabel("Potentiometer Voltage")
scope = Scope(ax)

# uses rd_data() as a generator to produce data for the update
func, the MCP3008 value is read by the plotting code in
# 40 minute windows for the animated screen display.
# Software overhead limits response speed of display.
ani = animation.FuncAnimation(fig, scope.update, rd_data,
interval=50,
blit=False)

plt.show()
```

Summary

- Experimental data recorded graphically as a plotting of y vs. time or as x vs. y can show numerous electronically generated waveforms and sensor readouts.

- Graphical data recordings can reveal signal drifting and signal deviations and display electrical, mechanical, and environmental influences on signal outputs not normally visible in numeric displays.

- Commercial SCADA plotting is easily configured, robust, and very flexible, while component-assembled systems are more constrained in display capability and must be calibrated manually.

- In Chapter 10, various methods of current control, an important aspect of experimental equipment configurations or design, are presented.

CHAPTER 10

Current Control

Current control and monitoring are significant portions of many experimental setups and scientific measurements. As demonstrated in the previous exercise, constant current control may be required to achieve specific results. Sensor measurements, motion control in scanning instruments, robotic manipulators, electroplating or amperometry, and heating control operations are just a few examples where current control is required. LEDs should be powered from constant current sources. It has been found that a batch of LEDs from one supplier when powered by a constant voltage supply consumed from 4 to 39 mA and with such a wide current difference could not be producing the same luminous or chromaticity outputs. Current control can vary from managing sensors of physical or chemical change, often requiring measuring milli- and microamps of DC current while heating, electro-deposition and motor control applications often involve controlling amperes of electrical current.

Current control can be implemented with discrete transistors as was done in Chapter 9; general-purpose integrated circuits such as operational amplifiers (op-amps), configured for current regulating; or application-specific integrated circuit (ASIC) chips produced specifically for either DC or AC current controlling applications.

This chapter is divided into three parts involving constant current DC supplies, control of larger currents, and control of potentially lethal, mains alternating current power. Simultaneous with the control of current, some of the limitations imposed by motors and ways to work around these limitations will be demonstrated. Inexpensive motors for experimental

© Richard J. Smythe 2021
R. J. Smythe, *Arduino in Science*, https://doi.org/10.1007/978-1-4842-6778-3_10

setups and for these exercises can be salvaged from obsolete computer equipment or obtained from electronics supply sources if required. Some of the limitations of motion control derived from rotating electric motors will be demonstrated, and the process of selecting the preferred motor for an experimental setup will be developed.

The technique of pulse width modulation (PWM) for current or power control is reviewed and demonstrated in both motor and incandescent lighting applications.

AC electronics, because of its cyclic nature, can be considerably more complicated than DC. In keeping with the simpler introductory nature of these exercises, only the non-inductive or completely resistive load applications will be considered. In strictly resistive applications, the root-mean-square (rms), peak-to-peak, or average AC values can be used as though they were DC values in most of the basic laws governing electronics. Higher-frequency and phase-sensitive AC electronics as encountered in advanced communications, induction heating, or spectroscopy are not dealt with in depth for these basic introductory exercises.

Constant Current Sources

A source of constant current as used previously is also found in numerous types of electronic circuits and in many experimental measurement instruments. As previously noted, constant current sources can be built from a pair of transistors as a "current mirror" or with an operational amplifier (op-amp) and some resistors. Although a discrete component current mirror is discussed in detail in most of the electronics books previously referenced, the operational amplifier is to be used in this exercise because of the simplicity of the design, the wide control range possible with the circuit, and its use of readily available and inexpensive components.

Operational amplifiers such as the LM741 used in this exercise are powered by dual-voltage supplies and must be balanced or properly biased for use. Figure 10-1 depicts the general schematic for the LM741–2N3906 PNP transistor, grounded load circuit that may be used to provide a constant current for a known load, as published in various references. The circuits depicted in Figures 10-1 and 10-2 can be assembled on a typical prototyping breadboard for testing, validation of circuit operation, and current control applications.

The circuit operating theory is explained in the following for the configuration in which the load is connected to ground and the current sense resistor is connected to the voltage supply. If the opposite situation is required, then an NPN transistor can be used to regulate the current (LF411 can be used as a direct replacement for the LM741).

Experimental

Hardware

A +/– dual-voltage power supply and a trim potentiometer are used to power and balance the op-amp. A power transistor, three appropriate biasing resistors, and a suitable adjustable resistor simulator of the expected experimental load are required to construct and validate the constant current supply. A typical implementation of the constant current op-amp circuit is detailed in the following descriptions of a test circuit assembled by the author. A 9-volt battery and four AA cells connected in series can make a 15 V DC supply. Connecting two 15-volt battery packs in series can be used to create the required bipolar supply of +/– 15 V with a center terminal ground. The bipolar power supply allows the op-amp output to be driven to positive or negative voltages. (See Figure 9-15 in Chapter 9.)

Circuit Schematic

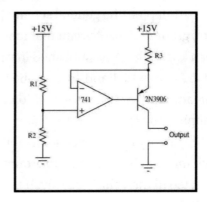

Figure 10-1. *A Typical Op-amp Current Control Circuit*

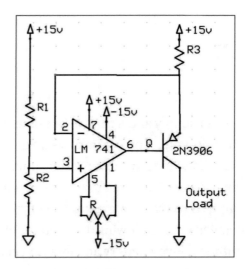

Figure 10-2. *Typical Circuit Implementation for Op-amp Balancing*

If a particular chemical analysis experiment such as a coulometric titration has a titration vessel that represents a 20 Ω load and a current of 20 mA is found to generate a reasonable time to reach the analysis end point, then the conditions for determining the resistor values needed to assemble the circuit depicted in Figures 10-1 and 10-2 are available.

From Ohm's law, to maintain a 20 mA current through a 20 Ω load will require a voltage of 0.40 V. The transistor typically has a 0.3 V drop across the PN junction, and hence the emitter should be held at 0.7 V. To convert 15 volts to 0.7 will require a divider with a numerical value of 0.0466; thus, R2/(R1 + R2) = 0.046. Any dual-voltage power supply between 12 and 18 volts can be used with the LM741, so the actual values of the resistors in the divider network and the current limiting R3 can be adjusted accordingly to maintain the desired op-amp reference voltage or set point, for the desired cell current flow. For a regulated current of 20 mA and from the power relationship of I^2R, we can estimate that 1/8-watt resistors in the regulated current-carrying portions of the circuit are adequate for the experiment at hand.

As a typical electrochemical cell load simulation, a 25 Ω, 30 W, adjustable tap, wire-wound resistor was used by the author. Adjusting the position of the center tap on the load resistance simulates a changing conductivity as may be encountered in an experimental electrochemical cell or a resistive heating element.

To begin the exercise, the experimenter can assemble the circuit according to the preceding schematics. After verification of the layout, temporarily ground the inverting and non-inverting inputs of the op-amp, adjust the trim potentiometer to its midpoint of travel, and apply power to the op-amp. While monitoring the voltage of the amplifier output, adjust the 10 kΩ variable resistance to obtain an amplifier output as close to 0 V as possible, either actually balancing the op-amp or positioning the trim potentiometer wiper at a low non-zero voltage value point that will result in system balance when the feedback loop is established during actual circuit operation.

The voltage divider formed by R1 and R2 creates a reference voltage V_{Ref} that is supplied to the non-inverting input of the op-amp. The op-amp will now try to keep the two inputs at the same voltage of V_{Ref} by varying the current through R3. The current flowing through the load, transistor, and R3 is controlled by the current injected into the base of the 2N3906 transistor. The entire current flowing through the load and transistor passes through R3 that must be of sufficient wattage to accommodate the required current variation that the constant current configuration may require. As the center tap of the load-modeling resistor is adjusted to provide simulations of changes in the simulated cell resistance, current measurements will confirm the circuit's ability to provide a nominal 20 mA current through the cell simulator as depicted in Figure 10-3.

Figure 10-3.   *Wire-Wound Load Simulator of a High-Current Test Circuit*

Item 1 in the preceding figure is the simulated variable resistance load consisting of a 25 Ω 30 W wire-wound resistor mounted vertically on a threaded rod. Item 2 is a 5 W current sensing resistor, while item 3 is a LM741 op-amp plastic DIP. Item 4 is a 2N3906 power transistor, and the items numbered 5 are the positive red, negative black, and green ground or neutral power supply leads. Item 6 is the trim resistor for op-amp balance or biasing.

Software

Page components and programmed software are not required for this portion of the exercise.

Observations

The wire-wound resistor produces a very coarse ohmic resistance when the position of the center tap is changed, but alteration of the load resistance value is sufficient to demonstrate the development of the required constant current source. The large-wattage simulated load is variable from the nominal 25 Ω measured between the main terminals and from about 20 to 10 Ω when repositioning the sliding tap on the exposed wire core turns. The large power resistor connected to the positive supply and supplying current to the transistor together with the variable load determines the current that can flow in the regulated circuit. When power is initially applied to the circuit, the observed current flow is high. As the electronics comes to a rough thermal equilibrium, the regulated current stabilizes at a final value close to the desired set point. Usually the circuit requires 15–30 minutes to reach a constant thermal value. Table 10-1 tabulates the stabilized currents measured with the author's breadboarded experimental simulation.

Table 10-1. *Load Resistance and Regulated Load Current*

Load Resistance (Ω)	Current (mA)
6.7	21.4
10.8	21.4
14.3	21.1
15.1	21.4
17.6	20.9
19.3	20.9
20.2	20.9
20.3	21.0

The load resistance in the preceding table is measured in ohms, and the current is measured in milliamps.

Discussion

The circuit operation can be explained in the feedback configuration by recalling that the op-amp drives its output in order to equalize the voltages at the inverting and non-inverting inputs so $V_{Sense} = V_{in}$. The current through the sense resistor is $I_{Sense} = V_{in} / R_{Sense}$, and since the current through the sense resistor flows through the transistor, the current through the load I_{Load} is V_{in}/R_{Sense} plus the very small base emitter current of the transistor.

For an intended current of 20 mA through a 20 Ω load, the table displays a 0.5 mA variation in an approximately 21 mA current seen through a load varying from 6.7 to 20.3 ohms. If an exact 20 mA current is required, the voltage divider could be experimentally trimmed to adjust the reference voltage to a value that regulates the transistor current to the desired level.

As discussed and demonstrated in Chapter 9 on the graphical display of data and as noted previously, thermal effects will cause the measured signal to drift until thermal equilibrium is established. If critical current control is required, then some form of thermal control or stabilization may need to be introduced into the experimental setup. Heat sinks, cooling air flows, insulations, or large metal thermal masses can be used to maintain or partially stabilize temperatures by either radiating or absorbing excessive heat.

Current regulation can also be achieved with dedicated integrated circuits such as the LM340/78xx series of integrated circuits from National Semiconductor. The integrated circuits however operate at specified, fixed voltages and are usually limited to 1-ampere total current. The actual current to be regulated is determined by appropriately valued sensing resistors. Specific configurations and limitations are detailed in the application sections of the manufacturer's data sheets for individual devices.

The operational amplifier power transistor circuit, assembled from discrete components, has the advantage of flexibility in being able to control currents at arbitrary voltages and load requirements. The op-amp power transistor configuration is also able to be used with the PNP "grounded load" configuration or with a "floating load" in which the sense resistor is grounded and an NPN transistor is connected to the power supply and floating load.

Op-amp characteristics and theory are found in most of the previously referenced textbooks and many introductory and in-depth online tutorials.

Control of Larger DC Currents

Introduction

Brushless Direct Current (BLDC) Motors (Motors Without Commutators or Sparking Brushes)

Larger DC current manipulation is encountered in experimental setups involving heating, pumping, mechanical movement, or motion control. For each type of motion to be controlled, there are usually several means of transforming electrical power into the desired physical motion or action. Solenoids move linearly in a back-and-forth motion as in robotics systems, while motors twist or rotate; and for the simpler applications of this work in which motors are required to drive and for liquid mixing or pumping, gas cooling, or perhaps rotational optical scanning operations, we shall focus on rotational motion control in motors. Further limitations consist of working with very small fractional horsepower motors designed for field or laboratory use with readily available, robust, 12 V lead acid battery systems or 12 V DC power supplies providing the required higher currents. (The physics and electro-mechanical aspects of motors and more powerful motor control are discussed in much more detail in the literature of robotics and mechanical, chemical, or electrical engineering.) In chemical analysis and a large portion of life sciences' laboratory work, flammable solvents are in constant use, and hence brushed DC motors should not be used in experimental operations unless certified as being explosion proof.

The heavier current required to drive a motor can be controlled by transistors that in turn can be controlled from much smaller base currents derived from integrated circuits. A variable 555 timer signal can be used to control a higher-current power transistor that in turn regulates the power applied to a motor to control the motor speed. In this portion of the exercises, a 555 timer will be used to generate a square wave pulse train whose duty cycle will be varied, in a controlled manner, to alter the time during which power is supplied by a power transistor to a fan motor capable of drawing up to 200 mA of current. The rotational speed of the fan motor will thus be controlled by a potentiometer in the 555 timer network. The fan disk rate of rotation will be measured optically with the LabJack counter, and a DAQFactory program will calculate the fan disk rotation speed for display on screen.

Experimental

Hardware

For the motor control circuitry, a breadboard will be required to mount a 555 timer and the passive components required to configure the IC into the astable mode. As can be seen in Figure 10-4, the author combined the mounting bracket for a 100 kΩ potentiometer, the heat sink for the TIP-122 power transistor, and the mount for the fan assembly with a brushless DC fan motor into a custom-drilled 1 in (2.5 cm) by 8 in (15 cm) piece of aluminum angle denoted as item 1. The heat sink–mount angle was bolted to an approximately 1/16 in (1 mm)-thick plate of 8 in by 6 in (20.4 cm by 15.2 cm) aluminum sheet denoted as item 1a, on which the breadboard was fastened with double-sided adhesive mounting tape (carpet tape). The simplest fan motors (brushless direct current, BLDC) have two leads for the DC power. Three- and four-lead fan motors are common with the added connections usually for the internal Hall sensors (magnetic field detectors) used for monitoring shaft positions. A photodiode and a phototransistor were fitted and fixed to two small ½ in (1.2 cm) by 1 in (2.5 cm) custom-drilled aluminum plates with room temperature vulcanization (RTV) silicone. Items numbered 4 are the sensor mounting tabs. Adhesive fillets on the back sides of the tabs held the sensor diodes firmly in place while not interfering with the optically active surfaces. As can be seen in Figure 10-4, the tabs were mounted on a corner of the fan motor frame with a bolt and a wing nut. The tabs were mounted with the narrow infrared optical beam generated by the photodiode pointing through the plane of rotation of the fan disk blades. The rotation of the seven-blade fan disk (item 2) thus chops the IR beam created between the photodiode and phototransistor seven times per motor revolution.

Figure 10-4. *Experimental Cooling Fan Current Load Testing Setup*

The two plates holding the optical beam source and detector are held in place on the author's setup with a bolt passing through the plates and motor frame, secured in place with a wing nut. Item 3 is an arm of the wing nut fastener that allows for easier alignment of the optical beam.

Power for the author's setup was supplied by a heavier +/−12 V, 2 A supply that was connected to a terminal strip mounted at the rear of the breadboard on the aluminum sheet metal base.

Many of the fan motors salvaged from obsolete or damaged computer equipment are used to power seven-blade disks. If the fans being used for these exercises do not have seven blades, enter the correct blade count into the DAQFactory variable value expression box as illustrated in Figure 10-7.

Circuit Schematic

In Figure 10-6, the 555 timer is configured in the astable mode to produce a continuous square wave format. A timer IC cycle starts with capacitor C discharged, pin 2 low, and output pin 3 high. With pin 3 high, C charges through the left side of R1 and left diode until pin 6 (threshold) reaches 2/3 V+ at which point pin 3 (output) and pin 7 (discharge) go low. With pin 3 low, the capacitor discharges through the right side of R1 and the right diode until C falls below 1/3 V+ at which point the output pin 3 and discharge pin 7 go high, and the cycle repeats. Thus, C charges through the left side of R1 while discharging through the right. By keeping the sum of the charge and discharge resistances at a constant value, the output signal wavelength is also constant, and only the duty cycle changes. The output frequency is fixed according to the formula

$$\text{Frequency} = 1.44/(R_{Varbl} * C_{Timing})$$

Figure 10-5 graphically displays the concept of the duty cycle and its relationship to the frequency or wavelength as marked by the red arrows. For power control applications such as driving a motor, the ability to rapidly turn the power on and off in terms of very fast pulsing widths provides a means of controlling the motor speed at the higher end of the power application range. However, if the load being supplied with power, via pulse width variation, is working at the lower end of the adjustment range, a longer frequency will provide a higher degree of resolution for the controlling of power applied. Heating circuits and low rotating speeds in stepper motors may require longer wavelengths or lower frequencies to provide an adequate span of control adjustment.

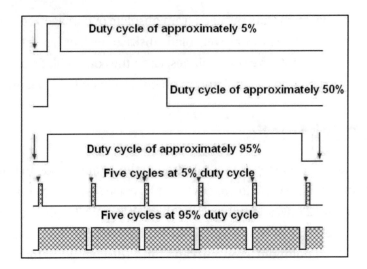

Figure 10-5. *Duty Cycle Concepts*

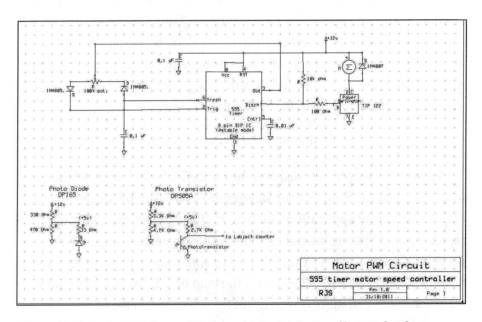

Figure 10-6. *A 555 Timer IC-Based Motor Controller with Photo Interrupter Circuit*

Software

Figure 10-7 depicts the properties Main tab for the variable value screen component used to display the fan rotation speed. The calculation that converts from the seven beam interruptions per fan disk revolution to the rotation speed of the fan motor is entered into the screen component's expression box. The various entries into the Variable Value Component tab of the child window, generate the RPM display box seen above the pop-up properties window.

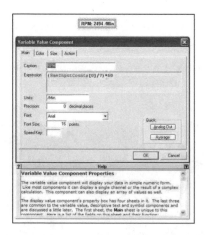

Figure 10-7. *DAQFactory Variable Value Component Configuration for Measurement of Fan Motor RPM*

There is no requirement for any scripting as the counter is read, reset, and entered once a second into the RawInputCounts channel. The value returned as RawInputCounts[0] is corrected for the number of fan blades on the disk and normalized to minutes.

Observations

With the potentiometer set to midrange, the two-wire fan motor spins at about 2950 rpm, and the speed can be varied from 3300 to approximately 100–150 rpm before the motor stalls.

During the initial development of the optical tachometer, the pulse train generated by the photodiode-phototransistor pair was unable to trigger the LabJack counter, and an increased signal strength was required. The power used to drive the photodiode-phototransistor pair was drawn separately from the +12-volt supply using the two voltage dividers shown in the schematic of Figure 10-6. The photodiode voltage divider produces a nominal 5 V, and the phototransistor voltage divider produces a nominal 6 V (5.91 V). Figure 10-8 shows an oscilloscope display of the optical beam chopper output.

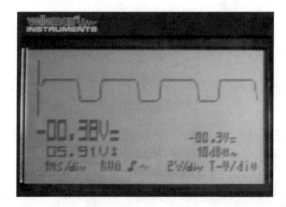

Figure 10-8. *Oscilloscope Display of Optical Beam Chopper Output*

A salvaged three-wire cooling fan motor from a large CPU chip was substituted for the two-wire system, and the high-end fan speed range was measured at 5,200 rpm. The fan speed with careful adjustment could be lowered into the 200 rpm range and occasionally into the 150 rpm range before the motor stalled.

The third wire on the chip cooling fan is usually the output from Hall effect sensors built into the motor. The Hall effect sensors detect changing magnetic fields, and the output from the third wire produces a series of small spikes created by the rotating magnetic fields that can be used to measure the motor's RPM.

Discussion

In this exercise, the pulse width modulation control of higher currents required to power a motor is being demonstrated. A limited pulse width modulation scheme based upon the astable configured 555 timer chip has been examined in Chapter 8, and the relatively constant frequency, variable duty cycle mode of power delivery is now being used with suitable diode modification to extend the range of the duty cycle while keeping the frequency or wavelength of the output square wave constant.

In Chapter 8, Figure 8-10, and in Figure 10-6, it can be seen that the capacitor charges through R1 and a portion of R2 but discharges only through R2, so the charging portion of the cycle can only be decreased to the value of R1, while the value of R2 can in effect be decreased to zero for the discharge portion of the cycle. Hence, the variation possible in the duty cycle is controlled by the value of R1.

In simplified terms, we can see that the PWM technique we are using to apply power to the BLDC motor changes the duty cycle from 100% down, literally, to 0%. An overall resulting voltage change from 12 V at 100% to 6 V at 50% duty cycle to in effect 0 V at 0% duty cycle is the reason for the erratic behavior at lower speed rotation. In the lower portions of the duty cycle, the 12 V power is not applied for a long enough period of time for the averaged power delivered, to be able to drive the motor, and it "stalls." In other words, the observed loss of control and stalling at low settings of the controlling potentiometer are the result of insufficient power being delivered to the motor. To achieve better control of low-speed motor operations, a different type of motor and power control will be required.

This 555 PWM, optical tachometer circuit, DAQFactory SCADA software display system was developed with a salvaged two-wire computer tower cooling fan. A second cooling fan from a more recent large CPU chip with a three-wire control circuit board connector was substituted into the breadboard setup for comparison. The third wire, usually yellow (see Figure 10-4), monitors the output from Hall effect detectors built into the rotor/stator portions of the motor. Hall effect sensors respond to changing magnetic fields and can be used to indicate the position of the magnets with respect to the coils to be energized in an electronic motor control system.

The chip cooling fan motor recovered from the author's obsolete equipment was a 2 1/4 in square (5.7 cm) seven-blade, 12 V, 180 mA unit that when powered through the red/black power leads has an upper speed of rotation in the 5,200 rpm range and stalls at rotation rates between 200 and 150 rpm.

As will be seen in later portions of this work, the recovery and reuse of fan motors can solve, inexpensively, practical problems that arise in some laboratory procedures.

Stepper Motors

BLDC motors requiring electronic control of the motor power come in two forms: the continuous duty type used to drive fans and a form known as stepper motors. Whereas the BLDC fan motor develops its maximum power at higher speeds with full applied voltage and stalls as the rotation rate decreases because of decreasing voltage/power levels, the stepper motor develops its maximum power when not rotating and loses power as its rotation rate increases. Stepper motors derive their name and utility from their ability to move or rotate in discrete "steps." By controlling the "stepping" action of the motor, exact rotational positioning and precise low-speed rotational rates, with significant torque, can be achieved.

Stepper motors are built in several forms and have different capabilities based upon the type of construction used to assemble the motor. There are numerous good tutorials available both online (Jones on Stepper Motors) and in the literature of both robotics and engineering for those experimental equipment development projects requiring more details.[1]

For the purposes of this current control exercise, we will limit our discussion and experimentation to the class of motors called bipolar, permanent magnet (PM) systems. These motors provide continuous low-speed rotation that has definite practical applications in robotics, simple physics, and chemical and biological laboratory procedures. Continuous rotation can be relatively easily implemented and controlled with ICs such as the 555 timer. Single stepping and oscillating in a back-and-forth stepping action require additional knowledge of both the motor windings, slightly advanced programming capabilities, and specialty hardware. The methods for implementing controlled rotation down to the point of single stepping are referred to in several of the exercises to follow, but oscillating and fractional circular rotation actions are not considered in this simple introductory section.

In order to keep the assembly of a motor power control unit in a simple, inexpensive, and familiar format, the electronic power control circuitry in this exercise is again based upon the adjustable, astable 555 timer circuit pulse generation but with some relatively simple additional digital logic circuitry. The 555 timer IC can be replaced by any computer or microcontroller capable of generating a low-voltage, adjustable duty cycle, square wave pulse train as used in PWM control.

Permanent magnet (PM) stepper motors are characterized by having a rotor shaft that does not spin freely as does the higher-speed BLDC fan motor. PM stepper motor shafts, when turned by hand, with the motor

---

[1] *Introduction to Mechatronics and Measurement Systems*, Alciatore and Histand, McGraw Hill, 466 pp, 2003, ISBN 0-07-240241-5

unconnected to a power source, "cog" or "step" between positions of equilibrium or rest. The number of steps required to make a full rotation indicates the "resolution" or degree of "fineness" with which the stepper motor rotation or oscillation can be controlled.

The stepper motor has been designed so individual coil windings can be separately energized, thus creating internal electromagnetic fields that, by rotation of the rotor, can establish an equilibrium position with the internal, permanent magnet magnetic fields. By energizing coils in a programmed sequence, the motor shaft can be made to rotate in any manner as determined by the programming. Programs in which the electromagnetic coils are energized in a sequential manner in order to smoothly rotate the motor shaft in either direction are the main focus of this simplified exercise.

Stepper motors turn at a much slower rate than conventionally wound, brushless motors and produce significantly more torque at lower speeds. Stepper motors do not move large volumes of air over their structure and hence concentrate much more heat around their outer metal cases.

Experimental
Hardware

A solid mounting is required for the stepper motor, speed control, forward/ reverse switch, and motor power connections. The power connections for the motor must have a means of interchanging the connections of the individual motor coil leads to the output power transistors of the electronic control circuitry. The integrated circuitry can be assembled on a breadboard for ease of construction, prototype development, and experimental demonstration. An experimental motor and hardware mounting frame assembled with hand tools from readily available materials is depicted in Figure 10-10 and described in detail in the following text.

Circuit Schematic

As noted, for the purposes of most experimental laboratory or field work, the control circuitry for a four-coil stepper motor need only drive the motor in smooth, controllable, clockwise or counterclockwise, low-speed rotation. The electronic supply should thus be able to produce a sequential series of four, adjustable width, current pulses with sufficient amperage to continuously step the motor through a full rotation of the rotor.

Some care must be exercised in assigning the power connections of the stepper motor to the output transistors of the electronic power controller. If the center tap in a five-wire motor or the taps in a six-wire motor are connected to the positive supply, then the ends of the "first" set of tapped coils should be connected to power output transistors 1 and 2 and the second set of coil ends to 3 and 4. If the motor does not rotate smoothly and respond as expected to the speed control potentiometer, then sequentially exchange the third and fourth coil connections and retest the motor. If the exchange does not correct the problem, exchange the first and second coil connections, retest, and if required reverse the second and third coil connections.

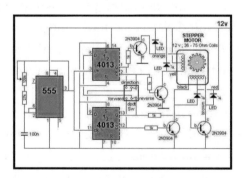

Figure 10-9. *A 555 Timer IC-Based Stepper Motor Controller*

In Figure 10-9, an astable 555 timer, controlled by a potentiometer, is used to generate an adjustable duty cycle pulse train. The pulse train is used to toggle (or power) a pair of D (data)-type flip-flops that have been configured as frequency dividers to produce the required series of four transistor base driving signals to create the required high-current power pulses. The data flip-flops are contained in a single CMOS 4013, 14-pin DIP that together with the 555 timer chip can be powered by the heavier-current 12 V power supply.

A stepper motor can be controlled by many different coil-energizing sequences that can create high-torque single or fractional step rotations, back-and-forth stepping motions, or smooth continuous rotations. The low-speed, high-torque, smooth continuous rotations are the motions with the most application in biological/chemical laboratory work, that is, stirring and pumping liquids. To achieve the correct sequencing of the motor coils by the four output transistors, the common center taps of the coils are connected to the positive supply. The energizing of a coil thus consists of grounding the end of a winding to enable current flows from the center tap to ground. The motor can thus be made to rotate by sequentially grounding the ends of the windings. The wiring color code on the motor being used for this exercise may be different than that displayed in Figure 10-9. Typical motors will have four connections to the ends of the windings and either a common connection to the center taps or two connections to the center taps, thus creating five- and six-wire, motor-to-power connections.

The current flow through the individual coils is limited by the resistance of the coils themselves. Reversing the direction of the DC current flow through the motor coils reverses the direction of rotation.

Motor rotation is created by sequentially energizing the internal windings of the motor to create a magnetic field. The transitory electromagnetic field interacts with the permanent magnetic fields causing the motor to rotate. Switching off the current to the energized coil then creates the back EMF induced into the coil by the collapsing magnetic field permeating the motor's internal windings. The switching transistors must be protected from the motor coils' higher-voltage back EMF, or their PN junctions will be destroyed. LEDs have been placed into the collectors of the switching devices of Figure 10-9 to both protect the output power devices and provide a visual confirmation of individual coil current passage.

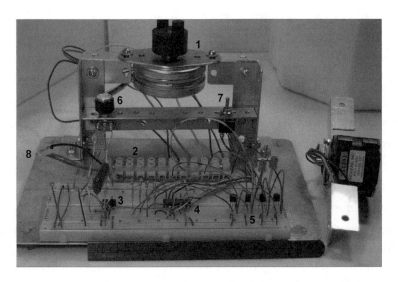

Figure 10-10. *A Stepper Motor Test Assembly*

Item 1 is a Copal Electra motor mounted on an aluminum ½ in (1.2 cm) right angle extrusion frame with an added black rubber shaft coupling to move and partially dampen the resonant frequency. A Howard motor can be seen to the right with mounting adapters. Item 2 is a terminal for motor winding wires and breadboard interfacing. Item 3 is the 555 timer chip, and the number 4 marks the position of the 4013 data flip-flop chip. Item 5 is the row of power transistors, and item 6 is the "speed" control potentiometer. Item 7 is the rotation direction switch, and item 8 is the high-current power input wires.

Software

Page Components Required

The pulse train used to toggle the 4013 D flip-flops and sequence the driver transistors can also be used to create a tachometer display for the rotation rate of the motor (see "Discussion"). The author's laboratory had 12 V permanent magnet, 75 Ω, four-phase (coil) stepper motors manufactured by Howard Industries, part number 1-19-4200, that were 3.6 degrees per step and SP-57B motors from Copal Electra, part number 85086780, with 36 Ω coil resistance and 7.5-degree step rotations. The Howard motors thus took an even 100 steps to complete a full rotation, while the Copal Electra motors only required 48. As with the fan motors, the rotation speed can be displayed on the screen with a DAQFactory variable value component. The rate can be calculated by counting the pulses applied to the flip-flop logic, in 1 second, then dividing by the number of steps required for a complete rotation, and normalizing to revolutions per minute. Scripting is not required as the calculation can be entered into the expression box for the variable value screen component displayed as the top line in Figure 10-7.

Observations

Moderate stepping speeds result in smooth rotation, while at low speeds the individual steps become visible. The use of LEDs as protection from the back EMF of the motor coils also serves as a pilot light for motor activity.

Both of the stepper motor types with rotors unloaded pass through certain rotational speeds that cause the motor and mounting structure to "resonate." The 3.6-degree Howard motor begins to vibrate at 113 rpm, generating a severe vibration at 100 rpm and a very loud, annoying audible buzz at 92 rpm, but runs smoothly and quietly at 85 rpm. When the ¼ in (0.6 cm) metal shaft coupling from a three-piece rubber "tee" motor drive connection was added to the Howard motor shaft, the motor displayed a greatly reduced in intensity, but still distinct, high-pitched vibration at 92 rpm and also displayed a lower intensity and deeper pitched vibration at 60 rpm and an even lower pitch and lower intensity resonance at 30 rpm. In any of the rotational speeds between the resonance "peaks," the motor ran smoothly.

The Copal Electra motor has an unloaded rotational speed range of 60–300 rpm and has a resonance "chatter" at 89–90 rpm. If the motor shaft is loaded with the drive connector coupling, the resonance speed moves up slightly into the 92–95 rpm range, and the motor completely stalls at 250 rpm.

Without the coupling on the rotor, it was impossible to squeeze the shaft hard enough to stall the motor, but with the additional leverage provided by the coupling base, the rotor could be stopped; and as the stalled rotor pulsed, the RPM indicator still recorded a 37 rpm equivalent pulse rate. The loss of torque with increasing RPM is evident with the Howard motor, but the Copal Electra with the added mass of the coupling stalls if speed settings for over 250 rpm are selected.

In addition to slow-speed mixing and blending in laboratory experimental work, stepper motors are also uniquely suitable for controlling the delivery rate from peristaltic pumps. By altering the value of the RC timing constant in the 555 astable configuration, the author's Copal Electra could be slowed to 5–6 rpm with a 1.0 uF capacitor and the 27 kΩ resistor of Figure 10-9; and by changing both the resistance and capacitor to 296 kΩ and 1 uF, the motor continuously single-stepped through its 48 increments at 1 rpm.

Discussion

The flexibility and desirable low speed properties available with stepper motors are achieved at the expense of significantly increased complexity in control circuitry. The required sequential generation of current pulses for smooth continuous motor rotation can be created with the D-type flip-flops as used in this exercise or with chips designed as shift registers such as the 74LS194 and CMOS 4035. Details for using the shift registers are available both online[2] and in the printed literature for the nominal ICs.

The design of stepper motors is such that maximum torque is created when the rotor is stationary. With the system created for this exercise, the rate of rotation can be slowed to 1 rpm at which rate each individual step of the motor takes 1/48 of a minute or 1.25 s. At the slow rate of 1 rpm, the Copal Electra motor used in the exercise is close to delivering its maximum available torque. Discrete, arbitrary time stepping or holding positions are useful in robotic control systems and require much more sophisticated programming capability in the power control system than is provided by the potentiometer-controlled 555 pulse generator used in this portion of the exercise.

Resonance is a problem with stepper motors, and continued operation of the motor while in a resonating mode will greatly reduce the service life of the motor by increasing the rate of mechanical deterioration of the rotating components. The motor should be operated off of the resonant speed, or if the resonant speed is important, then special mechanical mounting techniques, gearing, or changes in rotating mass may need to be built into the experimental apparatus to deal with system resonance.

The speed of rotation of the motor shaft can be measured electronically by using the DAQFactory, default data collection rate, of 1 second for the LabJack counter channel, applying the number of steps required for one revolution of the rotor shaft, and adjusting the values of

---

[2] http://www.electronics-tutorials.ws

the data to be displayed to the desired time units. The formula required to convert the pulse rate into a numerical display in a screen "variable value" component can be entered into the formula box of the screen component as seen in Figure 10-7. The use of the pulse rate to determine the motor shaft rotation speed uses an implicit assumption that the motor is not "slipping" as it rotates, which may happen at the higher end of the motor's rotation rate speed range or if the "load" being driven increases significantly. If slippage is a problem or the actual rotation of the experimental setup is to be monitored, then the photo interrupter tachometer method should be used on the moving load.

Stepper motors have their greatest utility at low-speed rotation or as rotatable positioning agents, and if lower speeds of rotation are required, the time constant of the 555 astable can be increased to widen the space between pulses applied to the flip-flops. The slower the speed of rotation, however, the more pronounced the "stepping" action of the motor's rotation.

Control of AC Current Sources

Introduction

Alternating current (AC) sources are often referred to as "mains." In North America, the mains or "household current" is supplied at a nominal 120 volts peak-to-peak or 115 V root-mean-square (rms) at 60 Hz, while in Europe and other areas of the world, it is 220 V (rms) at 50 Hz. A substantial number of the early alternating current supplies were generated by hydro-electric facilities where water turbines spun electric generators that created forward and reverse current pulses at these relatively low frequencies.

Low-voltage DC currents are virtually harmless, but "mains" voltages and currents easily start fires that burn buildings to the ground, cause severe painful burns, and produce potentially lethal electrical shocks.

In keeping with the lethal nature of high-voltage, high-current electrical energy, solid-state systems have been developed for both controlling the dangerous high power levels and isolating them from the low-voltage control circuitry.

The advantage of AC current, when properly isolated from the controlling circuitry, lies in the ability to power motors, illumination fixtures, and heating elements directly without any need for conversion into DC prior to usage. Mains or AC electrical power cycles from zero to a maximum forward value and then decreases back to zero rising to its maximum reverse value before decreasing back to the zero value, thus completing the cycle. AC power is usually controlled with thyristors or four-layer P-N-P-N semiconducting components fabricated into either of two types of device: the silicon-controlled rectifier (SCR) whose conduction can be regulated for half of the AC cycle or the triac that can control conduction for the full AC cycle. SCRs and triacs have limited frequency response and hence are used mainly at 50–60 Hz but are serviceable up to 400 Hz AC power frequencies. The SCR is a multilayered diode with a "gate" that allows the diode to be switched from a blocking to a conducting mode at any point in its normally conducting portion of the AC waveform. By placing two SCRs in parallel but conducting in opposite directions to form the silicon bilateral switch or triac, it becomes possible to control the forward and reverse cycles of the AC power waveform from the signals applied to a common gate.

As noted, both SCRs and triacs are diode-type devices, fabricated with gates that allow the circuit designer to control one or both directions of the passage of AC power cycles through the device itself and hence through the load. ICs have been developed that use photo-diodes optically coupled to a silicon bilateral switch to provide a means of optical isolation for separating gate control circuitry from the high-energy AC power flowing through the silicon switching devices. Optical isolator chips are available in two formats consisting of devices that transmit a control signal to randomly begin conducting and devices that are able to detect the zero-crossing point of the main power signal. If the AC power cycle is randomly "chopped," radio frequency interference (RFI) or more general electromagnetic interference (EMI) can be generated, and filters must be used for suppression of the unwanted radiation. Zero-crossing detector circuitry that turns the AC controlling device on and off only at the zero-crossing point minimizes the generation of significant RFI.

Random-phase or zero-crossing, optical isolation integrated circuitry operates from low-voltage DC sources, so if standard digital logic circuitry is to be used with triac control of mains AC power, then a source of the required DC power must be available. Batteries or the simple dedicated 5 V supply illustrated in Figure 10-11 may be used.

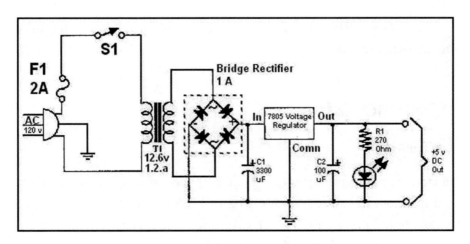

Figure 10-11. A Typical AC to 5-Volt DC Output Power Supply

The use of solid-state devices to control AC power provides the researcher with two methods for using the energy. In the first and simplest method, the full AC voltage can be applied to the load, and the time at which the full current is allowed to flow is varied. The second form of control involves varying the voltage applied to the load. The AC voltage cycles between 0 and 120, and the solid-state switching devices can be used to apply any portion in the cycle (between 0 and 120 volts) to the load, 60 times a second. The AC waveform is a sinusoidal phenomenon in which the voltage magnitude follows a sine curve. By selecting a portion of the waveform to apply a voltage to the load, the power control is called "phase angle control." Voltage variation is somewhat complex and should be used only when required. By applying the full AC voltage to the load and varying the time of full power application, the power delivered to the load can be controlled, and the radio frequency noise generated is greatly reduced and minimized when zero-crossing switching is used.

Pulse width modulation concepts introduced in Chapter 7 and applied previously in a motor control exercise are usually applied in DC power systems but can also be used to exert a rudimentary coarse control of AC power.

The optical isolators used in this portion of the exercise are random and zero-crossing units.

Experimental
Hardware

A 60 to 15 watt incandescent light bulb is a good visual demonstration load for this AC power control exercise. The socket for the bulb and a mounting bracket for holding a potentiometer control, while serving as a heat sink for the triac mount, along with a terminal block and the breadboard for mounting the controlling circuitry, should all be affixed to a sturdy wood or metal base as depicted in Figure 10-12. Recalling the dangers associated with AC mains voltages and currents, all of the wiring carrying mains power must be securely fastened, properly insulated, and covered according to local electrical building codes. Insulation on wires carrying mains power should be carefully cut to ensure no bare wire surface is exposed after the screw terminal connection on the terminal block is tightened. All exposed wire surfaces or soldered connections carrying mains power must be insulated with liquid plastic insulator, silicone sealant, or heat shrink tubing. *Never* power up any circuit with exposed conductors carrying mains current.

The numerical designations in the author's experimental setup (Figure 10-12) are explained in the following text.

Item 1 is a 60 W light bulb in an electrical code compliant receptacle properly mounted on a ¾ in (1.8 cm) high-density fiberboard. Item 2 is a 250 VAC terminal board with approved cord and plug (N.B. cover removed for clarity). Item 3 is a 400 VAC, 6 A, BTA06 STMicroelectronics, TO-220 tabbed triac on its heat sink, with heat-shrink wrapped conductors eliminating exposed conductor surfaces. Item 4 is the duty cycle control potentiometer, and item 5 is the optical isolation triac control ICs used in the demonstration exercises. The number 6 marks the position of the bipolar 555 timer, and item 7 is the 9 V battery power supply.

The 60 W bulb initially used as a visually active experimental load was subsequently replaced with a much cooler-surfaced 15 W bulb often used as an interior light in home appliances.

Figure 10-12. *An AC Current Control Test Apparatus with an Incandescent Light Bulb*

Circuit Schematic

Figure 10-13 is a typical block diagram representing an experimental setup for control of AC mains power with a triac and optical isolator.

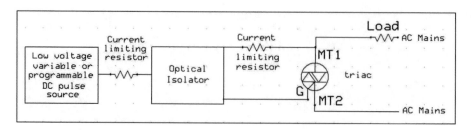

Figure 10-13. *Triac and Optical Isolator AC Current Control*

For this exercise, a manually controllable, DC pulse source can be assembled from a 555 timer configured for astable operation with its duty cycle controlled manually, through a potentiometer diode network, as used previously for a 90% range of duty cycle variation.

The circuit diagram in Figure 10-13 has been drawn in a configuration using the Fairchild semiconductor MOC 3022 that may be powered from either a 5 V supply or a 9 V battery when a suitable current limiting resistor is used in the MOC 3022 internal LED illumination circuit. Controlled AC power is applied to the load circuitry by energizing the low-voltage pulse generation circuit and then plugging in the AC power cord to the mains supply.

The circuit of Figure 10-13 has been drawn with a MOC 3022 random-phase optical isolator triac driver in place. The MOC 3061 zero-crossing device can be used in the same manner as depicted in Figure 10-14.

In order to conduct an important visual display of the resultant effects of the application of a pulse width variation technique to an AC current control, the circuit depicted in Figures 10-12, 10-13, and 10-14 should be built on a prototyping breadboard with the components in Figure 10-14.

After assembling and examining the effects on the light bulb filament of altering the duty cycle of the 555 timer with the 0.1 μF capacitor in the timing network, the capacitor should be changed to a 1.0 μF unit and the duty cycle varied over the available range again.

Although the circuit being assembled is for demonstration only, it is good practice to use low-leakage plastic film or ceramic capacitors in timing operations.

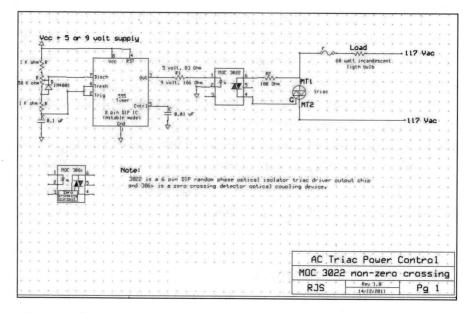

Figure 10-14. *A 5-Volt 555 Timer IC Control of Line Power*

Software

No screen display page components or scripting is required for this exercise.

Observations

A handheld multimeter able to measure frequency in Hz was used to measure the output frequency of the 555 timer circuit square wave that was found to be approximately 75–124 Hz for the 0.1 µF capacitor and 8–12 Hz for the 1.0 µF unit.

The initial setup assembled on a breadboard with a 0.1 µF in the timing circuit and using the MOC 3022 was able to vary the brightness of the lamp from about half power to full on. At the half-on power setting that was near the end of potentiometer rotation, the lamp flashed and flickered, and the timer output was found to erratically move between 75 and 82 Hz.

Replacement of the timing capacitor with a much larger 1.0 µF unit greatly lowered the 555 timer pulse rate frequency range from 12.6 Hz to 7.6 Hz. At the full rotation of the potentiometer to the 12.6 Hz position, the lamp is fully lit and does not flicker. Rotation of the potentiometer to the point at which the frequency meter reads 7.8 Hz causes a visually smooth decrease in the lamp luminosity and a concomitant increase in erratic lamp flickering until at the low end of the frequency range the lamp is essentially off but flickers with an erratic, very-low-level luminosity.

Although the PWM on/off power application of the AC line voltage through the optical isolator was able to roughly regulate the energy delivered to the lamp, the system does not function as a smooth lamp dimmer, but could work for non-lighting applications.

Discussion

A majority of the world's electric power grids carry energy created from rotating generators driven by water, steam, or more recently wind turbines. AC electrical energy can be passed through transformers for conversion to high-voltage forms for transmission over great distances and converted back into high-current relatively lower voltages forms for consumer use. Most of the world's power grids are operating at AC frequencies of 50 or 60 Hz.

For dissipative use as in incandescent or fluorescent lighting, heating, or turning electric motors, the AC power can often be used as received from the power distribution grid with minimal alteration.

Triac control of the power being applied to the incandescent bulb load in the demonstration circuit is controlled by the pulse rate delivered by the battery-powered 555 timer. The timing network used in the 555 timer astable mode of operation as shown in Figure 10-14 is able to allow the duty cycle to vary from approximately 5 to 95%. Thus, the power delivered to the load is variable over a considerable range but never turned fully off nor fully on.

For the simple purposes of non-inductive or strictly resistive usage of AC currents, the various forms of describing AC as rms (root-mean-square), peak-to-peak, or average can be used in the basic electrical calculation formulas but must be used consistently and cannot be mixed. If rms is used in Ohm's law, then all the values for voltage and current must be in unit values of rms.

If the lamp were replaced with a heating element inside a closed, insulated container, the heat produced could be crudely regulated by the on/off ratio controlled by the potentiometer that would in turn coarsely regulate the temperature. Recalling the graphic data of Figure 10-5, it can be seen that the span of the duty cycle is the span of control available by using pulse width variation.

Only very simplified AC circuit analysis and electromagnetic interference (EMI) are being examined in this exercise. AC electronics is frequency dependent and becomes very complicated as the frequency increases. In any experimental work involving higher frequencies such as is found in communications, induction heating, and nuclear magnetic or electron spin resonance spectroscopy, the literature must be consulted for much more specific and detailed information.

If circuits are to be protected from either generating or picking up EMI, they must be totally isolated from radiation by being completely encased in grounded metal boxes. If the circuits draw power from the grid, then the grounded metal boxes and their wiring must, for safety, conform to the local electrical building codes.

In most of the power control applications examined thus far, DC current has been involved, and hence there is no frequency component to be considered. However, an attempt to use PWM techniques with an alternating current power delivery at a fixed frequency of either 50 or 60 Hz immediately places limitations and restrictions on the nature of the PWM methodology.

In the circuit diagram depicted in Figure 10-14, a circuit has been built with a center-tapped potentiometer that can allow a resistance variation of approximately 50 kΩ. Examination of the expanded nomograph in Figure 9-1 suggests that for the 50 kΩ–0.1 μF combination, the experimenter should expect the timer to oscillate in the hundreds of Hz range.

Recall that the potentiometer diode arrangement is used to allow the variation of the duty cycle with only minor changes in the frequency of oscillation. If power is being delivered to the load through a triac device that is allowing current to flow in a manner oscillating at 50 or 60 Hz, then a tenth of a second the load will see five or six power cycles. If the 555 timer is turning the IR diode in the opto-isolator on and off hundreds of times per second, the triac will appear to be on for a substantial amount of the time.

If the frequency of the timer pulse train is lowered to 10 Hz, then the duty cycle variation can be made to span five or six power cycles of the power oscillating through the triac. Figure 10-15 depicts a tenth of a second time span in which the five power cycles are marked with the points that would switch the IR diode off at the nominal duty cycle settings.

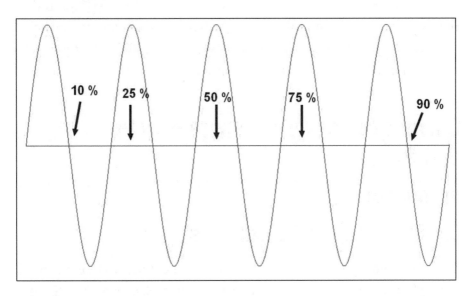

Figure 10-15. *A Tenth of a Second Graphical Representation of a 50 Hz AC Power Supply and a 10 Hz 555 Timer IC Variation of Output Duty Cycle*

As noted previously, at the higher frequency, the light bulb is brightly illuminated most of the time and can only be dimmed slightly and flickers erratically. At a frequency approximately ten times lower, the bulb can be dimmed over its entire range of illumination but flickers as the luminosity decreases to zero.

A further extension of the PWM method with AC systems is used in power control applications in which the frequency of the on/off switching is measured in seconds and minutes. Long time duration PWM power controls are often used in heating control applications where a large thermal mass exhibits a large time lag between the application of power to the heater element and an increase in temperature is seen in the mass being heated. AC-powered heating systems with large time delays can be calibrated and a PWM control system established.

A PWM system can be employed to precisely control the power delivered to a load through using semiconductors to pass only small portions of the power cycle to the load in a technique known as phase angle control. However, phase angle control involves establishing and coordinating the zero-crossing point in both of the power cycle and the PWM control signal that is beyond the simple introductory nature of this exercise.

Current Control with Raspberry Pi and Python

Introduction

Control of Larger DC Currents

As has been pointed out in previous exercises, the RPi has a limited ability to supply any sizable currents from the GPIO pins. Higher currents from external sources can however be controlled from some of the pins on the RPi array.

An excellent summary of current control hardware and circuitry is collected online.[3]

High-current DC, in the 30–60 A range, can be controlled with metal oxide semiconductor field effect transistors (MOSFETs) such as a FQP30N06L from ON Semiconductor or Fairchild. FET semiconductors often require a strong signal to enter into the conduction mode, and hence the experimenter using the GPIO array as a controlling source must make sure that the FET transistor selected is compatible with the 3.3 V available from the array pins. The L in the FQP30N06L indicates a device with a gate compatible with low-voltage control signals.

Moderate current handling capability can be realized with Darlington pair transistors schematically depicted in Figure 10-16.

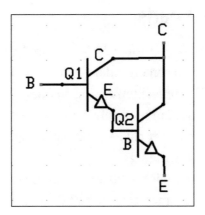

Figure 10-16. *NPN Darlington Pair Transistors*

Bipolar junction transistors (BJTs) are current control devices. The main current through the device flows between the collector and emitter. Current flow between collector and emitter is controlled by the much smaller base current. Amplification of the base current makes the BJT a sensitive device able to amplify very small, weaker signals from sensors

---

[3] https://elinux.org/RPi_GPIO_Interface_Circuits.

such as solar cells and thermocouples. The device fabricated from Darlington pair transistors is able to amplify the current in proportion to the product of the two amplification factors for the transistors in the pair. The dual-transistor assembly is also significantly more sensitive to base current than the single transistors used to create the device.

Two common Darlington pair transistors are the TIP 120 and 122 that are available as tabbed, three-terminal devices, in the TO-220 package. The devices are able to work at up to 60 and 100 V, respectively, and, with proper heat sinks, can operate with 5 A currents.

Experimental
Non-inductive Loads

To demonstrate a current control technique with the GPIO array of the RPi, a Python-tkinter GUI screen slider control will be used to manage the power from a 12 V supply illuminating an automotive incandescent lamp. The incandescent lamp is purely a resistive load and hence requires no diodes to bypass the destructive voltage spikes generated by inductive loads such as motor coil windings.

A TIP 122 Darlington pair transistor and a resistor were mounted on a prototyping board and connected to the 12 V battery power supply and the automotive lamp. The current control demonstration circuit is depicted in Figure 10-17.

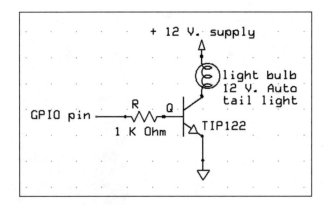

Figure 10-17. *Circuit for Incandescent Light Current Control*

The automotive lamp was found to draw 1.25 A from a 6 V source at a bright red heat that corresponds to a filament resistance of 4.80 Ω. The expected current draw at full power with a 12 V supply should thus be approximately 2.5 A well within the manufacturer's recommended 5 A capacity for the TO-220 package.

The Python-tkinter GUI slider control as created by Listing 10-1 is depicted in Figure 10-18.

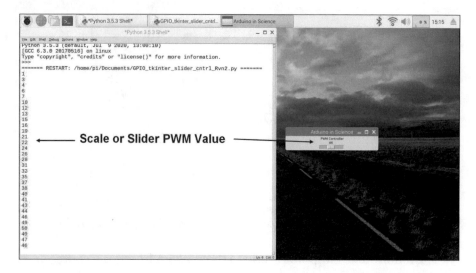

Figure 10-18. *A Python-tkinter GUI Sliding Power Controller for an Incandescent Lamp Load with Console Value Display of PWM Percentage*

Figure 10-19 is a detailed view of the tkinter scale or slider power control icon. Arrow captions and percentage numerical quantity identifiers have been applied to the image by the author while the text and immediate slider value number are created by the appropriate entries made in Listing 10-1. Extended detail has been added to Figure 10-19 to aid in describing the embedded features of the tkinter icon in the "Discussion."

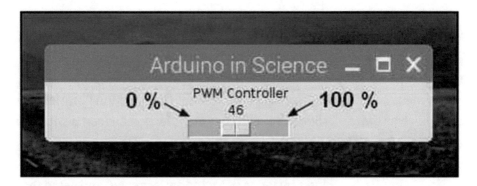

Figure 10-19. *A tkinter Scale or Slider Screen Icon Controller for the RPi.GPIO PWM Library Function*

Observations

The sliding scale widget depicted in Figure 10-19 performs as expected with the lamp filament completely off with the slider to the extreme left of the trough and at a yellow-red incandescence with the slider at the extreme right. The variations in filament intensity were similar to those observed in Chapter 7, Figures 7-7 and 7-9.

The scale or slider control must be moved slowly in order to follow the changing positional values. The icon has a much finer degree of control as detailed in the "Discussion" section.

Discussion

All circuitry wiring carrying hundreds of milliamps and amperes of currents should be properly connected with soldered joints or tight mechanical connections and insulated to prevent short circuits. High current discharges from short circuits even at low voltage can produce very high heat arcs that melt metals, ignite combustibles, and cause painful burns.

395

Tkinter is a Python library that enables the implementation of a number of icons for assembling an active, custom SCADA GUI for the RPi. A substantial amount of functionality is built into the icons available from the tkinter collection.[4]

In many tutorials on using tkinter and other GUI creation libraries, the icons such as buttons, sliders, scroll bars, and other screen icon devices are often referred to as "widgets" and given the symbol w in programming code.

In Listing 10-1, a tkinter instance of a window is created and set to the designator of master. The interior of the master window is scanned for mouse-activated events by the mainloop() function. Widgets are created on-screen or instantiated in code within the actively scanned area of the master window to accomplish the task at hand. If the widget in the window must communicate with the Python program in which the tkinter window is running, a "callback" function must be invoked to communicate with code outside the active area of the master window.

In simplified terms, it can be said that each widget is displayed inside a small window on the monitor display screen. The space inside the small window is scanned by the tkinter program looking for mouse click "events" that may occur within the frame. Mouse clicks or mouse button clicks can be used to drag the edges of screen objects to resize them, activate their display controls, and minimize, maximize, or exit from the program.

An ability to communicate with the Python code in which the tkinter window and widget are running allows the experimenter to gain access to the RPi serial port and as is detailed in Chapter 11 connect the screen widget to electro-mechanical systems for SCADA operations.

Figure 10-18 depicts the RPi screen obtained when Listing 10-1 is launched with the diagnostic print statement in the callback function active. The print statement causes the numerical position of the slider index that appears over the index line on the slider button to be printed

---

[4] effbot.org/tkinterbook/

to the Python console. The line containing the print statement in the scale or slider program's callback function can be commented out after code operation has been validated or when not needed for error tracing diagnostics.

Figure 10-19 has arrow captions that denote the two extreme values to which the indicator slide can be dragged with the mouse cursor and a clicked left mouse button. If the experimenter needs to finely set the PWM value from the screen icon, the index button can be dragged to the desired approximate position and then adjusted to the final desired position with the cursor tip. If the slider index button is to be increased in value by single digits, the cursor tip is placed on the top edge of the slider trough between the slider button and the 100% end of the slider scale and single-clicked for each desired single-digit increase in the index button position. If from the rough positioning the index value is to be decreased, the cursor tip is placed between the index slider button and the 0% end of the scale and single-clicked to the desired final position.

Power Control to Inductive Loads

Introduction

A RPi controlling a TIP 122 as depicted in Figure 10-17 can be used to control the power delivered to a brushless DC motor as depicted in Figure 10-4, but the coils in the motor are an inductive load and produce a back electromotive force (EMF) in the form of a voltage spike, when the magnetic field enveloping the coils collapses. To prevent the back EMF from destroying the PN junctions in the power transistor, a suitably sized diode should be placed in parallel with the load.

RPi PWM signals from the scale-slider GUI described previously could be used to replace the 555 timer–potentiometer power control to a transistor used to regulate the current delivered to a brushless DC motor and hence manage the speed of the motor as seen in Figure 10-4. A Python break beam RPM monitor could also be set up using the circuitry described in Chapter 8 to monitor the motor speed and thus duplicate the DAQFactory exercise in terms of the RPi-Python combination.

However, rather than perform a translation from one system to another, a very useful higher-current delivery demonstration that does not use PWM can be developed with the RPi and Python to power stepper motors.

Experimental

Stepper motors can be inexpensively controlled from the RPi with a single ULN2803 or ULN2804, eight–Darlington pair array IC ($3 CDN). A ULN280n consists of an eight–Darlington pair array of power transistors, in an 18-pin, dual in-line package. (DIP) The IC array has been fabricated with the bypass diodes already in place for use in driving inductive loads.

Each of the Darlington array transistor pairs is an "open collector" configuration in which the transistor is acting as an on/off switch. In the open collector configuration, the device to be powered is connected to the positive side of the power supply and the open collector of the transistor. The emitters of all the pairs share a common connection to the negative or "ground" terminal of the RPi GPIO array and the #9 pin on the ULN280n IC as seen in Figure 10-20. Toggling the GPIO pins between high and low switches the current flow through the motor coils and indicator LEDs on and off.

As has been repeatedly suggested in numerous previous exercises, the circuitry in which the ULN2803 is to be used should be built up, tested, and validated from basic first principles to a completed working final electronic power controller configuration. The RPi program should be developed to run a series of four LEDs connected to the ULN280n prior to being used in an attempt to connect to and power an actual stepper motor.

A standard application of the ULN280n IC array has been modified with the addition of four LEDs to the basic circuit used for the control of a stepper motor. A four-LED array aids visually in assembling and validating the stepwise implementation of this complex system.

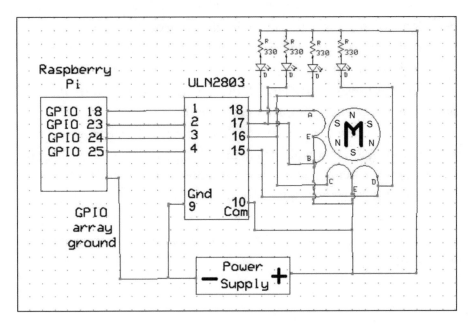

Figure 10-20. *Schematic for Stepper Motor Control with a ULN2803*

Figure 10-20 is a semi-schematic diagram of a connection in which the RPi GPIO array is interfaced through a power controlling IC to an illustrative stationary four-coil, multiple permanent magnet rotor, stepper motor.

As can be seen in the preceding figure, the toggling of GPIO 18 with a Python code taking the #1 pin on ULN2803 high and then low will cause a current pulse through the A-E stationary coil creating a magnetic field and illuminating the first diode. A transient pulse of current through the coil will create a localized magnetic field that will cause rotor rotation to a position in which the nearest permanent magnetic pole of the opposite sign aligns with that of the transient in the stationary motor coil. If the Python code controlling the GPIO array now delays for a short period of time to allow for rotor rotation and field alignment before repeating the logic high/low toggling action on GPIO 23 to pulse a current through coil E-B and illuminate the second diode, a second "step" of rotor rotation will occur. Repetition of the toggling action interspersed with short time delays for GPIO array pins 24 and 25 will illuminate the third and fourth diodes as the stepper motor shaft completes one rotation.

In simplified terms, it can be said that to control the stepper motor from the RPi GPIO array with the circuit of Figure 10-20, the experimenter must assemble a Python program to sequentially illuminate the LED array as described in Chapter 3 and in Listings 10-2 and 10-3 provided at the end of this chapter.

Figure 10-21 depicts one of the author's experimental configurations on a prototyping board.

Figure 10-21. *Experimental Setup for Stepper Motor Driver Python Program*

In Figure 10-21 item 1 is a Model 3 Raspberry Pi with the appropriate GPIO input pins connected to the first four channels of the ULN2803 black DIP mounted in the center of the prototyping board (item 2). The power control IC output pins are in turn connected to the four input pins of the stepper motor wiring harness seen in the upper right-hand corner of the prototyping board, while four additional wires power the green LED array seen in the upper left-hand corner of the board. An arrow points to the illuminated LED in the array. Listing 10-2 is presented as a diagnostic utility that illuminates a designated LED, but in reality, with the circuit of Figure 10-20, it "single-steps" the stepper motor. Listing 10-3 written as a continuous "single stepping" extension of Listing 10-2 in reality provides fundamental control over stepper motor actions from the RPi GPIO array.

Item 3 is a USB hub with a thumb drive, and item 4 is a low-power 28BYJ-48 geared stepper motor. The slowly moving motor shaft has a transparent tape "flag" with black pen marker lines to aid in displaying shaft rotary motion. Also seen in the figure is a GPIO pin position and identification aid that helps in pin location during the complex hookup wiring as seen in Figure 10-21.

Figure 10-22 displays a very inexpensive ($19 CDN) board-mounted stepper motor and IC driver. A 28BYJ-48 motor (item 1) on the board is widely used by hobbyists and can be used for this exercise. The small stepper motor module is widely available from most hobby or electronics stores and online suppliers. Item 2 is the motor wiring harness, and item 3 is the array of input pins to connect to the GPIO array on RPi.

Figure 10-22. *A Commercially Available SMT Stepper Motor Driver Module*

Although presented in a very simplistic manner, stepper motor control is not a trivial matter; and in keeping with the introductory nature of this work, the investigator is referred to the written and online literature for the explanations and computer code for dealing with the advanced topics of stepper motor controls as listed in the "Discussion" section of this topic.

A four-unit, D cell battery pack, charged with four alkaline cells, was initially used by the author to provide a 6 V output and a 12,000 mAh rating to power a larger stepper motor during wiring validation and rotation testing. Subsequently a geared stepper motor (approx. 1:64, actually 63.6839:1) commonly used in robotics and available from numerous mail-order sources as a model 28BYJ-48 ($5 USD) was used to develop the motor driver programs in the code listings for this exercise. The small stepper can be powered with 5–12 V and is reportedly capable of 15 rpm with a DC coil resistance of 50 Ω that at 5 volts should draw 1/10 A well within the RPi 5 V output current capability of slightly below an ampere. The motor weighs 30 gm and is encased in a metal housing with two screw mount lugs for easy positioning on experimental setups.

Observations

In keeping with the previously noted philosophy that a working complex system is assembled from simpler, tested, and operationally validated sub-components, the following procedure was invoked.

After an initial configuration of the ULN2803, the motor, and the GPIO array physical pin connections in accordance with that depicted in Figure 11-20, the LED illumination program of Listing 10-2 was run with a 2-second delay once for each of the GPIO values of 18, 23, 24, and 25 (array physical pins 12, 16, 18, and 22; recall the array is counted across not along the row). As each GPIO connection was enumerated, the corresponding LED illumination was visually confirmed to validate the RPi GPIO connection to the appropriate motor coil leads.

After the system validation with the individual LEDs, the second program of Listing 10-3 using a while loop to step through the four coil connections was launched with the same 2 s delay as used previously to validate the correct sequential activation of the motor coils and confirm the rotation of the stepper motor.

A 2 s time delay produces a very small step in the highly geared motor, but decreasing the time delay to 1/8 of a second induced a slow but distinct stepping action.

Discussion

Listings 10-2 and 10-3 are rudimentary codes that are designed to demonstrate to the investigator how a stepper motor works and is controlled. To expand motor applications, the experimenter can reverse the motor's continuous rotation by sequentially activating the coils in the reverse manner than is presented in the rotation programs. To drive the stepper motor into a positional service in which the rotor steps a fixed number of increments in a clockwise or counterclockwise rotation, the correct coil-energizing code can be enclosed in a Python do loop construct.

There are a significant number of different actions that can be programmed into a stepper motor that are beyond the simple codes presented here to implement forward and reverse continuous rotation and speed variation that are detailed in the large engineering and robotics literature on stepper motors that should be examined for more complex stepper motor applications.

For applications or experimenting with larger stepper motors such as those salvaged from obsolete equipment, a separate power supply and heavier current draws may be required to achieve motor rotation. The GPIO array can be used to activate either Darlington pair transistors or heavier MOSFET devices, but both of these types of transistor must be protected with bypass diodes to avoid semiconductor destruction by the back EMF from the motor coils. Heavier current draws by larger systems may also require heat sinks for the semiconductors in use.

Control of AC Currents

Introduction

Python and the RPi can be used to demonstrate the limited PWM control of AC electrical energy with the same, very inexpensive ICs used with the DAQFactory programs as listed previously. Multiple ampere triac devices capable of over 400 VAC operation and optical isolation devices can be obtained from mail-order houses for less than $2. An incandescent light bulb powered from the 110 V AC line can be used as an electrical load for the RPi demonstration as illustrated in Figure 10-12 with these inexpensive components.

For safety and compliance with the law, all wiring involving line electrical energy must be completely covered or insulated when assembled in accordance with local electrical wiring and building codes.

Experimental

Figure 10-23 depicts the circuit to be used to control the AC power delivered to the incandescent light bulb load. The BTA06 triac should be mounted on a heat sink sufficient for the passage of current that will be used in the load selected for the exercise. Small incandescent lamps for the interiors of domestic cooking ovens can be obtained in small wattages down to 15 watts.

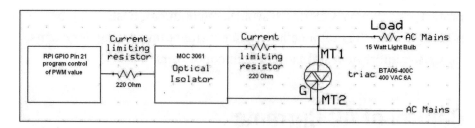

Figure 10-23. *110 VAC Line Control for Raspberry Pi*

The circuit of Figure 10-23 has replaced the 555 timer and potentiometer of Figure 10-13 used in the DAQFactory line power control exercise with the pulse width modulation control function available from the RPi. The GPIO pin has sufficient power to not only drive the triac gate but also simultaneously drive an optional LED "pilot" light and its current limiting resistor connected to the GPIO 21 pin and ground immediately before the 220 Ω resistor protecting the input to the MOC 3061.

As noted, the RPi.GPIO library contains the functions necessary to apply a PWM signal from the GPIO array with sufficient power to illuminate a 5 mm LED. An internal LED in the MOC 3061 is used to turn on the triac and thus pass power to the lamp filament to light the bulb.

Listing 10-1 is the PWM program for this power control. The listed program generates the scale or slider widget depicted in Figures 10-18 and 10-19, and the duty cycle is determined by the scale or slider horizontal position.

A RPi.GPIO library implementation of a PWM power control operation involves the selection and setting of a number of variable parameters. The operator must select the frequency of the PWM pulse train and the initial duty cycle of the control signal and manually insert the selections in the two lines of code listed in the following. Once the selections are entered into the code, the program can be run, and the slider button will apply the custom configured PWM power control signal to the triac controlling the power illuminating the lamp:

> pwm = GPIO.PWM(18, 500) # PWM signal on pin 18
> set to 500Hz

> pwm.start(0) # initial starting value for the duty
> cycle

To demonstrate the difference between PWM power control with DC and AC power supplies, the slider or scale program is run starting with a typical default PWM frequency of 500 Hz. When the slider icon is displayed, the lamp should be cycled through its 0–100% power cycle, and the effects realized with the power control technique noted.

To accumulate more data to evaluate the effect of the different PWM frequencies on the AC power delivered to the lamp, the frequencies of the PWM signal can be manually halved from the line frequency approximation of 64 Hz down to 8 Hz, and notes on the effects seen on the light bulb illumination can be collected.

Observations

Table 10-2 tabulates the semi-quantitative effects seen in the illumination of the small AC-powered light bulb at the various nominal PWM frequencies.

Table 10-2. *110 VAC Light Bulb Luminous Output at Nominal PWM Frequency*

Light Meter Deflection - 15 watt AC Bulb			
PWM Hz	Nominal Power Applied		
Frequency	1%	50%	100%
64	6 mm	14 mm	14 mm
32	3 mm	11 mm	14 mm
16	0	10 mm	14 mm
8	0	7 mm	14 mm

Luminosity was semi-quantitatively measured with a photographic light meter by measuring the dial indicator displacement from its zero position at a fixed distance from the illuminated light bulb.

Discussion

A PWM frequency variation study is possible with the RPi and the RPi.GPIO library because the PWM frequency is software and not hardware controlled.

As can be seen from Table 10-2, the optimum correlation between PWM frequency and power delivery to the light bulb appears to occur between 16 and 32 Hz.

Attempts to apply PWM control methods to a 60- or 50-cycle AC power source are only coarsely effective when the PWM signal wavelength is equal to or larger than the wavelength of the power delivered to the load.

As indicated by the data tabulated in Table 10-2 and depicted in Figure 10-15, when the PWM signal is applied to an AC power source with a wavelength shorter than that of the control signal, the PWM function can exert a coarse control over the power delivered to the load. A low-intensity lamp flicker at low PWM values can be caused by the control signal turning the power signal on at its maximum point in the power cycle. As the length of the PWM signal increases, the power signal is able to cycle through one or more complete cycles; and as observed in the experiments, the flicker or flashing dies out as the PWM signal approaches 100% duty cycle.

The investigator will see both light flickering of variable intensity and flickering from completely off to full on evident in virtually all the PWM frequency variation experiments conducted. The lack of coordination between the phase angles of the two signals creates completely random flickering and cyclic pulsing of the lamp intensity in the very responsive low-mass lamp filament.

As noted previously, in order for the PWM signal to be used to modulate or control the application to the load of only a portion of the AC waveform called phase angle control, complex additional circuitry must be in place to detect and coordinate the zero-crossing point of both the power supply wave and the PWM signal. A variation of PWM control of an AC power source can be used for heating and other long-term applications where multiple full power cycles are applied to the load in timed pulses.

Code Listings
Raspberry Pi–Python Codes

Listing 10-1. A Horizontal Sliding Current Control Icon

```
# A Horizontal Sliding Current Control Icon for the Raspberry
  Pi GPIO Array
# In RPI.GPIO pin 18 in BCM numbering or pin 12 in BOARD
  numbering has
# a PWM function of 0-100%. A slider is a standard Tkinter icon
  with a
```

```
# call back function to send slider position data 0 to 100%
  back to the python
# program running the RPI.GPIO library to adjust / alter the
  PWM values.
#
from tkinter import *
import RPi.GPIO as GPIO
import time
#
# library set up
GPIO.setmode(GPIO.BCM)
GPIO.setwarnings(False)
GPIO.setup(18,GPIO.OUT)
pwm = GPIO.PWM(18, 500) # PWM signal on pin 18 set to 500Hz
pwm.start(0) # initial starting value for the duty cycle
#
# tkinter scale or slider control icon set up
#
# set up call back function to process the slider value. Print
  statement
# in callback is a development/error diagnostic utility
#
def Val(val):     # callback function definition (outside Tk()
                    window instance)
    val = w.get() # the get function reads the slider value
    print(val)    # diagnostic utility comment out when not
                    in use
    pwm.ChangeDutyCycle(val) # RPI library function to alter
    the PWM power applied to the load
#
```

```
master = Tk()      # window instance
master.title("Arduino in Science")  # a title for the main
                                        window that holds the
                                        widget
w = Scale(master, from_=0, to=100, orient=HORIZONTAL,
label="PWM Controller", command=Val)  # creates widget, scale,
                                        text and names callback
                                        function
w.pack()           # display scale or slider icon instance
#
mainloop()         # main loop over window construct.
GPIO.cleanup()     # reset GPIO pins to low.
```

Listing 10-2. RPi GPIO Pin Identification Utility

```
# Locate Physical Pins and GPIO Designations with LEDs

import RPi.GPIO as GPIO

import time
#
GPIO.setmode(GPIO.BCM)

GPIO.setwarnings(False)
#
GPIO.setup(25, GPIO.OUT)

GPIO.output(25, GPIO.HIGH) # caution open collector - ULM2803

time.sleep(2)

GPIO.output(25, GPIO.LOW)
```

Listing 10-3. Continuous Stepper Motor Rotation

```
# Illuminate LEDS repeatedly in sequence

import RPi.GPIO as GPIO

import time
#
GPIO.setmode(GPIO.BCM)

GPIO.setwarnings(False)
#
# A while loop repeats the cycle till terminated from the
  keyboard
#
while True:

    # illuminate the first LED on GPIO 18

    GPIO.setup(18, GPIO.OUT)

    GPIO.output(18, GPIO.HIGH)

    time.sleep(0.125)

    GPIO.output(18, GPIO.LOW)
    #

    # illuminate the second LED on GPIO 23

    GPIO.setup(23, GPIO.OUT)

    GPIO.output(23, GPIO.HIGH)

    time.sleep(0.125)

    GPIO.output(23, GPIO.LOW)
    # illuminate the third LED on GPIO 24
```

```
GPIO.setup(24, GPIO.OUT)

GPIO.output(24, GPIO.HIGH)

time.sleep(0.125)

GPIO.output(24, GPIO.LOW)
# illuminate the fourth LED on GPIO 25
GPIO.setup(25, GPIO.OUT)

GPIO.output(25, GPIO.HIGH)

time.sleep(0.125)

GPIO.output(25, GPIO.LOW)
```

Summary

- Constant current sources are required for numerous electronic and experimental science operations.

- Exacting DC current control can be achieved in the analog format with discrete electronic components or integrated circuits and in the digital format with pulse width modulation techniques.

- Sinusoidal AC current control uses solid-state devices functioning as controlled diodes passing selected portions of the sine wave power profile to the load as determined by device gate activation.

- Precise current control is required to regulate typical loads such as continuous motor rotation speeds or activate discrete inductive, stepper motor actions.

- – Exercises demonstrating the problems inherent in using basic DC pulse width modulation techniques as AC power controls are presented as a prelude for understanding advanced microcontroller techniques using a PWM variant to control mains power.

- – In Chapter 11, the microcontroller is introduced, and its ability to function as a "smart" I/O device and sensor interface is presented.

CHAPTER 11

Microcontrollers and Serial Communications

During the 40 years in which the 555 timer, 741 op-amp, and Exar XR-2209 have been in production, complete central processing units (CPUs) for digital computing have been developed in the form of microprocessors. Microprocessors have in some circumstances been used to create far more flexible control systems, with fewer parts than were available with the legacy, discrete, multiple-chip-based assemblies.

A microprocessor is a computer central processing unit in an IC chip format, while a microcontroller could be considered to be a "micro-miniature computer" designed for embedded applications. An embedded system is usually one dedicated to a specific task, may be written in the assembly or the C language for optimum speed and efficiency, and may have limited I/O capabilities. A microcontroller contains a microprocessor, memories, and programmable input/output peripherals, all combined to form a single unit either in a printed circuit board format or as an IC chip.

Microprocessors have been in use for many years, and Parallax Inc.'s "BASIC Stamp" and the PIC series of microprocessors from the Microchip company are two of the systems that have been available to the advanced

© Richard J. Smythe 2021
R. J. Smythe, *Arduino in Science*, https://doi.org/10.1007/978-1-4842-6778-3_11

hobbyists and specialists for many years. Both the Stamp and PIC series of microcontrollers require some detailed knowledge of computer science and electronics to be used in nontrivial applications.

Readily available constantly improving, inexpensive microprocessor chips, advances in software, and Internet growth have led to the establishment of sizable "online" communities of physical computing enthusiasts. Physical computing interest has grown to the size where commercial enterprises are able to supply the rapidly growing Internet-based online communities with circuit boards and integrated circuitry. In forums, individual community members exchange ideas and information, thus developing "open source" systems for which members contribute both written code software and hardware configuration developments to improve and expand the applications for the systems at hand.

Interest in physical computing in which a PC is used to control electro-mechanical systems has grown to the point at which online, open source physical computing platforms have come into being permitting both the non-engineering or new computer experimentalist to begin to create and use microcontroller devices to control electro-mechanical systems.

An open source platform called the Arduino project from Italy has been specifically developed in which the Atmel series of microprocessor chips has been used to build a series of very small and inexpensive microcontroller circuit boards. Originally conceived to provide non-specialists with the ability to endow design, artistic, and hobbyist projects with interactive capabilities, the system has also become a popular rapid prototyping technique for the trained or experienced electro-mechanical developers and serious experimental researchers.

A microcontroller is able to accept coded instructions, process those instructions, and manipulate its on-chip input and output peripherals, to perform the task required by the coding. Usually the coded instructions are written and then assembled on a host PC running a program known as an "integrated development environment" (IDE). Error-free code developed in the IDE is then transferred (or uploaded) into the microcontroller via a USB connection for actual execution.

The Arduino project has produced several circuit boards that use the ATmega series of 8-bit microprocessor chips, together with clock oscillators and additional circuitry to form a USB-accessible, programmable microcomputer. The boards are programmed from a PC-hosted IDE based upon the Processing programming language. Both the Arduino and Processing language projects are open source creations with freely downloadable software, tutorials, projects, and online help from user forums. The systems are fully supported by numerous textbooks, manuals, and commercially available hardware sources and, through the online forums, are constantly advancing and evolving.

As of the time of this writing, the most recent Arduino board release is the Uno revision 3. Figure 11-1 depicts an original Uno board that uses an Atmel AT328 (8-bit) microprocessor, flash, SRAM (static random-access memory), and EEPROM (electrically erasable programmable read-only memory) with a 16 MHz clock and serial port I/O. The clock speed provides time resolution into the microsecond range, and the serial port I/O can be accessed by the COM (serial communications) ports of the PC hosting DAQFactory. Variations of the Uno board are available with Microchip PIC 32-bit microprocessors that use significantly greater clock speeds, have greatly extended I/O capabilities, and are completely compatible with the code previously developed for the Arduino 8-bit systems. (In Figure 11-1, note the socket mounting of the main chip. Newer devices are all surface mount technology (SMT).)

Microprocessors provide flexibility and are able to provide programmed timing functions in both input and output modes that greatly improve the control and reading of sensors or motion control devices.

An open source platform concept is extremely useful for experimental science. A microprocessor chip supported by various I/O interfacing circuitry, a crystal-controlled clock, and other supporting hardware, all mounted on a very small, inexpensive, readily available circuit board, can function as a "smart" peripheral. Smart peripherals can greatly augment both the sensitivity and range of data collection through high-speed time averaging that often reveals trends, which might otherwise remain hidden from the experimenter.

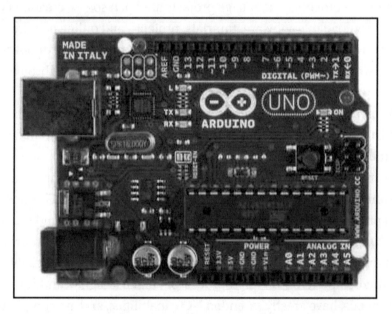

Figure 11-1. *The Arduino Uno Microcontroller*

An open source concept also brings many minds from different disciplines to focus on a single problem, and the advantage that this brings to the increase in the development of knowledge is virtually unmeasurable. In the following exercises, the basic ability of the microprocessor to read sensors and control motion devices will be demonstrated as a basis for more complex and focused applications in actual experimental scientific measurements. After establishing the communications link between the

Arduino monitoring a simple light-dependent resistor (LDR) and the host computer, the ability of the microprocessor to expand the functionality of experimental inquiry through such concepts as digital signal processing and increased timing capability will be demonstrated.

In preparation for subsequent experimental measurements and assembly of laboratory apparatus, the basics of two-way serial communications with simple electro-optical light detection and PC graphical display of streamed sensor data will be developed in this chapter.

Experimental: Microprocessor to Host PC Communications – "Uploading"

Before proceeding with this exercise, the reader should be familiar with the fundamentals of microprocessors and their applications. As noted, the Arduino project is an excellent place for those without a background in physical computing or electronics to begin to learn and apply the basic skills required to use microprocessors. There are sufficient books, tutorials, and project descriptions available at the open source website that, if read or reviewed, will enable the experimental researcher to become comfortable in designing and creating microprocessor-controlled experimental setups.

The current exercise is predominantly concerned with interfacing a microprocessor with a PC running or hosting the DAQFactory SCADA software. Once the interface is established, the flexibility of microprocessors will be evident as analog-to-digital converted data is streamed out to the PC on the serial connection between sensor and PC for supplementary data processing and very flexible graphical data display.

To begin assembling the utilities required to use the microprocessor, download and expand the compressed files from the Arduino website for the operating system in use (Windows and RPi for the author). Install the drivers for the Uno board on the PC hosting the DAQFactory software.

Once the PC is able to see the Uno board, launch the IDE for the Arduino and run the "Blink" test software, termed a "sketch," to ensure the basic hardware-software connection between PC and Uno board is functional.

To transfer data from the Uno board to the PC and ultimately into the DAQFactory software for graphical display, a serial communications protocol must be established between the software of the two computing devices. The communications protocol must operate both ways permitting data to be "uploaded" to the PC-hosted DAQFactory software from the Uno board and to "download" to the UNO instructions and control commands from the PC DAQFactory software. The bidirectional data transfer is conducted by the USB connected between the PC and Uno board. The two software "ends" of the USB are the communications (COM) ports on either of the two systems. Care must be exercised to ensure that the microcontroller is communicating with the correct COM port being used by the software on the PC. The PC usually has several COM ports, while the microcontroller may have only one.

COM port communication consists of passing ones and zeros back and forth between the PC and the peripheral. Since the electrical pulses that make up the binary information are transmitted and received in a linear fashion, one after another, the data transmission is called serial. The more sophisticated and powerful PC is termed the host/master, and the smaller dedicated microcontroller is termed the client/slave. Binary information is uploaded from client/slave to host/master and downloaded from host/master to client/slave. All binary information transfer between the two devices is conducted under a standard set of rules called a "serial protocol." There are many standard serial protocols in use, and it is possible to create a simple special serial protocol if required. The DAQFactory software manual contains an entire chapter on serial communications, and a separate "Serial/Ethernet Communications Guide" is available from the AzeoTech website. By following these guides with the suggested code, the experimentalist will be able to create and configure a simple protocol to receive streamed data in the "On Receive" event of their user protocol as seen in Figure 11-7. Once the ability to receive streamed data has been established and is made available as a named DAQFactory channel, the powerful statistical and graphics capabilities of DAQFactory can be used to display the incoming data. There are several methods that DAQFactory can use to implement serial communications that will be developed in later portions of this manuscript.

As the Uno-type boards are functioning as a "smart" sensor or peripheral and may be moved around between different fixed location workstations, mobile wireless laptops, notebooks, or other computing devices, different COM ports may be required to support the serial communications. COM port selection can be managed from the Tools menu on the Arduino IDE, while the location of the COM port being used on the PC can be located with the operating system utilities such as "Device Manager" in Windows-based systems.

As noted in Chapter 8 on counting and timing, there is a limit to the response time of the DAQFactory software. If the Arduino board software produces a stream of data that is too fast for DAQFactory to process, the cursor response of the main screen becomes sluggish and erratic. To slow a data stream that is too fast, a delay statement can be entered into the main loop of the Arduino sketch to moderate the transmission rate of the outgoing data.

The Arduino IDE monitor does not display the data streaming from the Uno board to the PC when the DAQFactory program is receiving the stream. The stream arriving at the PC can be displayed graphically or "broadcast" for entry into a spreadsheet such as Excel.

In the primary portion of this exercise, a light-dependent resistor will be used to provide an analog, varying input for the Arduino Uno board that will be passed through an analog-to-digital converter (ADC) and then serially transmitted to the host for a virtually real-time-based, graphical display by the DAQFactory software.

Hardware

A USB microcontroller board, such as an Arduino Uno, will be used to monitor the output from a 5 V biased voltage divider, formed by a light-dependent resistor and a 10 kΩ resistor. The Arduino is providing the 10-bit A/D converted value in the very small 2.75 in (7 cm) × 2 in (5 cm) × 0.5 in (1.2 cm) circuit board rather than the much larger robust 4 in (10.3 cm) × 6 in (15.2 cm) × 1 in (2.45 cm) LabJack.

Circuit Schematic

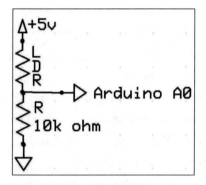

Figure 11-2. *An LDR Biasing Circuit*

The 5 V supply and ground are derived from the Arduino board. Analog-to-digital conversion is accomplished by connecting the junction of the sensor and resistor to the first analog input pin A0 (A zero) on the microcontroller. The analog signal is converted into a digital value between 1023 and 0 (1024 or 2^{10} data points). The light-dependent resistor is a thin flat strip of cadmium sulfide semiconductor mounted on a flat plane, encased with a protective transparent coating. Cadmium sulfide photo resistors are available from many local, mail-order, or online electronics supply sources and are usually priced in the $1–2 range.

Software

The software for this "upload" portion of the exercise is divided into two parts. The first programs the Arduino board, and the second provides the "strip chart recorder" graphical output display from the DAQFactory program.

Listing 11-1 (all listings are at the end of the chapter) provides a copy of the Arduino sketch that monitors the voltage at the LDR–10 kΩ resistor junction. (A sketch is the Arduino documentation name for the set of program instructions assembled and validated in the integrated development environment (IDE) program running on the PC or RPi that the microcontroller will follow.)

In essence the Arduino code reads the junction voltage value with the A0 input of the system's 10-bit A/D converter and then prints the value to the Arduino COM 3 port with a line feed instruction after each value, every 500 ms.

In order for the DAQFactory program to be able to read the data placed on the COM 3 port by the Arduino, a port identified as "com_3" must be created and configured in the SCADA graphing software.

The author's DAQFactory program channel table was configured with the channel name "ArduinoStream" that was set to receive data from the device called com_3. The com_3 port had been named, configured, and then set up according to the following sequence of selections depicted in Figures 11-3 to 11-8.

Initially the Quick menu of Figure 11-3 is used to start the configuration process.

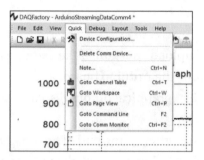

Figure 11-3. *Quick Device Configuration*

Selecting the Device Configuration option brings up the Device Configuration window of Figure 11-4.

Figure 11-4. *Device Configuration Window*

From the window of Figure 11-4, the New Serial selection is made to bring up the Ethernet / Serial Device port configuration window as seen in Figure 11-5.

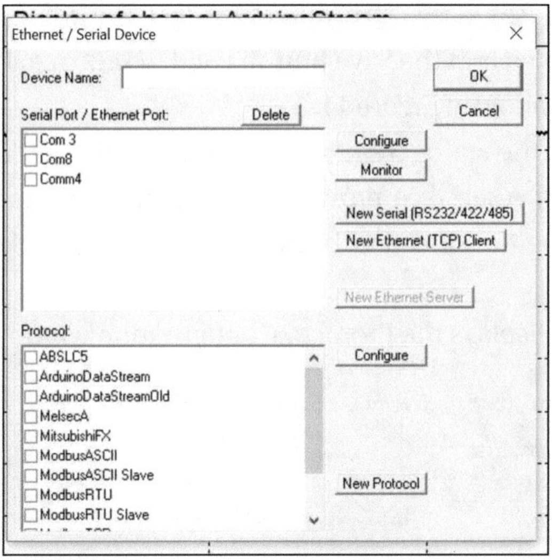

Figure 11-5. *Serial Device Naming and Configuration Selection*

In the window of Figure 11-5, the new com device must be named with a DAQFactory-acceptable name (names must begin with letters and can contain only letters, numbers, and the underscore). After having entered an acceptable name, the Configure button must be clicked to bring up the Serial Port Configuration window as seen in Figure 11-6.

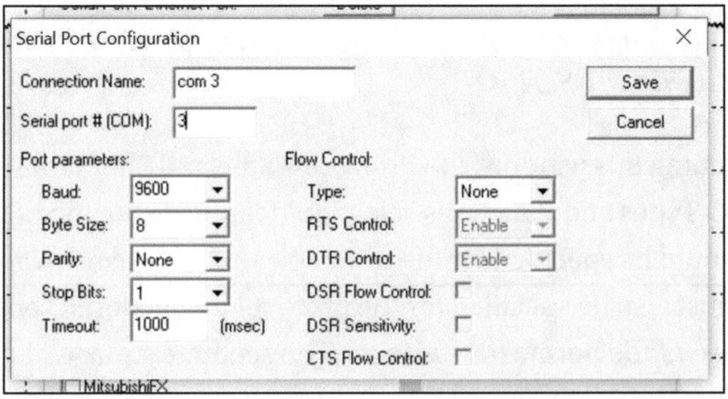

Figure 11-6. *Serial Port Configuration Window*

For the purposes of this introductory exercise, the default options should be accepted and the Save button used to return to the Ethernet / Serial Device window of Figure 11-5.

To complete the connection between the Arduino serial port and the DAQFactory port, a serial communications method or protocol must be specified with the New Protocol button of the Ethernet / Serial Device window.

Figure 11-7 displays the Protocol Configuration window.

Figure 11-7. *The Protocol Configuration Window and "On Receive" Event Data Parsing Script*

On opening this window, the Protocol Name and File Name are blank, and the I/O Types and Functions selection defaults to the top of the list. A name should be specified for the protocol, and a file name with the location must also be specified for the protocol that is stored separately from the rest of the normal documents. The separate storage of the protocol allows sharing of the protocol but also means the protocol has to be moved if the host computer is updated or changed.

To complete the connection in which the Arduino is independently streaming out data, a script must be prepared to be executed each time a complete entity of data arrives on the com_3 port. The script is entered into the "On Receive" selection of the I/O Types and Functions list. The complete code is in Listing 11-2.

Once the com port protocol has been created and saved, the Channel Table View can be used to fill in the entries required to establish the channel to receive the streamed Arduino data as depicted in Figure 11-8.

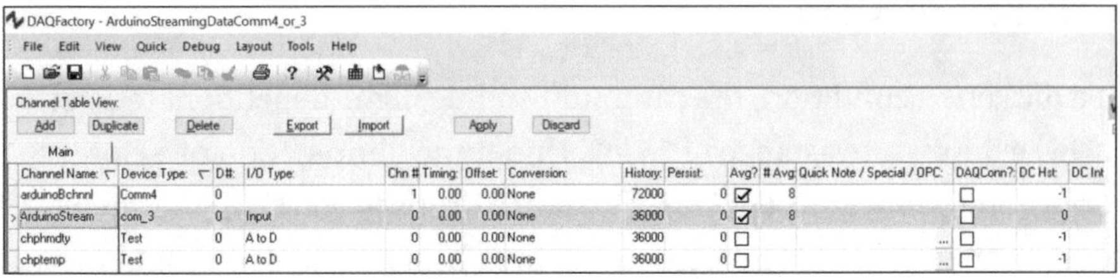

Figure 11-8. *Creation of the Channel for Streamed Data*

With the filling in of the entries in the Channel Table View and the clicking of the "Apply" button seen in Figure 11-8, the channel should begin filling with timestamped data.

The data can be viewed in tabulated form by expanding the Channels heading in the workspace panel and double-clicking the desired channel to bring up the Channel details window with five tabs. Selecting the Table tab will display the timestamp and data arriving at the port with the most recent values at the top (see Chapter 6, Figure 6-14). The Graph tab displays a graph of the data. The Event tab displays any code that may be applied to data manipulation of the channel values. The Main and Details tabs contain numerous named channel configurations and options.

Page Components Required

Channel data can be displayed with a two-dimensional or 2D graph screen component expanded to use as much of the screen as possible. A suitable display is seen in Figure 11-9 with the time axis set to a 5-minute interval (300 seconds) and the Arduino ADC converter values received, scaled from 0 to 1000 units on the charted output.

Observations

In a darkened condition, the cadmium sulfide, light-dependent resistor (LDR) exhibits a resistance of 75 kΩ. Under the illumination of a close, very strong white LED, the LDR resistance drops to 250 Ω. In the circuit configuration depicted in Figure 11-2, the observed voltage should vary from approximately 0.6 to 5 V as the lighting changes from darkness to intense brightness. The Arduino ADC is a 10-bit device that will scale the voltage to 1024 units or 4.9 mV/division at 5 V input. A 5-volt input is realized when the LDR resistance drops virtually to zero or under very strong lighting conditions. The configuration in which the LDR and fixed resistor are assembled causes the graphical trace to rise upward in proportion to the intensity or brightness of the light falling on the detector. The graphical display thus mirrors what the eye sees as higher illumination is toward the top of the graph and deepening darkness causes the trace to decrease. The simple plotting of the streamed Arduino data is not linear with illumination. (See "Discussion.")

Variations in the light falling on the Arduino-mounted LDR caused the response changes depicted in Figure 11-9.

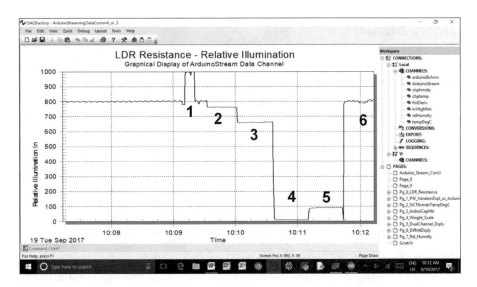

Figure 11-9. *Graphical Recording of Illumination Variation on Arduino-Mounted LDR*

In Figure 11-9 a strong LED when shone on the LDR saturated the monitoring system in section 1. In section 2 the overhead lights were turned off, and in section 3 the room lights were turned off, leaving only the diffused window light to illuminate the detector. Section 4 was recorded with a cover placed over the LDR in the darkened room, and section 5 measured the light leakage into the cover when the room lights were turned back on. Section 6 shows the reproducibility of the monitor when normal room lighting was restored.

Although the response of the LDR is quick and sensitive, rapid, flickering obstruction of the light falling on the LDR causes the display to lag behind the lighting changes.

Discussion

The speed at which the clock on the microprocessor runs provides access to the higher speeds required to monitor some rapidly occurring physiochemical events in the experimental sciences. However, the serial port is easily able to receive data at a rate far above that at which the computer screen can be updated. If the rate of data being streamed into the PC port is too high, the cursor response will slow, and it has actually frozen the cursor on the author's system. If the data rate is too high, the Arduino may have to be slowed with a delay statement in the microprocessor's main loop. Alternatively the data can be streamed into the DAQFactory program and the logging functions used to store data in files at up to 20 points per second (20 Hz) for later retrieval and examination. The LabJack devices (model U3) are able to sample at full resolution at data rates up to 2500 samples/s. Data streamed or collected at these rates must be saved in memory for processing after the closure of the data stream.

A light-dependent resistor is a thin film of semiconductor deposited beneath a protective transparent covering. Ambient light falling on the detector causes electrons to be knocked from the semiconducting material, and the resistance of the device drops as current flows through the strip and the circuit connected to its two leads. The dark resistance for the author's setup is usually measured in the range of 75 kΩ or higher, while under strong illumination, the resistance may fall to only several hundreds of ohms. LDRs can be obtained with dark resistances into the megohm range and usually exhibit a green spectral response similar to that of the human eye.

Cadmium sulfide is one of the more common and inexpensive light-dependent resistors. When the circuit shown in Figure 11-2 is used to create a varying voltage and the signal is connected to the analog input pin A0 of the Arduino board, a 10-bit analog-to-digital converter provides a numerical value with a 1 in 1024 part resolution of the input analog signal to the USB–COM port serial output.

Configuring a light-sensitive resistor in a voltage divider circuit provides a very simple method for conversion of light intensity into a measurable voltage. However, the conversion is not linear.

In the circuit of Figure 11-2, the LDR has been connected to the 5 V supply and a 10 kΩ "pull-down" resistor connected between the LDR and ground. The analog voltage observed at the LDR–pull-down resistor junction is given by the voltage divider equation

$$V_{analog} = V_{+5} * (R_{pull\ down}/(R_{LDR} + R_{pull\ down}))$$

A typical cadmium sulfide LDR may vary from a dark resistance of 75 kΩ to a 1 kΩ resistance in bright light. An Excel spreadsheet can be used, as illustrated in Figure 11-10, to calculate and display a plotting of the analog voltage output for variations in the resistance of the LDR as depicted in the circuit drawn in Figure 11-2.

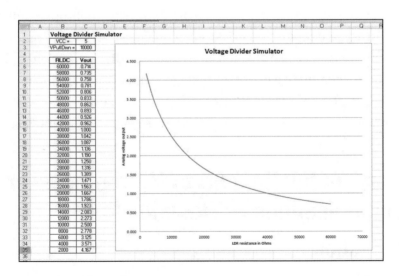

Figure 11-10. *Analog Output of a 10 kΩ–LDR Voltage Divider Circuit*

The curvature seen in Figure 11-10 is typical of that seen when the sensor is between the voltage source and the grounded pull-down resistor. The curve will be the same exponential shape but inverted for a circuit in which the sensor is connected between ground and a pull-up resistor to the positive voltage supply. Each curve generated for an individual LDR and fixed value resistor will be slightly different because of the manufacturing variations in both the photocell and resistance. The preceding curve is best represented by a logarithmic curve of the form $y = -1.053\ln(x) + 12.173$ with a variance of $R^2 = 0.9939$.

As can be seen in Figure 11-10, there are two areas in which the curvature of the analog output decreases and starts to trend toward linearity. In the upper left-hand quadrant of the plot, there are high analog output changes being caused by small changes in the LDR resistance. In the lower right-hand quadrant of the plot, large changes in the LDR resistance are making small changes in the low value of the voltage output. The experimenter may wish to change the value of the pull-up or pull-down resistor and replot the curve shown previously to find the optimum conditions for using a resistive sensor in a voltage divider configuration. For accurate quantitative use of the voltage divider configuration for sensor measurements, the investigator should calibrate the system at hand with as many data points as possible over the sensor range of interest.

Experimental: Host PC to Microprocessor Communications – "Downloading"

Introduction

In the first portion of this exercise, data has been harvested by the microprocessor and sent to the host computer for real-time graphical display, archival storage, and possible production of a hardcopy format.

In this section the host computer and microprocessor will be configured for the Arduino to receive commands from the host via the serial port. The host will be configured with a DAQFactory control screen containing buttons that will activate a LED and start a very simple script to cycle a LED on and off several times.

Hardware

For simplicity an LED and an appropriate current limiting resistor are inserted into a prototyping board and connected in series between pin 13 and ground on the Arduino board.

Software

The author's DAQFactory program for the graphical display of streamed Arduino data was used to provide a fresh blank page on which several buttons were installed as illustrated in Figure 11-11.

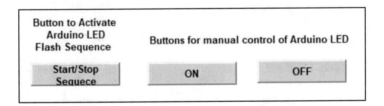

Figure 11-11. *Buttons for Control of Arduino LED*

Each of the buttons labeled ON and OFF was configured as described in previous exercises. For simplicity, in situations where a simple action is required from the downloaded instruction, the Quick Sequence selection was made from the action list as shown in Figure 11-12.

By clicking the highlighted Quick Sequence entry, the text screen of Figure 11-13 is opened, and the required instructions can be entered.

Figure 11-12. *The Quick Sequence Selection*

Figure 11-13. *The Quick Sequence Text Entry Panel*

Quick Sequences do not appear in the listings of formally programmed sequences accessed by expanding the Sequences menu option in the workspace. The linking of the single line of Quick Sequence text to transmit an "H" or "L" is all that is required to activate the ON/OFF button when the Arduino code of Listing 11-4 receives the command to alter the LED status.

A sequence programmed to effect a series of on/off actions for transmission can be prepared in the normal manner for the DAQFactory software. The leftmost button in Figure 11-11 flashes the Arduino LED on and off five times at 3-second intervals in accordance with Listing 11-3.

Observations

When the buttons on the DAQFactory control screen are clicked, the LED on the Arduino board is activated or inactivated in accordance with the button labels.

Discussion

When working through the "downloading" commands exercise, each piece of the communications link can be independently tested as the system is built up. The LED and its current limiting resistor can be tested by loading and running the required sketch and sending an uppercase H or L from the Arduino serial port. The LED will light and extinguish as instructed.

The serial port display must be closed on the Arduino for the port to be available for use by the DAQFactory program. Once the connection is made from the screen button code to the Arduino, any attempts to use the port by the Arduino in troubleshooting will invoke a "port in use" error response from the Arduino. The Arduino must be shut down and rebooted to regain access to the port.

The DAQFactory side of the two-way link and the correct operation of the Arduino sketch can be also be confirmed by accessing the com_3 monitor (com3 in earlier programs) in DAQFactory and manually transmitting an uppercase H with the entry box and Send button on the monitor window. The manual transmission should activate the Arduino-mounted LED, and a manual transmission of the uppercase L should then turn the LED off.

The two port monitors accept and transmit H/L, but the scripting commands must use the quotation marks to designate "H" and "L" as the uppercase ASCII characters.

Raspberry Pi and Arduino

In the previous exercises, the Raspberry Pi has used different libraries for its GPIO pin array to communicate with the outside world. Each of the three libraries has different abilities and limitations that can virtually be eliminated by using the Arduino microcontroller as a smart peripheral.

Recall that Arduino programs are written in the integrated development environment (IDE) that is a program downloaded from the Arduino website. RPi and Arduino communicate on the USB that should not be connected when the IDE program is downloaded and installed with the terminal entry

```
$ sudo apt-get install arduino
```

On completion of the software installation, the USB cable can be connected, and from the Tools menu in the IDE, select Board and set the type to Arduino Uno. The serial port option / dev / ttyACM0 should be selected to complete the configuration process.

The safest and simplest way to communicate between the RPi and the Arduino is via the USB connection. (See "Discussion.")

Figure 11-14 illustrates the microcontroller start menu on the RPi after the installation of the Arduino IDE.

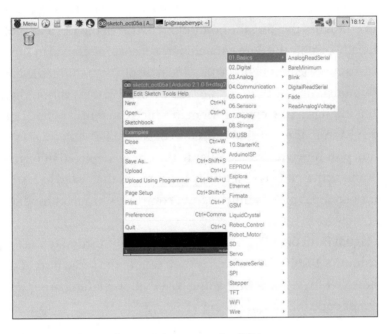

Figure 11-14. *The Arduino Menu on the RPi*

Examination of the menu entries in Figure 11-14 reveals that a very large body of open source code has been written for the Arduino microcontroller allowing it to interface to both hardware and software. A USB connection between the RPi and the Arduino makes much of this analog and digital interfacing code accessible to the computational power of the RPi.

Experimental

With configuration complete, the Blink program can be selected through Examples ➤ Basic, compiled and uploaded to the Arduino, which should then flash the LED once per second.

Once the LED on the Arduino flashes as programmed, the simple process to interface the two devices is complete and validated.

One of the more important experimental aspects of the Arduino-RPi connection lies in using the computing power of the RPi as a plotter to graphically display the data collected by sensors interfaced to the Arduino. A simple example of the graphical display capabilities available can be demonstrated by plotting the signal from a LDR as various lighting conditions change in the environment in which the sensor is positioned.

Five volts from the Arduino is used to bias the LDR with a 5.49 kΩ 1% metal film, pull-down resistor similar to the circuit depicted in Figure 11-2. The Arduino active code is essentially the same as that listed in Listing 11-1 with minor changes in only the program comments to accommodate the different pull-down resistor value.

The signal from the LDR can be digitized by connection to the A0 input of the Arduino's 10-bit ADC, which is then sent to the serial port of the microcontroller for viewing or reading by a Python plotting program. The serial plotter code is listed in Listing 11-5.

Observations

After configuring the LDR sensor and the Arduino and starting the plotting program on the RPi, the trace of Figure 11-15 was recorded. On initial start-up, the plotter program creates a small window on the right-hand side of the display with the interactive screen on the left. The streaming printed column of numbers and characters seen on the left of the interactive screen are the transmitted characters and the numbers to be plotted. (See "Discussion.")

As noted in Chapter 9, the matplotlib plotting programs are displayed with a panel of buttons beneath the lower left-hand corner of the active display for invoking several functions such as scale expansion, stepping forward and back in frames, or saving the plot as applicable for the type of data being displayed.

Recall that the timing markings on the graphical plotting display must be calibrated for quantitative use.

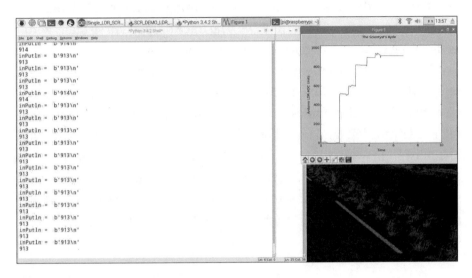

Figure 11-15. *Plotting Data from Arduino*

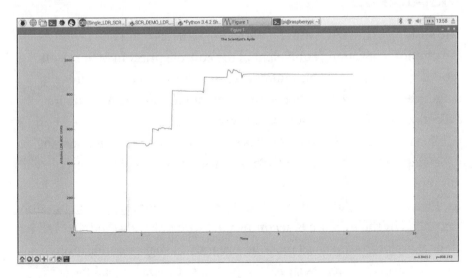

Figure 11-16. *Recorder Tracing of Room Lighting Intensity Variations Monitored by a Light-Dependent Resistor*

In Figure 11-16 the full-screen option button has been used to expand the recorded plot from the small window visible in Figure 11-15. At the extreme left of the plot, the tracing was recording the room light leaking under the cover placed over the LDR. The trace dropped to virtually zero as the room window was covered and the room lighting was turned off. The first large displacement at about a minute and a half was due to the uncovering of the window. The second step-up was due to the turning on of the overhead incandescent light at about two-and-a-half minutes, followed by the left- and right-hand desk lamps at three and four minutes. The maximum trace value was created by shining a bright LED light on the sensor from a distance of about an inch (2.5 cm). Exact relative times since session start and expanded sections of the trace can be accessed with the aid of the tool buttons beneath the lower-left corner of the display. (See Chapter 9.)

Discussion

The flashing of the LED with the Blink program has often been cited as the physical computing equivalent of the console printout of the "Hello World!" program run by all students when learning a new computer language. In essence the RPi is sending commands to the Arduino for execution. The free, open source software that has been developed and published for the Arduino and RPi is substantial and requires constant reviewing for the experimentalist or investigator to remain up-to-date with this rapidly evolving technology.

Plotting of the data generated by the sensor connected to and possibly controlled by the Arduino is accomplished with a slightly modified version of the matplotlib strip chart recorder program. A slight modification of the original code is necessary for the plotter to be able to read the serial port. Serial port transmissions involve patterns of 1's and 0's that have to be translated into transmissible packets of data, received and parsed back into numerical values for plotting. Arduino is programmed and operates in the C language, while the RPi uses Python. As an aid to configuring the parsing code and validating the data transmission prior to plotting, the characters received by the Python end of the serial connection are printed out "as received" on the console display and then printed again in the format suitable for recognition as the data for plotting. The print statements can easily be commented out when the software is performing as intended.

In normal usage the matplotlib strip chart recorder program has variables and labels identified in the comments for x, y, and time axis scaling. Axis labeling may also need to be modified to plot and identify the data at hand.

The RPi and Arduino are both capable of using 3.3- or 5-volt power supplies, and for some applications using direct serial communications, a voltage level adjusting circuit may be required to avoid damage to electronic components. Level adjusting circuits are detailed in several published and online sources.[1]

Code Listings

Listing 11-1. Arduino Code

```
// Single LDR readings with serial transmission for DAQFactory
   SCR display.
// The voltage at the junction of an LDR biased by +5 v and
   with a 10K ohm
// resistance to ground is monitored by the AO input.
```

[1] 1) elinux.org/RPI_GPIO_Interface_Circuits
    2) *Raspberry Pi Cookbook* 2nd Edn., Monk, O'Reilly Media Inc., ISBN 978-1-491-93910-9
    3) *Electronics Cookbook*, Monk, O'Reilly Media Inc., ISBN 978-1-491-95340-2

```
//
//
void setup()
{
  // initialize serial port
  Serial.begin(9600);
}
//
void loop()
{
  // read A0
  int val1 = analogRead(0);
  // read A1
  // print to serial port
  Serial.println(val1);
  //Serial.print(" ");
  // delay
  delay(500);
 }
```

Listing 11-2. DAQFactory "On Receive" Serial Port Parsing Script

```
if (strIn == Chr(13))
   private string datain = ReadUntil(13)
   Channel.AddValue(strDevice, 0, "Input", 0,
StrToDouble(DataIn))
Endif
```

Listing 11-3. DAQFactory Sequence Code for Writing to com_3 Port

```
 for (Private.Counter = 0, Counter < 5, Counter ++)
   device.com_3.Write("H")
   delay(3)
```

```
    device.com_3.Write("L")
    delay(3)
endfor
```

Listing 11-4. Arduino Code to Be Run on DAQFactory Screen
Button Command

```
//Simple DAQFactory - Arduino Serial Communications Program,
  Mar. 3, 2012
//An LED with an appropriate CLR is connected between pin 13
  and ground on the Arduino
//The pgm below waits for an incoming character. If the
  character is an upper case H, the LED is
//turned on. If the character is an upper case L the LED is
  turned off. The state of the LED is
//thus determined by the nature of the character in the serial
  import buffer.
//
//
const int ledPin = 13;          // the pin with the LED and CLR
int incomingByte;               // a variable to hold the
incoming data
//
//
void setup(){
  Serial.begin(9600);           // initialize communication
  pinMode(ledPin, OUTPUT);      // set the pin function
}
//
void loop() {
  // check for incoming serial data
  if (Serial.available() > 0) {
```

```
    // read the last byte in the serial buffer
       incomingByte = Serial.read();
    // if the byte is H (ASCII 72), turn on the LED
    if (incomingByte == 'H') {
      digitalWrite(ledPin, HIGH);
    }
    // if character is an L (ASCII 76) turn the LED off
    if (incomingByte == 'L') {
      digitalWrite(ledPin, LOW);
    }
  }
}
```

Listing 11-5. RPi-Python Code for Reading and Plotting Serial Port Data

```
# A Strip Chart Recorder for Raspberry Pi with Serial Input
# SCR Plotting of changing LDR data from room environment.
  LDR data from 5 volt
# 5.49 K 1% MFR pull-down cct on A0 and output on Arduino
  serial port for plotting
#
import matplotlib
import numpy as np
from matplotlib.lines import Line2D
import matplotlib.pyplot as plt
import matplotlib.animation as animation
import time
import serial
#
#
```

```
#
class Scope:
    def __init__(self, ax, maxt=10, dt=0.02):
        """maxt time width of display"""
        self.ax = ax
        self.dt = dt
        self.maxt = maxt
        self.tdata = [0]
        self.ydata = [0]
        self.line = Line2D(self.tdata, self.ydata)
        self.ax.add_line(self.line)
        self.ax.set_ylim(0.0, 1024.0)  # y axis scale
        self.ax.set_xlim(0, self.maxt)

    def update(self, y):
        lastt = self.tdata[-1]
        if lastt > self.tdata[0] + self.maxt: # reset the arrays
            self.tdata = [self.tdata[-1]]
            self.ydata = [self.ydata[-1]]
            self.ax.set_xlim(self.tdata[0], self.tdata[0] +
            self.maxt)
            self.ax.figure.canvas.draw()

        t = self.tdata[-1] + self.dt
        self.tdata.append(t)
        self.ydata.append(y)
        self.line.set_data(self.tdata, self.ydata)
        return self.line,
#
```

```python
ser = serial.Serial("/dev/ttyACM0", 9600)
#
def rd_data():
    while True:
        inPutln = ser.readline()
        print("inPutln = ", inPutln)
        line = int(str(inPutln)[slice(2,-3)]) # convert arduino
                                                    serial output
                                                    stream
        # to a Python string, parse out the numerical symbols
            and convert to a value
        print(line)
        yield (line)

fig = plt.figure()
fig.suptitle("The Scientyst's Ayde", fontsize = 12)
ax = fig.add_subplot(111)
ax.set_xlabel("Time")
ax.set_ylabel("Arduino LDR ADC Units")
scope = Scope(ax)

# uses rd_data() as a generator to produce data for the update
  func, the Arduino LDC
# value is read by the plotting code in 10 minute windows for
  the animated
# screen display. Software overhead limits response speed of
  display.
ani = animation.FuncAnimation(fig, scope.update, rd_data,
interval=50,
blit=False)
plt.show()
```

Summary

- Microcontrollers can be considered as smart interfaces in the SCADA architecture that use serial port communications to up- and download instructional commands and data between the host computer and remote processes.

- Microcontrollers can greatly augment the digital signal processing and I/O capabilities of the host computer.

- A microcontroller and a single-board computer can form the basis of one of the least expensive SCADA implementations available.

Extensive use of the microcontroller and the techniques and software described in the previous ten chapters of this book are applied to the tasks of implementing experimental determinations in the next work of this series, *Arduino Measurements in Science.*

List of Abbreviations

A/D	analog to digital
ADC	analog-to-digital converter
AGM	absorbed glass mat (a form of lead acid battery)
AMR	anisotropic magnetoresistance
API	application programming interface
ASCII	American Standard Code for Information Interchange
ASIC	application-specific integrated circuit
AO	analog output
AWG	American wire gauge
BCD	binary-coded decimal
BJT	base junction transistor (either an NPN or a PNP)
BLDC	brushless direct current (a type of DC-powered motor)
BMS	battery management system
BoB	breakout board (adapter to use SMT IC with a prototyping board)
C4D	capacitively coupled contactless conductivity detection
C and C++	a compact efficient programming language and a variation for Windows applications

(continued)

© Richard J. Smythe 2021
R. J. Smythe, *Arduino in Science*, https://doi.org/10.1007/978-1-4842-6778-3

CCC	constant current charging
cGLP	current good laboratory practice (a QA/QC protocol)
CLR	current limiting resistor
CMOS	complementary metal oxide semiconductor
CNTRL	Ctrl key
COM	serial communication port
cps	cycles per second
CPU	central or computer processing unit (a term used to describe the main processor chip)
CPVC	chlorinated polyvinyl chloride
CR	carriage return (in printer control code)
CSA	Canadian Standards Association
CSM	current shunt monitor (an ASIC for current measurement)
CSS	chip slave select (in four-line SPI data transmission protocol)
CSV	comma-separated values (a common file data storage format)
CV	computer vision
DHCP	Dynamic Host Configuration Protocol
DI/O	digital input/output
DIP	dual in-line package
D/L	download
DMM	digital multimeter
DPM	digital panel meter
DSP	digital signal processing

(*continued*)

DUT	device under test
DVM	digital voltmeter
EEPROM	electrically erasable programmable read-only memory
EMF	electromotive force
EMI	electromagnetic interference
EPS	electric potential sensors
ERH	equilibrium relative humidity
ESD	electrostatic discharge
FFT	fast Fourier transform or flicker fusion threshold
FOV	field of view
FID	flame ionization detector
FSD	full-screen display or full-scale displacement
GND	ground
GPIO	general-purpose input/output
GPR	ground penetrating radar
GPS	global positioning system
GPU	graphics processing unit
GUI	graphical user interface
HAT	hardware added on top (RPi add-on boards)
HDMI	high-definition multimedia interface
HMI	human-machine interface

(continued)

HTML	HyperText Markup Language
HTTP	HyperText Transfer Protocol
HTTPS	Secure HyperText Transfer Protocol
I^2C or I2C	inter-integrated circuit (data transmission protocol)
ICAP	inductively coupled argon plasma (also ICP, a spectroscopic source)
ICFT	input capture feature of the timer (ATmega328)
IDE	integrated development environment
IEPE	integrated electronics piezo-electric (vibration sensors)
IMS	ion mobility spectroscopy (plasma chromatography)
IMU	inertial measurement unit
INS	inertial navigation systems
INU	inertial navigation unit
I/O or IO	input/output
IP	Internet protocol
IR	infrared
ISR	interrupt service routine (programming code)
ISRC	internal stray resistance and capacitance (on a circuit board or IC chip)
ITO	indium tin oxide
LAN	local area network (of computers)
LCD	liquid crystal display
LDR	light-dependent resistor
LED	light emitting diode

(continued)

LF	line feed (in printer control code)
LFP	lithium iron phosphate (a lithium ion battery chemistry)
LiMH	lithium metal hydride (a type of rechargeable battery and chemistry)
LSB	least significant bit
MA	moving average (a form of DSP)
MAC	media access control
mAh	milliampere hours (sometimes as mAhr)
mcd	millicandela (a measure of light intensity)
MEMS	micro-electro-mechanical systems
MHz	mega-Hertz (a frequency of millions of cycles per second)
MISO	master in slave out (four-line SPI data transmission protocol)
MOSFET	metal oxide semiconductor field effect transistor
MOS	metal oxide semiconductor
MOSI	master out slave in (four-line SPI data transmission protocol)
MPCLC	multiple plate capacitor load cell
MPPT	maximum power point transfer
MSB	most significant bit
N.C.	normally closed (relay or switch normal configuration, often NC)
NiMH	nickel metal hydride (a rechargeable battery chemistry)
NIST	National Institute of Standards and Technology
NMR	nuclear magnetic resonance (a form of spectroscopy and the basis for medical imaging)
N.O.	normally open (relay or switch normal configuration, often NO)

(*continued*)

NPN	a base junction transistor consisting of a P type of semiconductor between two N types
NTC	negative temperature coefficient (a term used with thermistors)
OCV	open circuit voltage
OH-MPCLC	over had multiple plate capacitor load cell
OS	operating system
PC	personal computer (IBM/Microsoft Windows OS)
PCB	printed circuit board
PDIP	plastic dual in-line package
PE	polyethylene (a plastic)
PGA	programmable gain amplifier
PID	photo ionization detector or proportional, integral, derivative (a control algorithm)
PIN	an intrinsic PN junction used in high-sensitivity photo diodes, a thick light-sensitive layer
PIR	passive infrared (an infrared sensor)
PLC	programmable logic controller
PM	permanent magnet
PNP	a base junction transistor consisting of an N type of semiconductor between two P types
PV	photo-voltaic
PVC	polyvinyl chloride (a plastic)
PVDF	polyvinylidene di-fluoride (an inert plastic polymer)
PWD	pulse width difference

(continued)

PWM	pulse width modulation
PZT	lead zirconate titanate
RMB-PUM	right mouse button pop-up menu
RC	resistor-capacitor (electronic circuit time constant elements or radio controlled)
RE	rare earth
REM	rare earth magnet
RF	radio frequency
RFI	radio frequency interference
RGB	red, green, and blue (the three basic colors used in LED displays)
RH	relative humidity
rms	root mean square (a measurement form used with AC or sinusoidal power signals)
RPi	Raspberry Pi
RPM	revolutions per minute (a measure of rotation speed)
RTC	real-time clock
RTD	resistance temperature device
RTV	room temperature vulcanization (a term used to describe a silicone sealant/adhesive)
SAR	successive approximation register (a type of ADC)
SBC	Single-board computer
SC	specific conductivity
SCADA	supervisory control and data acquisition
SCC	short circuit current

(*continued*)

SCL(K)	the clock line designation in four-line SPI data transmission protocol
SCR	silicon controlled rectifier or strip chart recorder
SD	secure data (a plug-in digital data storage media/card)
SDA	I^2C serial protocol for slave data
SHE	standard hydrogen electrode
SLI	starting lighting ignition (a form of lead acid battery)
SOIC-8	small outline integrated circuit eight-pin SMT-defined package format
SIP	single in-line package (an IC with only a single row of power I/O pins)
SMBUS	System Management Bus (a simple one-wire serial communications protocol)
SMT	surface mount technology
SoC	state of charge or system on a chip
SPAD	single-photon avalanche diode
SPC	statistical process control
SPI	serial peripheral interface
SRAM	static random-access memory
SS	slave select
SSR	solid-state relay
TCR	temperature coefficient of resistance
TEC	thermoelectric conversion or converter
TEG	thermoelectric generator
TIA	trans-impedance amplifier
TIG	tungsten inert gas (a form of welding)
ToF	time of flight (a form of distance measurement or mass spectrometry)

(continued)

tpi	threads per inch
TTL	transistor-transistor logic
UART	universal asynchronous receiver-transmitter (serial data transmission protocol or IC)
UAV	un-manned aerial vehicle
ui /UI	user interface
URL	universal resource locator (an Internet address)
USB	Universal Serial Bus
UTC	universal time coordinates
VCO	voltage-controlled oscillator
Vdd	voltage drain (usually the positive supply)
VLS	visual light systems (a communications technique)
VOM	volt-ohm meter
VRSLA	valve-regulated sealed lead acid (a form of battery)
Vss	voltage source supply (usually ground potential)
VVC	variable value component (a GUI screen numerical display of DAQFactory software)

List of Suppliers

Chapter	IC or Part	
1	LabJack U3-HV	`https://Labjack.com/support/datasheets/u3`
	LabJack U12-HV	`https://Labjack.com/support/datasheets/u12`
	chipKIT	`https://reference.digilentinc.com/reference/microprocessor/uc32/start`
	Arduino RedBoard	`www.sparkfun.com/products/13975`
	Arduino (BlueBoard)	`www.arduino.cc/`
	CD4050	`www.ti.com/lit/ds/symlink/cd4049ub.pdf`
2	MCP3008	`www.microchip.com/wwwproducts/en/MCP3008`
4	2N3904/2N3906	`www.onsemi.com/pub/Collateral/2N3906-D.PDF` and `www.onsemi.com/pub/Collateral/2N3903-D.PDF`
6	ADC0804	`www.ti.com/lit/ds/symlink/adc0804-n.pdf`
	MCP3201	`ww1.microchip.com/downloads/en/devicedoc/21290d.pdf`
7	TIP 122	`www.onsemi.com/pub/Collateral/TIP120-D.PDF`
8	LM555	`www.ti.com/lit/ds/symlink/lm555.pdf`

(continued)

© Richard J. Smythe 2021
R. J. Smythe, *Arduino in Science*, https://doi.org/10.1007/978-1-4842-6778-3

Chapter	IC or Part	
9	CMOS 555	www.ti.com/lit/ds/symlink/lmc555.pdf
	Bipolar 555	www.st.com/resource/en/datasheet/ cd00000479.pdf
	Exar XR-2209	www.maxlinear.com/ds/xr2209v202.pdf
10	LM741	www.ti.com/lit/ds/symlink/lm741.pdf
	LF411	www.ti.com/lit/ds/symlink/lf411.pdf
	CD4013	www.ti.com/lit/ds/symlink/cd4013b.pdf
	MOC 3022	www.mouser.ca/datasheet/2/239/MOC302-1175440.pdf
	BTA06	www.st.com/resource/en/datasheet/ bta06.pdf
	MOC 3061	www.mouser.ca/datasheet/2/308/ fairchild%20semiconductor_ moc3061m-1191638.pdf
	FQP30N06L	www.onsemi.com/products/discretes-drivers/mosfets/fqp30n06l
	ULN2803	www.ti.com/lit/ds/symlink/uln2803a.pdf
11	LDR	www.farnell.com/datasheets/77395.pdf or www.resistorguide.com/photoresistor/

Index

A

AC current
   advantage, 380
   circuit analysis, 388
   circuit schematic, 384, 385
   experimentation, 405–407
   50 Hz and 10 Hz 555 timer IC
      variation, 389
   5-volt 555 timer IC control of
      line power, 386
   5-volt DC output power
      supply, 381
   hardware, 382, 383
   110 VAC bulb output, 408
   110 VAC line control, 406
   hydro-electric facilities, 379
   introduction, 405
   mains/household current, 379
   observations, 386, 387, 407
   optical isolator chips, 381
   potentiometer diode
      arrangement, 389
   power control
      applications, 388, 390
   power grids, 387
   PWM frequency, 408
   random flickering and cyclic
      pulsing, 409
   random-phase/zero-
      crossing, 381
   SCR, 380
   software, 386
   solid-state devices, 381
   test apparatus, 384
   timer pulse train, 389
   timing network, 387
   triac and optical isolator, 384
ADC0804, 163–167
Aliasing, 331
Analog-to-digital conversion
   (ADC), 19, 46, 155, 421
   ADC0804, 163–167
   adjustable analog signal
      source, 160
   binary array, 154
   circuitry, 160
   coding
      decimal-to-binary
         conversion via serial
         connection, 190–192
      decimal-to-binary sequence
         codes, 185, 186, 188
      diode array illumination,
         195–197
      GPIO pin array, 206
      GPIO pin values to zero, 207

© Richard J. Smythe 2021
R. J. Smythe, *Arduino in Science*, https://doi.org/10.1007/978-1-4842-6778-3

H

M

Printed in the United States
by Baker & Taylor Publisher Services